KILL
M.O.D.O.K.
HEAD TRIPS

M.O.D.O.K. CREATED BY STAN LEE & JACK KIRBY

COLLECTION EDITOR MARK D. BEAZLEY
ASSISTANT EDITOR CAITLIN O'CONNELL
ASSOCIATE MANAGING EDITOR KATERI WOODY
ASSOCIATE MANAGER, DIGITAL ASSETS JOE HOCHSTEIN
MASTERWORKS EDITOR CORY SEDLMEIER

SENIOR EDITOR, SPECIAL PROJECTS JENNIFER GRÜNWALD
VP PRODUCTION & SPECIAL PROJECTS JEFF YOUNGQUIST
RESEARCH & LAYOUT JEPH YORK
BOOK DESIGNER STACIE ZUCKER

SVP PRINT, SALES & MARKETING DAVID GABRI
DIRECTOR, LICENSED PUBLISHING SVEN LARSE
EDITOR IN CHIEF C.B. CEBULSKI
CHIEF CREATIVE OFFICER JOE QUESADA
PRESIDENT DAN BUCKLEY
EXECUTIVE PRODUCER ALAN FINE

M.O.D.O.K.: HEAD TRIPS. Contains material originally published in magazine form as CAPTAIN AMERICA (1968) #133, INCREDIBLE HULK (1968) #287-290, SUPER-VILLAIN TEAM-UP/MODOK'S 11 (2007) #1-5, FANTASTIC FOUR IN...ATAQ DEL M.O.D.O.K.! (2010) #1, MARVEL ADVENTURES THE AVENGERS (2006) #9, M.O.D.O.K. ASSASSIN (2015) #1-5, TALES OF SUSPENSE (1959) #93-94 and IRON MAN ANNUAL (1970) #4. First printing 2019. ISBN 978-1-302-92074-6. Publish by MARVEL WORLDWIDE, INC., a subsidiary of MARVEL ENTERTAINMENT, LLC. OFFICE OF PUBLICATION: 135 West 50th Street, New York, NY 10020. **Printed in the U.S.A.** DAN BUCKLEY, President, Marvel Entertainment; JOHN NE Publisher; JOE QUESADA, Chief Creative Officer; TOM BREVOORT, SVP of Publishing; DAVID BOGART, Associate Publisher & SVP of Talent Affairs; DAVID GABRIEL, VP of Print & Digital Publishing; JEFF YOUNGQUIST, VP of Production & Spec Projects; DAN CARR, Executive Director of Publishing Technology; ALEX MORALES, Director of Publishing Operations; DAN EDINGTON, Managing Editor; SUSAN CRESPI, Production Manager; STAN LEE, Chairman Emeritus. For informati regarding advertising in Marvel Comics or on Marvel.com, please contact Vit DeBellis, Custom Solutions & Integrated Advertising Manager, at vdebellis@marvel.com. For Marvel subscription inquiries, please call 888-511-5480. **Manufactur between 10/4/2019 and 11/5/2019 by LSC COMMUNICATIONS INC., KENDALLVILLE, IN, USA.**

10 9 8 7 6 5 4 3 2 1

HEAD TRIPS

TALES OF SUSPENSE #93-94
WRITER STAN LEE
PENCILER JACK KIRBY
INKER JOE SINNOTT
LETTERERS ARTIE SIMEK & SAM ROSEN
COVER ART GENE COLAN (#93); JACK KIRBY (#94)

CAPTAIN AMERICA #133
WRITER STAN LEE
PENCILER GENE COLAN
INKER DICK AYERS
LETTERER SAM ROSEN
COVER ART MARIE SEVERIN

IRON MAN ANNUAL #4
WRITER BILL MANTLO
PENCILER GEORGE TUSKA
INKER DON PERLIN
COLORIST PHIL RACHELSON
LETTERER JOHN COSTANZA
COVER ART AL MILGROM

INCREDIBLE HULK #287-290
WRITER BILL MANTLO
PENCILER SAL BUSCEMA
INKERS CHIC STONE, JIM MOONEY, JOE SINNOTT & CARLOS GARZON
COLORIST BOB SHAREN
LETTERERS JIM NOVAK, JOE ROSEN & MICHAEL HIGGINS
COVER ART RON WILSON & AL MILGROM (#287); RON WILSON & JOE SINNOTT (#288); AL MILGROM (#289-290)

SUPER-VILLAIN TEAM-UP/ M.O.D.O.K.'S 11 #1-5
WRITER FRED VAN LENTE
PENCILER FRANCIS PORTELA
INKER TERRY PALLOT
COLORIST GURU-eFX
LETTERER BLAMBOT's NATE PIEKOS
COVER ART ERIC POWELL (#1); MARKO DJURDJEVIĆ (#2-5)

FANTASTIC FOUR IN... ¡ATAQUE DEL M.O.D.O.K.!
WRITER TOM BELAND
ARTIST & COLORIST JUAN DOE
LETTERER DAVE LANPHEAR
COVER ART JUAN DOE

MARVEL ADVENTURES THE AVENGERS #9
WRITER JEFF PARKER
PENCILER JUAN SANTACRUZ
INKER RAUL FERNANDEZ
COLORIST IMPACTO STUDIOS' ADRIANO LUCAS
LETTERER DAVE SHARPE
COVER ART CAMERON STEWART & GURU-eFX

M.O.D.O.K.: ASSASSIN #1-5
WRITER CHRISTOPHER YOST
PENCILER AMILCAR PINNA
INKERS TERRY PALLOT WITH AMILCAR PINNA (#1) & ED TADEO (#2)
COLORIST RACHELLE ROSENBERG
LETTERER VC's TRAVIS LANHAM
COVER ART DAVID LAFUENTE & JOHN RAUCH

ASSISTANT EDITORS: ANN NOCENTI, NATHAN COSBY & ALANNA SMITH
EDITORS: STAN LEE, ARCHIE GOODWIN, AL MILGROM, CARL POTTS, MARK PANICCIA, ALEJANDRO ARBONA, DANIEL KETCHUM & JON MOISAN

EXECUTIVE EDITOR (¡ATAQUE DEL M.O.D.O.K.!): TOM BREVOORT
FRONT COVER ART: SAL BUSCEMA, CHIC STONE & VERONICA GANDINI

TALES OF SUSPENSE
featuring
IRON MAN
AND
CAPTAIN AMERICA
APPROVED BY THE COMICS CODE AUTHORITY
MARVEL COMICS GROUP
12¢ IND.
93 SEPT
DON'T MISS THE VILLAINY OF... HALF-FACE!

POWER VS. POWER!
BACK AGAIN!! STRONGER THAN EVER! THE TITANIUM MAN!

CAPTAIN AMERICA, LIVING LEGEND of WORLD WAR II
"INTO THE JAWS OF...A.I.M.!"
IN ALL THE WORLD, THERE IS BUT ONE GIRL WHOM CAPTAIN AMERICA TRULY LOVES--ONE MYSTERIOUS, VALIANT AGENT OF SHIELD-- WHOSE VERY NAME IS STILL UNKNOWN TO HIM! LAST ISH WE SAW HOW CAP UNWITTINGLY PLACED HER IN THE DEADLIEST PERIL WHEN HE ATTEMPTED TO RESCUE NICK FURY-- AND NOW, DESPITE THE MAGNITUDE OF THE ODDS AGAINST HIM--THE STAR-SPANGLED AVENGER FIGHTS BACK--!
ALL FURY KNEW ABOUT AIM'S LOCATION IS THAT THEY'RE BASED IN A GIANT SUB--SOMEWHERE IN THESE WATERS!
S.H.I.E.L.D.
AND, IF ANY-ONE CAN FIND IT, I WILL--USING SHIELD'S LONG-DISTANCE MINI-CRUISER!
FACE IT, FAITHFUL ONE... STAN (THE MAN) LEE and JACK (KING) KIRBY WERE BORN TO BRING YOU CAPTAIN AMERICA!
AIDED, OF COURSE, BY JOE SINNOTT, INKER, AND ARTIE SIMEK, LETTERER!
1

SWIMMING TIRELESSLY, CEASELESSLY--HIS EQUIPMENT COATED WITH A SPECIAL, NEW RADAR-BLOCKING CHEMICAL SCREEN--CAP FINALLY SIGHTS--
THE SUB--NESTLED WITHIN THAT DEEP, UNDERWATER RAVINE!
BUT, IF I SEE THEM--
THEIR OBSERVERS MUST HAVE SPOTTED ME, TOO!
I CAN ALMOST FEEL THEIR EYES UPON ME NOW!
A.I.M.

AND, AS THOUGH SUITING ACTION TO THE LONE SWIMMER'S THOUGHTS--
FZZZAAP!
ANOTHER VICTIM FOR AIM!
THE EYES OF MODOK ARE EVERYWHERE!

THE CYLINDER'S THIN, IONIC VALVE HEAD WILL PENETRATE ANY WATERPROOF DEVICE KNOWN TO MAN--!

--INSTANTLY PUMPING A NULLIFYING GAS THRU ITS ARMOR-PIERCING NOZZLE--!
2

WITHIN SECONDS, THE SUBJECT LAPSES INTO TOTAL HELPLESSNESS--

PLUNGING INTO AN ALL-ENGULFING SEA OF ENDLESS NIGHT--!

DRIFTING DEEPER--DEEPER INTO A NAMELESS, SILENT LIMBO--

UNTIL--!

HE'S HURLED INTO REALITY LIKE AN EXPLODING METEOR!!

NOW, BEFORE HE FULLY REGAINS HIS SENSES--LET US WRENCH HIS ACCURSED SHIELD FROM HIS GRASP!

WELCOME, CAPTAIN AMERICA!
MODOK WELCOMES YOU TO THE SUPREME WORLD OF-- AIM, REBORN!
3

MODOK? WHO IS MODOK?
THE ONE WHO WILL SOON BE RULER OF ALL--EVEN AS HE NOW RULES THE INVINCIBLE FORCES OF ALL-MIGHTY AIM!
TIME ENOUGH TO WORRY ABOUT THAT LATER! FIRST--I'VE GOT TO FIND A WAY TO BREAK FREE!
I'M BEING DRAWN TO A CONDUCTIVE BASE PLATE BY SHEER MAGNETIC FORCE!
AIM REBORN IS AS DIABOLICALLY INVENTIVE AS EVER BEFORE!

AND NOW, BEFORE WE DISPOSE OF YOU PERMANENTLY--
HERE IS ANOTHER AGENT OF SHIELD--WHO SHALL JOIN YOU IN YOUR FINAL DEFEAT!
CAPTAIN AMERICA!! THEY--THEY CAPTURED YOU, TOO?!!
THE GIRL!! THE ONE I CAME TO RESCUE! THANK HEAVEN SHE'S STILL ALIVE!

YOU FOOL!! WHY DID YOU DO IT?? YOU KNEW IT WAS HOPELESS!! WHY DID YOU COME? WHY DID YOU SACRIFICE YOURSELF??
MY LIFE IS OF NO IMPORTANCE! I WAS PREPARED TO DIE! BUT YOU--YOU'RE MORE THAN ONE EXPENDABLE AGENT--YOU'RE A LIVING SYMBOL--!

YOU'RE THE GREATEST--MOST WONDERFUL MAN I'VE EVER KNOWN--!
LISTEN CLOSELY--I'M WEARING SPECIAL ANTI-POLAR COVER-ALLS--THEY CAN REVERSE THE MAGNETIC FIELD WHICH HOLDS YOU--
I'LL PRETEND TO KISS YOU GOODBYE! AS SOON AS I TOUCH YOU--DROP TO THE FLOOR!!
NO MATTER WHAT HAPPENS TO US--AT LEAST WE'LL MEET OUR FATE TOGETHER!
NOW, CAP--NOW!!

IT'S A TRICK!!
SHIELD KNEW ABOUT OUR MAGNETIC BOND--SHE'S BEEN WEARING ANTI-POLAR MATERIAL!!
SHE FREED HIM!!
FIRE!! SHOW THEM NO MERCY!
THANKS, LITTLE LADY! NOW, I'LL TAKE OVER--!
4

SPUKUKK!

BUH-KOW!
THWOOSH

BLAM!

YOU--PUT FOUR OF THEM--OUT OF ACTION--IN AS MANY SECONDS!!
I SHOULD HAVE MOVED FASTER-- BUT THAT GAS SLOWED ME DOWN!
HOLD ONTO THAT BLASTER YOU PICKED UP--AND LET'S GO!!
WE'VE GOT THINGS TO DO!
NO ONE GETS MY SHIELD AWAY FROM ME!
5

SECONDS LATER, IN AN ADJACENT CHAMBER--
IT IS USELESS!
NOT EVEN MY TITANIUM BLADE CAN PIERCE THE SHIELD!
THE HYDRAULIC PRESSURE DRILL IS EQUALLY POWERLESS AGAINST IT!
ENOUGH! WE MUST HAVE SUFFICIENT WISDOM TO ADMIT DEFEAT!
WE ARE TOTALLY UNABLE TO DAMAGE THE ACCURSED SHIELD OF CAPTAIN AMERICA!

WHATEVER IT IS COMPOSED OF, THE SUBSTANCE WAS NEVER MINED HERE ON EARTH!
IT IS UNDOUBTEDLY SOME SORT OF ALIEN, EXTRA-TERRESTIAL METAL!
WE MUST REPORT OUR FINDINGS TO MODOK--AT ONCE!

SORRY, MASKED MAN!! THERE'LL BE A SLIGHT DELAY!
THWOP!

AND NOW--SINCE YOU WERE ALL SO INTERESTED IN MY SHIELD--
I'LL GIVE YOU A LITTLE DEMONSTRATION OF HOW EFFECTIVE IT CAN BE!
ZAK

HE FIGHTS LIKE A RAGING, UNLEASHED TIGER--BUT THE ODDS ARE STILL TOO GREAT AGAINST HIM!
I'LL CREATE A DIVERSION FOR HIM--BY FIRING AT THE ELECTRONIC WALL CIRCUITS JUST AHEAD!
6

THE CIRCUITS HAVE BEEN IGNITED!!!
SUMMON THE EMERGENCY FIRE DETAIL-- BEFORE THE ENTIRE SHIP GOES DOWN IN FLAME!!!
GOOD WORK, LADY!! BUT, WHERE DO WE GO FROM HERE?
QUICKLY --FOLLOW ME--!!

AIM HAS THE MOST ADVANCED SCIENTIFIC APPARATUS OF ANY CRIMINAL ORGANIZATION ON EARTH!
THEY'LL HAVE THE FIRE UNDER CONTROL IN MINUTES--AND BE AFTER US AGAIN!
IN FACT, I HEAR THEIR SHOCK TROOPS BEING MUSTERED NOW!
WE'VE GOT TO TAKE COVER!
LEAD ON, LITTLE GIRL! I LIKE YOUR STYLE!

THEY'LL BE PAST US SOON--THEN I'LL FIND THEIR EMERGENCY ESCAPE HATCH AND HAVE YOU OUT OF HERE BEFORE THEY KNOW IT!
NO! I CAN'T LEAVE UNTIL MY MISSION IS COMPLETED!
THERE IS SOMEONE --OR SOME THING-- NAMED MODOK-- WHICH MAY BE THE GREATEST MENACE THE WORLD HAS EVER KNOWN--!

IT WAS MY ASSIGNMENT TO LEARN WHAT MODOK IS--AND I MUST DO IT--EVEN IF IT COSTS ME MY LIFE!
BUT IF YOU HURRY, THERE'S STILL A CHANCE FOR YOU TO ESCAPE--BEFORE THE SHOCK TROOPS RETURN!
ARE YOU MAD? DO YOU THINK I COULD GO--AND LEAVE YOU HERE ALONE?
NOW THAT I'VE FINALLY FOUND YOU AGAIN-- DO YOU THINK I'LL EVER LET YOU OUT OF MY LIFE?!!
YOU MUSTN'T SPEAK THAT WAY! NOT NOW! NOT WHEN--WAIT!!
LISTEN!! SOMETHING'S HAPPENING-- UP AHEAD--!
WE'VE GOT TO GET CLOSER!
THEY'RE WAITING TO SPEAK--TO MODOK!!
7

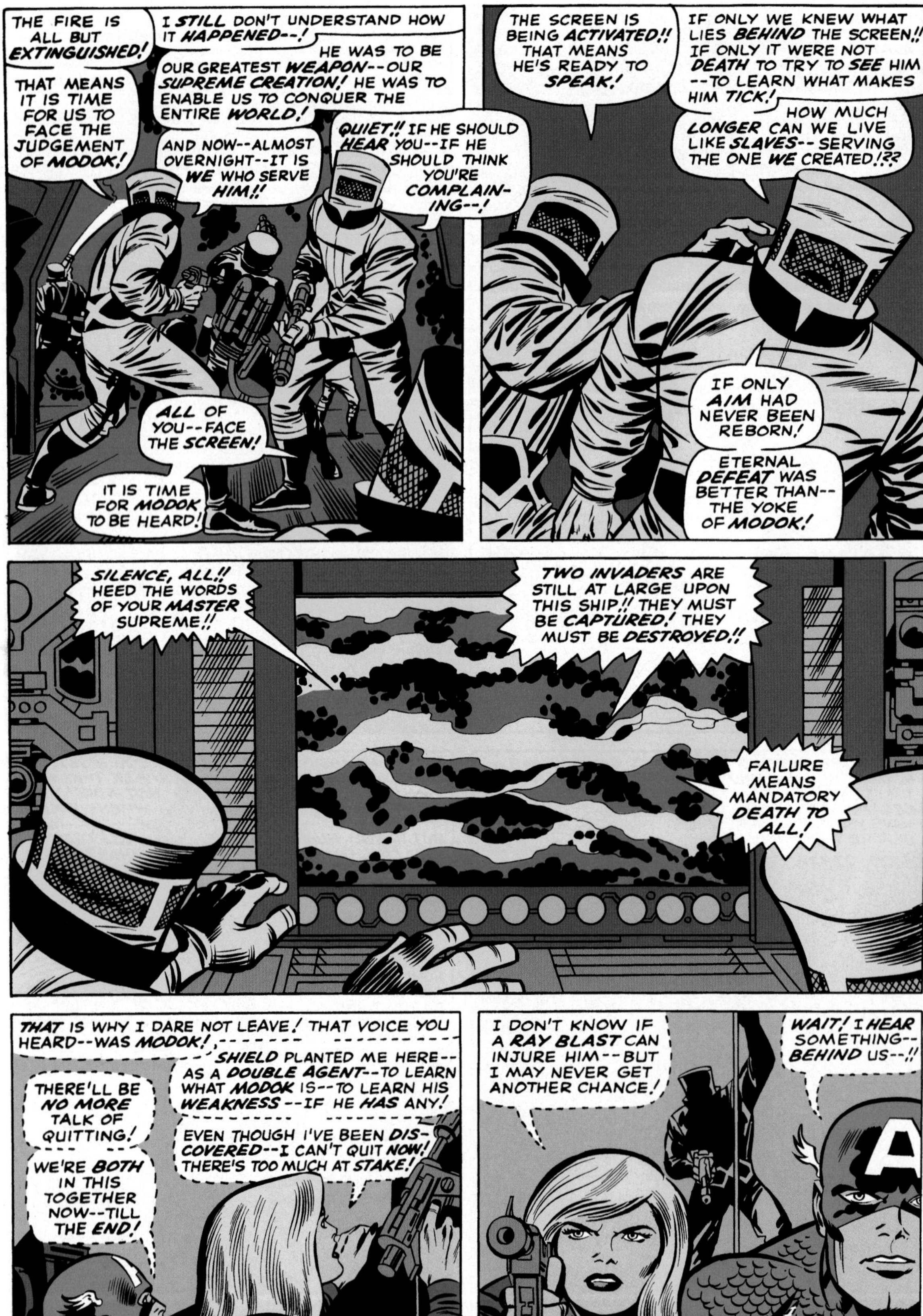

THE FIRE IS ALL BUT EXTINGUISHED!
THAT MEANS IT IS TIME FOR US TO FACE THE JUDGEMENT OF MODOK!
I STILL DON'T UNDERSTAND HOW IT HAPPENED--!
HE WAS TO BE OUR GREATEST WEAPON--OUR SUPREME CREATION! HE WAS TO ENABLE US TO CONQUER THE ENTIRE WORLD!
AND NOW--ALMOST OVERNIGHT--IT IS WE WHO SERVE HIM!!
QUIET!! IF HE SHOULD HEAR YOU--IF HE SHOULD THINK YOU'RE COMPLAIN-ING--!
ALL OF YOU--FACE THE SCREEN!
IT IS TIME FOR MODOK TO BE HEARD!

THE SCREEN IS BEING ACTIVATED!! THAT MEANS HE'S READY TO SPEAK!
IF ONLY WE KNEW WHAT LIES BEHIND THE SCREEN!! IF ONLY IT WERE NOT DEATH TO TRY TO SEE HIM --TO LEARN WHAT MAKES HIM TICK!
HOW MUCH LONGER CAN WE LIVE LIKE SLAVES-- SERVING THE ONE WE CREATED!??
IF ONLY AIM HAD NEVER BEEN REBORN!
ETERNAL DEFEAT WAS BETTER THAN-- THE YOKE OF MODOK!

I'LL THROW UP MY ARMS--
CATCH HIS ATTENTION--
MAKE HIM FIRE AT ME--
SO THAT SHE'LL BE--
UNHHH!!
I CAN'T!! I CAN'T FIRE AT MODOK NOT WHILE YOU'RE IN DANGER--!

OH, CAP!! I-I WAS TOO LATE!!
HE HIT YOU WITH A PARALYZER RAY!! YOU SACRIFICED YOURSELF--FOR ME!
CAN--HARDLY SPEAK--BUT--MUST TELL YOU--
ESCAPE--WHILE YOU CAN--JOB IS--TOO BIG FOR ONE GIRL!
FURY--WILL SEND--OTHERS!--FORGET ABOUT ME! GET AWAY--GET AWAY--!

I CAN'T!! I CAN'T LEAVE YOU!
I'VE NEVER SEEN YOU--WITHOUT YOUR MASK--AND YOU DON'T EVEN KNOW MY NAME!
YET--I FEEL AS THOUGH SOME MYSTERIOUS BOND--IS LINKING US TOGETHER--FOREVER!
NO!! SAVE YOURSELF!! YOU MUST!! YOU MUST--!!
IT'S TOO LATE! YOUR FATE IS MY FATE NOW--AND I'M NOT AFRAID!

IT'S THE ONE WHO BETRAYED US!! SEIZE HER!
WHATEVER YOU DO TO ME--OR TO CAPTAIN AMERICA--DOESN'T MATTER!
SHIELD KNOWS THAT AIM IS REBORN!! AND THEY KNOW ABOUT--MODOK!
9

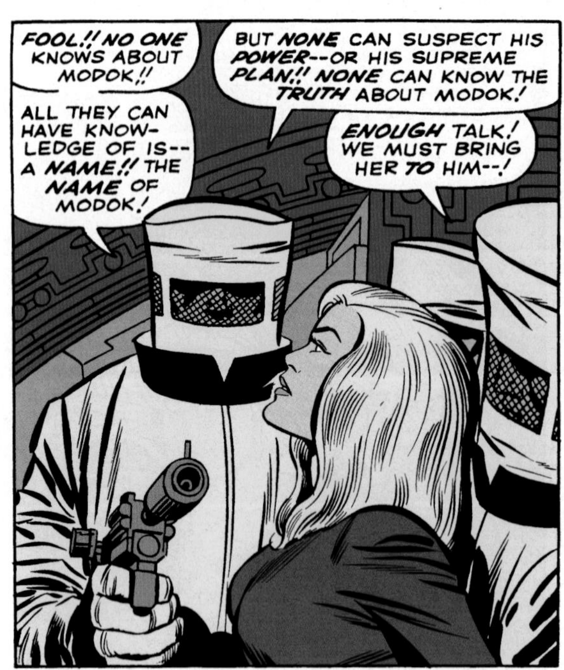
FOOL!! NO ONE KNOWS ABOUT MODOK!!
ALL THEY CAN HAVE KNOWLEDGE OF IS--A NAME!! THE NAME OF MODOK!
BUT NONE CAN SUSPECT HIS POWER--OR HIS SUPREME PLAN!! NONE CAN KNOW THE TRUTH ABOUT MODOK!
ENOUGH TALK! WE MUST BRING HER TO HIM--!

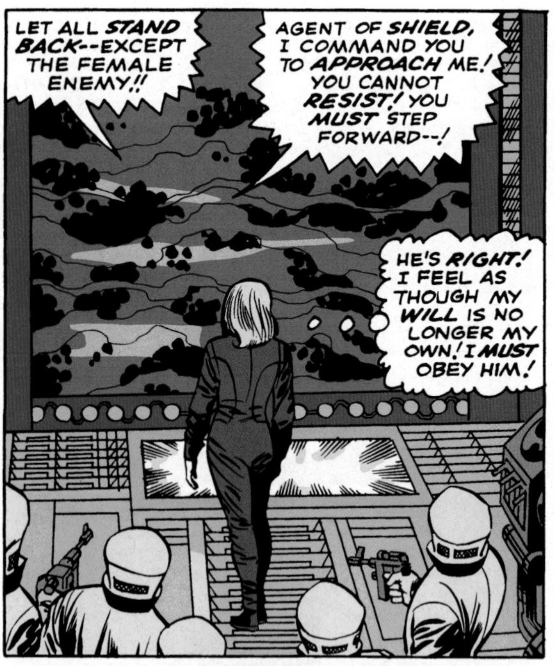
LET ALL STAND BACK--EXCEPT THE FEMALE ENEMY!!
AGENT OF SHIELD, I COMMAND YOU TO APPROACH ME! YOU CANNOT RESIST! YOU MUST STEP FORWARD--!
HE'S RIGHT! I FEEL AS THOUGH MY WILL IS NO LONGER MY OWN! I MUST OBEY HIM!

THE FLOOR PANEL BELOW ME--IT'S BEGINNING TO GLOW--WITH SOME STRANGE, RADIANT LIGHT--

I'M STARTING TO SINK--TO DESCEND INTO THE FLOOR ITSELF--!
MODOK IS DOING IT!! BUT--HOW?? WHY??
WHERE--IS HE TAKING ME--??

AND--ONLY A FEW YARDS AWAY--THE TORTURED EARS OF CAPTAIN AMERICA HEAR THE GIRL'S FINAL SCREAM--AS HE LIES MOTIONLESS--HELPLESS--UNABLE TO LIFT A FINGER--
HAVE I--FAILED HER--JUST AS I FAILED BUCKY--THOSE LONG YEARS AGO??
BUT THEN--IN THE SPACE OF A SINGLE, ANGUISHED HEARTBEAT--

YOU HAVE TOO OFTEN ESCAPED US IN THE PAST--!
YOU WILL NOT ESCAPE US AGAIN!!

THUS, WITHOUT ANY FURTHER ADO, CAPTAIN AMERICA--
--YOU NOW SHALL DIE!
NEXT
IF THIS BE MODOK!

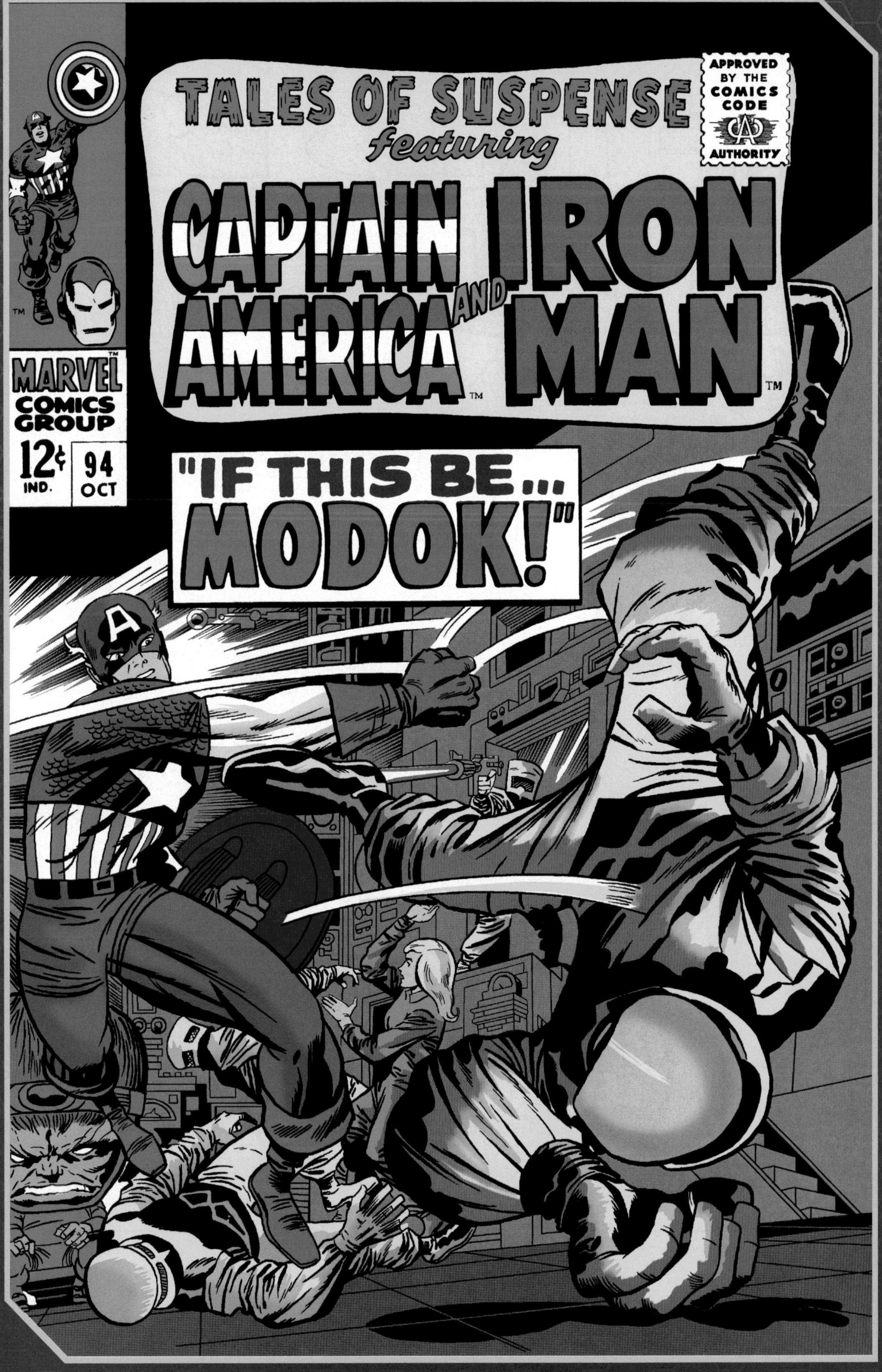
TALES OF SUSPENSE
featuring
CAPTAIN AMERICA AND IRON MAN
APPROVED BY THE COMICS CODE AUTHORITY
MARVEL COMICS GROUP
12¢ IND.
94 OCT
"IF THIS BE... MODOK!"

CAPTAIN AMERICA, LIVING LEGEND of WORLD WAR II
"IF THIS BE... MODOK!"
WITHOUT ANY FURTHER ADO, CAPTAIN AMERICA...
...YOU NOW, SHALL DIE!!
THE EVIL ORGANIZATION KNOWN AS A.I.M. NOW LIVES AGAIN! ONLY CAPTAIN AMERICA CAN RESCUE THE LOVELY AGENT OF SHIELD WHO HAS BEEN CAPTURED WHILE TRYING TO LEARN AIM'S GREATEST SECRET--THE IDENTITY OF MODOK!
BUT, CAP HIMSELF IS NOW A PRISONER OF AIM, REBORN--!
FROM THE TITANIC TYPEWRITER AND PEERLESS PENCIL OF
STAN (THE MAN) LEE and JACK (KING) KIRBY
EMBELLISHED BY: JOE SINNOTT
LETTERED BY: SAM ROSEN
IS THIS THE END OF CAPTAIN AMERICA? SOMEHOW WE DOUBT IT! LET'S TURN THE PAGE AND SEE IF WE'LL NEED A REPLACEMENT..

STOP!! HAVE YOU FORGOTTEN MODOK??
HIS ORDERS ARE THAT ONLY HE MAY GIVE THE COMMAND TO DISPOSE OF A PRISONER!
MODOK! MODOK!! HOW MUCH LONGER MUST WE SERVE THE ONE WHOM WE OURSELVES CREATED?
WATCH YOUR TONGUE!! MODOK'S EARS ARE EVERYWHERE!
NO! IF WE ARE EVER TO REBEL--IT MUST BE NOW!
NOW.. WHILE MODOK IS BUSY INTERROGATING THE FEMALE AGENT OF SHIELD!

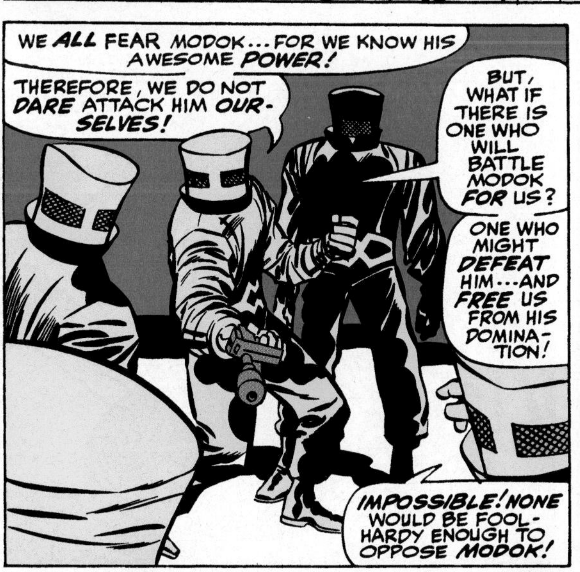
WE ALL FEAR MODOK... FOR WE KNOW HIS AWESOME POWER!
THEREFORE, WE DO NOT DARE ATTACK HIM OUR-SELVES!
BUT, WHAT IF THERE IS ONE WHO WILL BATTLE MODOK FOR US?
ONE WHO MIGHT DEFEAT HIM---AND FREE US FROM HIS DOMINA-TION!
IMPOSSIBLE! NONE WOULD BE FOOL-HARDY ENOUGH TO OPPOSE MODOK!

CAPTAIN AMERICA WOULD DO IT---IN ORDER TO SAVE THE GIRL!
AND, WHETHER HE SUCCEEDS OR NOT IS UNIMPORTANT!
WHAT DOES MATTER IS..WHILE MODOK BATTLES THE AVENGER, WE WILL BE FREE TO FOLLOW OUR OWN PLAN!
AIM
EXCELLENT!! WE'LL DO IT!

QUIET NOW... WHILE I CONTACT HIM--!
WE HAVE TAKEN CAPTAIN AMERICA PRISONER! DO YOU WISH TO STUDY HIM BEFORE HE IS.. DISPOSED OF?
I SO DESIRE! BRING HIM TO ME!

IT WORKED!..ONCE THEY MEET, THERE MUST BE A BATTLE!
EVEN IF IT MEANS PLAYING INTO AIM'S HANDS..I'VE GOT TO RESCUE THE GIRL FROM MODOK!... I DARE NOT FAIL!
2.

I'M SINKING... DOWNWARD..!
THEY'RE DISPERSING THE MOLECULES OF THE FLOOR... AS THEY DID WITH---HER!

ONLY THE INVENTIVE GENIUS OF AN OUTFIT LIKE AIM COULD HAVE CREATED SUCH A METHOD OF BRIDGING SPACE!
IF ONLY THAT SAME GENIUS WASN'T DEDICATED TO EVIL!

THE PARALYSIS RAY THAT HELD ME MOTIONLESS IS GONE!
I CAN MOVE AGAIN... I CAN FIGHT-- THE SAME AS EVER!

THIS TIME.. IF I DON'T COME OUT ON TOP... I'LL HAVE ONLY MYSELF TO BLAME!
WHOEVER... OR WHATEVER MODOK IS... HE MUST HAVE A WEAK SPOT...
AND, IF HE DOES.. I'LL FIND IT!

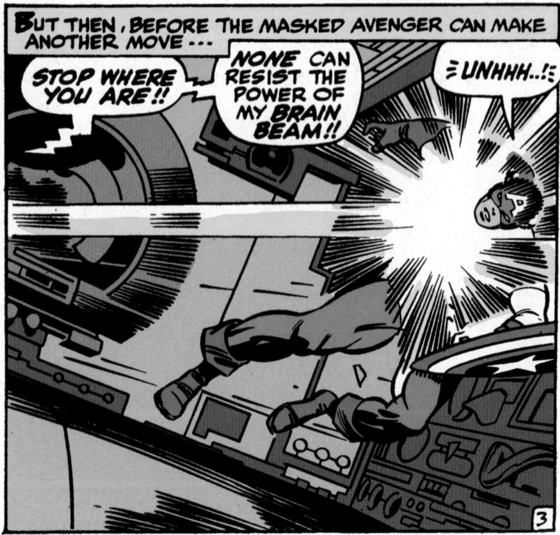
BUT THEN, BEFORE THE MASKED AVENGER CAN MAKE ANOTHER MOVE---
STOP WHERE YOU ARE!!
NONE CAN RESIST THE POWER OF MY BRAIN BEAM!!
UNHHH..!
3

I AM MODOK!!
ONCE, I WAS A MERE HUMAN GUINEA PIG FOR THE SCIENTISTS OF AIM!
BUT, THEY DID THEIR JOB TOO WELL.. AND NOW--
I AM THEIR MASTER!!
CAP.. BE CAREFUL! HIS BRAIN IS HIS WEAPON!
HE CAN USE IT TO CONTROL... TO FIGHT.. AND, IF HE DESIRES... TO DESTROY!!

I AM AWARE THAT YOU SEEK TO GOAD ME INTO ACTION --- HOPING TO FIND A WEAK CHINK IN MY MENTAL ARMOR!
BUT, YOU WILL FIND INSTEAD THAT I DO MORE THAN TALK A GREAT FIGHT---
MY INVINCIBLE MIND BEAM IS THE GREATEST SINGLE WEAPON EVER UNLEASHED!!

SEE HOW EASILY IT CAN BE ANCHORED TO YOUR SHIELD.. LIFTING YOU HELPLESSLY INTO THE AIR--!
COULDN'T DODGE!! --HIS BEAM IS.. TOO FAST!
BUT THERE ARE MANY TYPES OF MIND BEAMS..

FOR EXAMPLE.. THIS---IS AN INFALLIBLE STUN-SHOCK BEAM--!

---WHICH CAN BE INSTANTLY FOLLOWED BY A SIMPLE BLAST CAPABLE OF SHATTERING A STEEL FLOOR---
---AND THEN HURLING THE PIECES AT ANY TARGET I SO DESIRE!
SO FAR YOUR SHIELD HAS PROTECTED YOU---
BUT, LET US SEE WHAT HAPPENS NEXT..!

A HEAT BEAM.. MAKING THE FLOOR RED HOT BENEATH MY FEET!
BUT I CAN'T GIVE IN! I'VE GOT TO KEEP DODGING---KEEP FIGHTING---
SOONER OR LATER HE'LL MAKE A SLIP..!! AND WHEN HE DOES..!

WHILE, IN ANOTHER CHAMBER OF THE HIDDEN SUBMARINE---
IT IS WORKING EXACTLY AS PLANNED!
CAPTAIN AMERICA IS PUTTING UP A MASTERFUL DEFENSE.. OCCUPYING ALL OF MODOK'S ATTENTION!
THEREFORE, THE MOMENT HAS COME..FOR US TO.. ATTACK!
5.

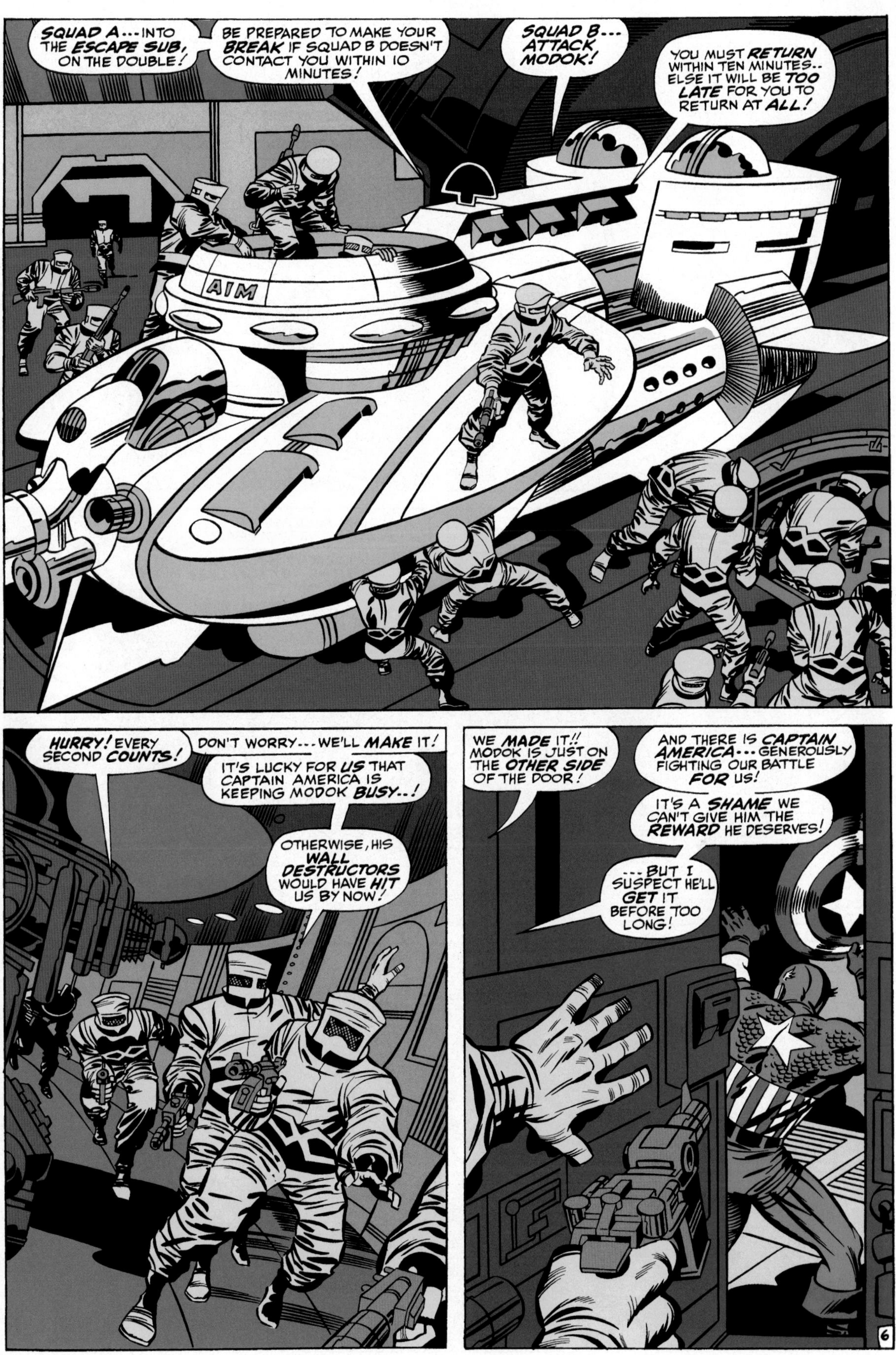

SQUAD A... INTO THE ESCAPE SUB, ON THE DOUBLE!
BE PREPARED TO MAKE YOUR BREAK IF SQUAD B DOESN'T CONTACT YOU WITHIN 10 MINUTES!
SQUAD B... ATTACK MODOK!
YOU MUST RETURN WITHIN TEN MINUTES.. ELSE IT WILL BE TOO LATE FOR YOU TO RETURN AT ALL!
AIM

HURRY! EVERY SECOND COUNTS!
DON'T WORRY... WE'LL MAKE IT!
IT'S LUCKY FOR US THAT CAPTAIN AMERICA IS KEEPING MODOK BUSY..!
OTHERWISE, HIS WALL DESTRUCTORS WOULD HAVE HIT US BY NOW!

WE MADE IT!! MODOK IS JUST ON THE OTHER SIDE OF THE DOOR!
AND THERE IS CAPTAIN AMERICA... GENEROUSLY FIGHTING OUR BATTLE FOR US!
IT'S A SHAME WE CAN'T GIVE HIM THE REWARD HE DESERVES!
...BUT I SUSPECT HE'LL GET IT BEFORE TOO LONG!
6

MEANWHILE, THE ONLY THOUGHT ON CAPTAIN AMERICA'S MIND IS--- SMASH MODOK!!
NOTHING STOPS HIM!
PERHAPS IF I THROW MY SHIELD...FAST ENOUGH--!

HAVE YOU NOT YET LEARNED--?
NOTHING MOVES FASTER THAN THE SPEED OF THOUGHT!
HE STOPPED IT.. WITH ONE SINGLE MIND BLAST!

---ONLY ONE THING LEFT TO DO--!
I'LL TACKLE HIM EMPTY-HANDED!!
CAP.. WAIT!! LOOK OUT... BEHIND YOU--!!

A SUDDEN FUSILADE OF SHELLS---OVER MY HEAD!!
IF YOU HADN'T STOPPED ME IN TIME--BY TACKLING ME THE WAY YOU DID--!!
SPTOK!

BUT, LOOK!! THE SHOTS WERE REALLY INTENDED FOR MODOK!
IT WAS MY BATTLE WITH HIM THAT GAVE THEM THE CHANCE THEY NEEDED!!
THEY CAUGHT HIM BY SURPRISE-- AND THEIR ATTACK WORKED!! HE'S DONE FOR!
7.

KEEP FIRING!! MAKE SURE HE'S FINISHED!!
ENOUGH! DON'T WASTE ANY MORE TIME ON MODOK!
LET'S GET CAPTAIN AMERICA OUT OF THE PICTURE... WHILE WE CAN!

I'VE GOT NEWS FOR YOU CLOWNS..!
YOU CAN'T!!
STAY BEHIND ME, LADY! THIS TIME I KNOW WHAT I'M FIGHTING..
SO IT'S GONNA BE MY INNING NOW!

SPANG!

KHBONNK!
8.

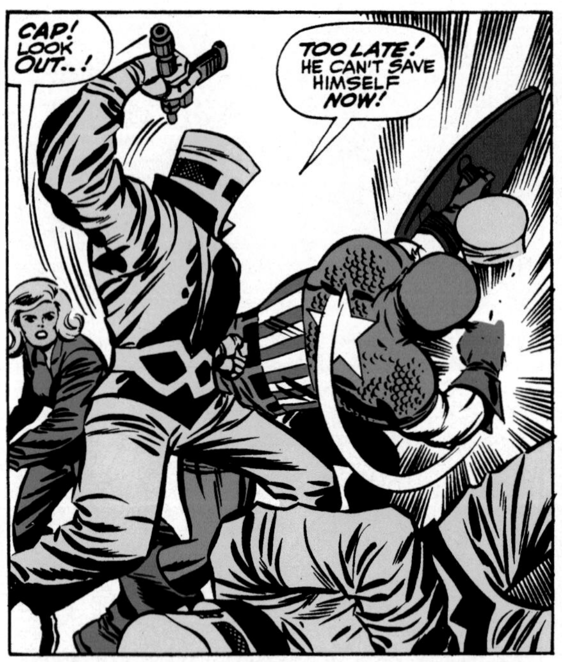
CAP! LOOK OUT..!
TOO LATE! HE CAN'T SAVE HIMSELF NOW!

MAYBE HE CAN'T---
BUT I CAN!
FZAT!

GOOD GOING, GIRL!
BUT, OUR JOB ISN'T OVER YET!
IF THEY'VE REVOLTED AGAINST MODOK, THE OTHERS MUST BE MAKING A GETAWAY!
AND WE'RE GONNA STOP THEM!

BUT, AT THAT VERY MOMENT...
THE TEN MINUTES ARE UP! THEY HAVEN'T RETURNED!
WE CAN AFFORD TO WAIT NO LONGER!
EVERYTHING IS IN READINESS FOR INSTANT DEPARTURE!

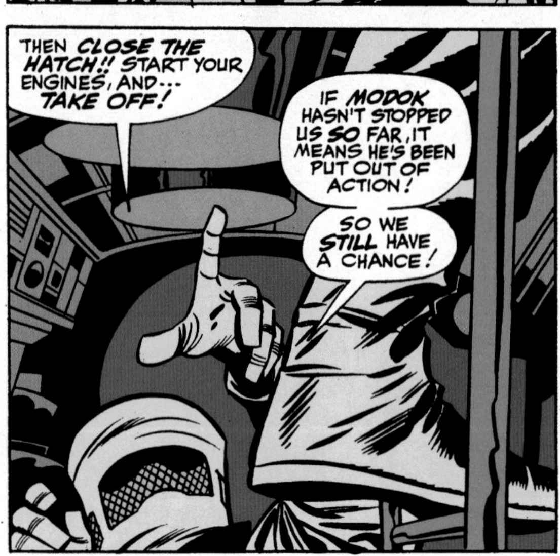
THEN CLOSE THE HATCH!! START YOUR ENGINES, AND... TAKE OFF!
IF MODOK HASN'T STOPPED US SO FAR, IT MEANS HE'S BEEN PUT OUT OF ACTION!
SO WE STILL HAVE A CHANCE!

THE HATCH!! IT WON'T CLOSE!!
WAIT! WHAT'S THAT?!!
THE SHIELD OF CAPTAIN AMERICA!!
HE'S FREE AGAIN... AND HE'S FOUND US!!
9.

WHILE, IN ANOTHER PART OF THE SUB, A DYING FIGURE SUMMONS HIS LAST REMAINING VESTIGE OF POWER...
MODOK... MUST NOT DIE --- LIKE ANY HELPLESS BEING--!
FOR... ONCE I POSSESSED.. THE POWER... TO CHANGE THE WORLD!.!

THEREFORE.. I MUST PERISH -- IN A MANNER.. BEFITTING.. THE MASTER SUPREME!!
MEN MUST TALK.. OF MY LAST FEW SECONDS -- FOR AS LONG AS -- LEGENDS ENDURE..!
AND... SO THEY SHALL..!

I'VE REACHED... THE EMERGENCY DETONATOR!!! NOW -- IF I CAN -- INCREASE..THE PRESSURE..!

AND, AS MODOK'S UNCANNY MENTAL PRESSURE BEGINS TO MOUNT...
..A SMALL, SPEEDY ESCAPE SUB STREAKS FROM THE MOTHER SHIP SEEKING THE SAFETY OF THE DEEP..!

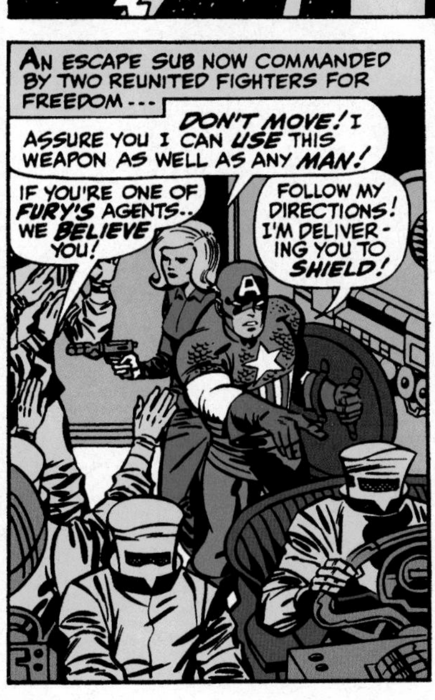
AN ESCAPE SUB NOW COMMANDED BY TWO REUNITED FIGHTERS FOR FREEDOM ---
DON'T MOVE! I ASSURE YOU I CAN USE THIS WEAPON AS WELL AS ANY MAN!
IF YOU'RE ONE OF FURY'S AGENTS.. WE BELIEVE YOU!
FOLLOW MY DIRECTIONS! I'M DELIVERING YOU TO SHIELD!

YOU SAVED MY LIFE... YET, I'VE NEVER EVEN TOLD YOU MY NAME! NOR HAVE I EVER SEEN YOUR FACE.. BENEATH THAT MASK!
HOW STRANGE... IT TOOK MODOK TO BRING US TOGETHER AGAIN! AND NOW --- WE DON'T EVEN KNOW IF HE'S ALIVE --- OR DEAD!
LISTEN!! THAT EXPLOSION --- FROM AFAR!

I THINK YOU CAN FORGET ABOUT MODOK NOW!
YOUR QUESTION HAS JUST BEEN.. ANSWERED!
NEXT
THE DEATH OF A LEGEND!
10

CAPT. AMERICA
15¢ 133 JAN

APPROVED BY THE COMICS CODE AUTHORITY

CAPTAIN AMERICA

THE POWER OF-- BULLDOZER

MARVEL COMICS GROUP

EXTRA! THE ORIGIN OF MODOK!

MAD-NESS IN THE SLUMS!

CO-STARRING: the FALCON!

CAPTAIN AMERICA, LIVING LEGEND of WORLD WAR II
MADNESS IN THE SLUMS!
IN THE HIDDEN HEADQUARTERS OF AIM (ADVANCED IDEA MECHANICS), THE MONSTROUS MODOK SUMMONS TWO FEARFUL, TREMBLING AIDES---
FEATURING: THE FALCON AND THE TERRIBLE THREAT OF THE BULLDOZER MAN!
BY: STAN LEE AUTHOR GENE COLAN ILLUSTRATOR DICK AYERS EMBELLISHER SAM ROSEN LETTERER
THE ANDROID BUCKY BARNES THAT WAS SUPPOSED TO DESTROY CAPTAIN AMERICA HAS FAILED!
AND WELL YOU KNOW MODOK'S PRICE FOR FAILURE!
4282

MASTER, NO! IT WAS NOT OUR FAULT!
WE HAVE BEEN LOYAL, MODOK! YOU MUST BE MERCIFUL!
WE DID NOTHING BUT CARRY OUT YOUR ORDERS!

WHAT?!! YOU DARE SPEAK TO ME OF MERCY?
TO ME-- WHO HAS SUFFERED AT THE HANDS OF AIM MORE THAN ANY LIVING BEING HAS EVER SUFFERED BEFORE?!!
THIS IS THE MERCY OF MODOK!

ZAK

SO COULD I ALSO DESTROY CAPTAIN AMERICA!
BUT IT WOULD BE TOO SIMPLE -- IT WOULD BE TOO QUICK!
TOO MANY TIMES HAS HE BESTED ME-- FOILED ME!
TOO MANY WOUNDS DO I CARRY TO LET HIM OFF SO EASILY!
HE MUST BE MADE TO SUFFER AS I HAVE SUFFERED--
AS ALL HAVE MADE ME SUFFER!
2.

WHEN I THINK OF HIM-- SO STRAIGHT, AND TALL, AND HANDSOME..
AND THEN I SEE--- MYSELF!

I HATE HIM ALL THE MORE-- FOR HE IS WHAT I WAS-- WHAT I CAN NEVER BE AGAIN!

NEVER! NEVER! NEV

"I'LL NEVER FORGET THAT DAY-- THAT HORRIBLE, UN-BELIEVABLE DAY-- WHEN I WAS BROUGHT BEFORE THE AIM SCIENTIST SUPREME--"
NO! NO! I'VE DONE NOTHING! NOTHING!
SILENCE! THE SUPREME ONE NEEDS A VOLUNTEER--
AND YOU ARE HE!

PLACE HIM IN THE ALTERATION CHAMBER!
NO! NO!
DON'T! YOU CAN'T-- YOU MUSTN'T!

YOUR CRIES ARE USELESS! YOUR FATE IS SEALED!
3.

YOU ARE A NOTHING-- A NOBODY-- ONE OF THE COUNTLESS, NAMELESS AGENTS OF AIM!
ON
BUT, WHEN WE HAVE FINISHED--

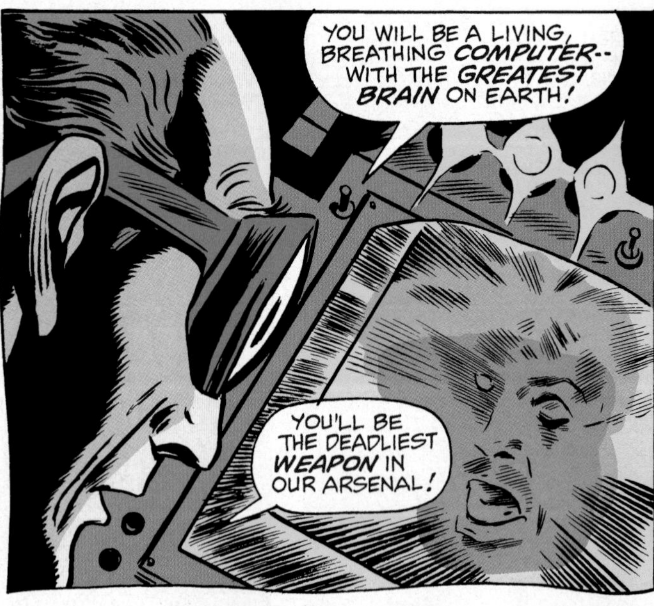
YOU WILL BE A LIVING, BREATHING COMPUTER-- WITH THE GREATEST BRAIN ON EARTH!
YOU'LL BE THE DEADLIEST WEAPON IN OUR ARSENAL!

24 HOURS LATER--
IT IS DONE!
WE HAVE CREATED THE ULTIMATE INTELLI-GENCE!

WE'LL CALL HIM MODOK-- SINCE HE IS A MENTAL ORGANISM, DESIGNED ONLY FOR KILLING!
BUT-- LOOK AT HIM! HE HAS BECOME A FREAK--AN INHUMAN MON-STROSITY!

WHAT AM I? WHAT HAVE YOU DONE TO ME? WHAT HAVE YOU DONE?
YOU ARE NOW MODOK-- YOU ARE THE MOST POWERFUL BRAIN ALIVE!
WITH YOU SERVING THE CAUSE OF AIM, NOTHING CAN EVER STOP US!
4

"BUT, IN THEIR CRUELTY, THEIR BLINDNESS, THEY HAD MADE ONE FATAL ERROR--"
THEY'VE MADE ME STRONGER THAN THEY KNOW!
I HAVE THE POWER TO MENTALLY DESTROY THEM ALL!
THEREFORE-- IT IS THEY WHO SHALL SERVE MODOK!
AND THOSE WHO REFUSE-- MUST DIE!

WITH A SINGLE BRAIN BLAST, I INSTANTLY SLEW THE SCIENTIST SUPREME!
WITHIN THE HOUR, THE FORCES OF AIM WERE MINE TO COMMAND!
BUT STILL I REMAIN A GROTESQUE AND PITIFUL FREAK--- IMPRISONED IN A NIGHTMARE FORM!

AND NOW, ALL MY HATRED-- ALL MY LOATHING-- IS CENTERED ON ONE MAN-- THE MAN WHO IS EVERYTHING THAT I AM NOT! THE MAN WHO STANDS FOR EVERYTHING I DO NOT!
CAPTAIN AMERICA! --THE MAN I MUST DESTROY!

I CAN STILL RECREATE THE SCENE OF A FEW DAYS AGO--WHEN HE SURVIVED THE ATTACK OF THE ANDROID BUCKY BARNES, WHOM I HAD SENT TO KILL HIM!

LITTLE DID HE DREAM I WAS MENTALLY VIEWING THE ENTIRE AFFAIR-- UNTIL THE TIME HE BURIED THE FALLEN ANDROID!
TO THINK THAT I, MODOK, SHOULD HAVE TO VIEW MY OWN FAILURE!*
NO WONDER MY SOUL CRIES OUT-- REVENGE! REVENGE!
*WE WATCHED IT ALL TOGETHER, LAST ISH--REMEMBER?: STAN.
5

NOW, USING MY MATCHLESS CYBERNETIC POWER, I MUST MENTALLY FIND MY COSTUMED FOE!

ALL I NEED DO IS THINK OF HIM--- AND LET MY MIND FLOW FREE--

AN IMAGE FORMS! I SEE THE TEEMING STREETS OF NEW YORK'S HARLEM---

AND THERE HE IS-- WITH HIS ONE-TIME FRIEND AND ALLY-- THE FAST-MOVING, FIGHTING FALCON!

IT DOES NOT MATTER THAT I CANNOT HEAR THEIR WORDS!
I HAVE FOUND HIM-- THUS, IT IS TIME TO STRIKE!
THE FOOLS! THEY SEEK TO MAKE THEIR WORLD A BETTER PLACE--
--LITTLE DREAMING THAT THEIR TIME HAS JUST RUN OUT!
FOR, I HAVE EVOLVED MY PLAN-- AND THIS ONE CANNOT FAIL!
6

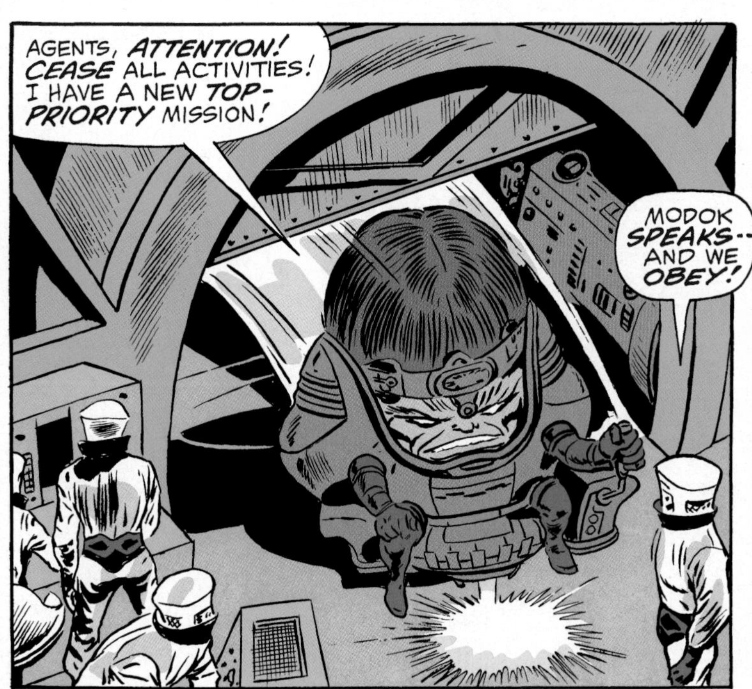
AGENTS, ATTENTION! CEASE ALL ACTIVITIES! I HAVE A NEW TOP-PRIORITY MISSION!
MODOK SPEAKS-- AND WE OBEY!

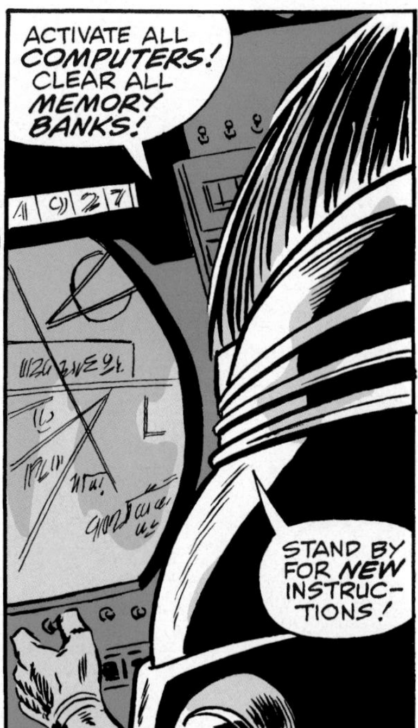
ACTIVATE ALL COMPUTERS! CLEAR ALL MEMORY BANKS!
STAND BY FOR NEW INSTRUCTIONS!

MOVING, PLANNING, COMPUTING-- FASTER THAN ANY MERE MACHINE-- THE MYSTERIOUS MODOK SETS HIS SUPER-HUMAN BRAIN TO WORK, AS HIS OBEDIENT AGENTS CARRY OUT HIS EVERY COMMAND--

THEN, IN A MATTER OF HOURS---
PREPARATIONS ARE COMPLETE!

THE MASTER HAS REDESIGNED THE ALL-POWERFUL ALTERATION CHAMBER!
NOW HE WILL CREATE A MONSTER --OUT OF LIFELESS CLAY!
7.

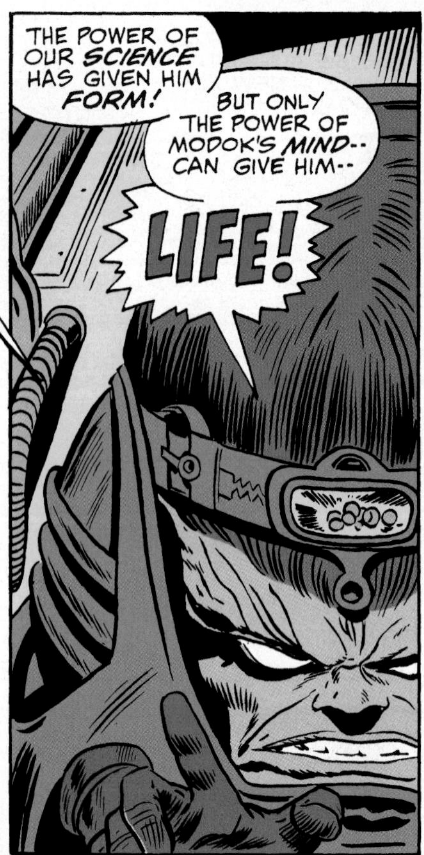

HE MOVES! HE BREATHES! THE MASTER HAS SUCCEEDED!

THE DIE IS CAST! CAPTAIN AMERICA AT LAST IS DOOMED!

8

ALL IS IN READINESS! PREPARE TO LAUNCH!
THE VICTIMS WAIT-- AT TARGET ZERO!

MASTER! THE CARGO IS ABOARD!
THE TIME IS COME!
LET ALL STAND BACK!

LAUNCH!
BRRRR

AND SO IT'S DONE!
NOTHING CAN SAVE THE MASKED AVENGER NOW!

AIM
AIM
NOTHING CAN SAVE HIM-- OR ANY OTHER MAN WHO WALKS THE EARTH--
--FROM THE POWER OF --MY LIVING BULLDOZER!
9.

HOW DOES MODOK PLAN TO DISCREDIT CAPTAIN AMERICA BY USE OF THE BULLDOZER?
IT IS NOT FOR US TO KNOW!
OUR TASK IS MERELY TO DELIVER HIM TO HIS DESTINATION!

WE HAVE ARRIVED!
HERE, ON THIS LONELY STRETCH OF NEW JERSEY MARSHLANDS, NONE WILL REACH US IN TIME TO INTERFERE!
THE PROGRAMMING IS PERFECT! HE BEGINS TO STIR!
AIM

AT NEWARK AIRPORT--
UNIDENTIFIED AIRCRAFT--- DOWN IN THE MARSHLANDS!
WHAT IN BLAZES CAN IT BE?

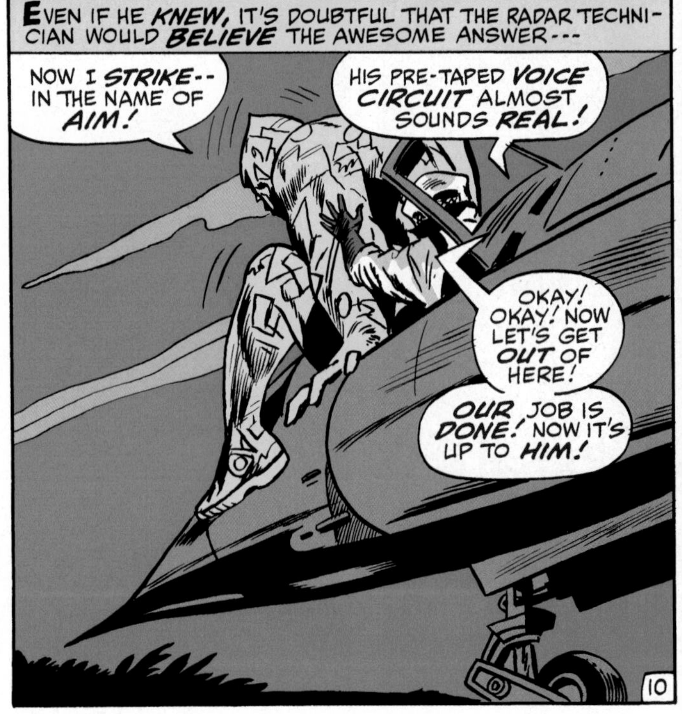
EVEN IF HE KNEW, IT'S DOUBTFUL THAT THE RADAR TECHNICIAN WOULD BELIEVE THE AWESOME ANSWER---
NOW I STRIKE-- IN THE NAME OF AIM!
HIS PRE-TAPED VOICE CIRCUIT ALMOST SOUNDS REAL!
OKAY! OKAY! NOW LET'S GET OUT OF HERE!
OUR JOB IS DONE! NOW IT'S UP TO HIM!
10

MINUTES LATER, AT THE ENTRANCE TO THE LINCOLN TUNNEL ---
I MUST PASS THRU THE TUNNEL!
NOTHING MUST KEEP ME FROM REACHING MY GOAL!
PKOW!
HE'S THREE STORIES HIGH-- WITH FISTS LIKE BATTERING RAMS!
I HOPE THAT GOAL OF HIS IS FAR FROM HERE!

AND JUDGING BY THE WAY HE DOESN'T EVEN FEEL MY BULLETS--
I'M BETTING HE REACHES IT EASY!
SPTANG!

OUR GUNFIRE'S USELESS! WE MIGHT AS WELL LET 'IM GO!
THEY'LL STOP 'IM AT THE OTHER SIDE!
PTHOOM!
KRAK!
I WOULDN'T BET ON IT, JOE!

BUT HOW, HOW, HOW DO YOU STOP-- THE UNSTOPABLE?
I HAVE REACHED THE AREA CALLED HARLEM!
NOW I MUST DO AS MODOK COMMANDS!

WHILE NEARBY---
WHY HAVE YOU ALLOWED ME TO SEE YOU WITHOUT YOUR MASK?
FOR A GOOD REASON, SAM--
11.

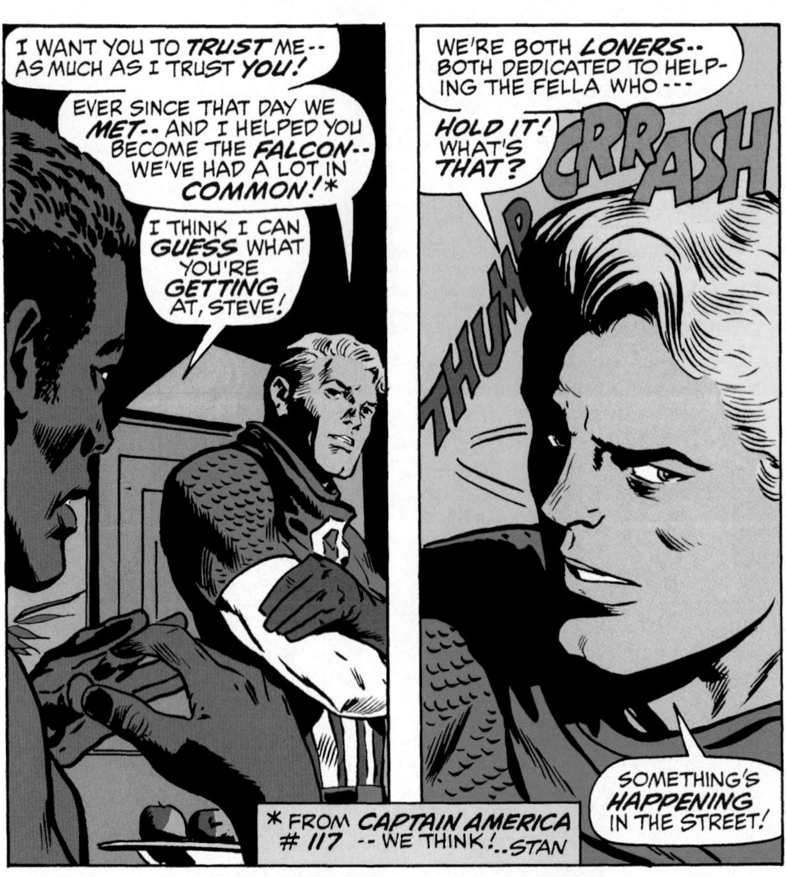
I WANT YOU TO TRUST ME-- AS MUCH AS I TRUST YOU!
EVER SINCE THAT DAY WE MET-- AND I HELPED YOU BECOME THE FALCON-- WE'VE HAD A LOT IN COMMON!*
I THINK I CAN GUESS WHAT YOU'RE GETTING AT, STEVE!
* FROM CAPTAIN AMERICA #117 -- WE THINK! ..STAN
WE'RE BOTH LONERS-- BOTH DEDICATED TO HELPING THE FELLA WHO---
HOLD IT! WHAT'S THAT?
CRRASH
THUMP
SOMETHING'S HAPPENING IN THE STREET!

THE AREA'S BEEN COOL FOR WEEKS!
I DON'T GET IT, MAN!
RRRRRUMBLE
LISTEN! IT SOUNDS LIKE WALLS COLLAPSING!
BUT I DON'T HEAR ANY BOMBS!
12

WHATEVER IT IS-- IT'S BIG TROUBLE!
SO LET'S MOVE!
IT'S LIKE GIANT HANDS-- SHAKING THE BUILDING!
OKAY MISTER-- WE'RE OFF!

THIS WHOLE NEIGHBORHOOD'S A TINDER BOX! WHATEVER HAPPENS HERE COULD ENFLAME THE ENTIRE CITY!
WHATEVER IT IS-- IT SOUNDS LIKE IT'LL TAKE BOTH OF US TO HANDLE IT!
THAT'S WHAT I WAS GETTING AT BEFORE, SAM!
MAYBE IT'S AN OMEN!
13

IN THE NAME OF AIM-- I DESTROY THESE SLUMS!

IT'S A GIANT FIGURE-- SHATTERING STONE AND BRICK WITH HIS FISTS!

THE PEOPLE ARE CHEERING HIM! THEY THINK HE'S HELPING THEM!

RIGHT ON, BULLDOZER!

FOOL! YOU CANNOT STOP THE BULL-DOZER!
BTYOIING!

GET LOST, MASKED MAN! WE DON' WANT YA HERE!
THEM BUILDINGS DESERVE TO COME DOWN!
KEEP GOIN', BULL-DOZER! LET IT BE!

MODOK PLANNED IT THIS WAY! THEY THINK HE'S BEFRIENDING THEM!

LOOKS BAD, CAP! HE'S TOO MUCH FOR US!
IN MORE WAYS THAN ONE!
HE'S GOT THE PEOPLE ON HIS SIDE!

STAY BACK! LEAVE THE BULL-DOZER BE!
TAKE IT EASY, YOU GUYS!
YOU DON'T WANNA START A RIOT!

CAN'T BLAME THE BROTHERS! ANYTHING'S BETTER THAN THOSE HOVELS THEY HAVE TO LIVE IN!
BUT THEY'RE FOOLIN' THEMSELVES --AIM DON'T CARE ABOUT 'EM!
GO, RED-WING! YOU KNOW WHAT TO DO!
15

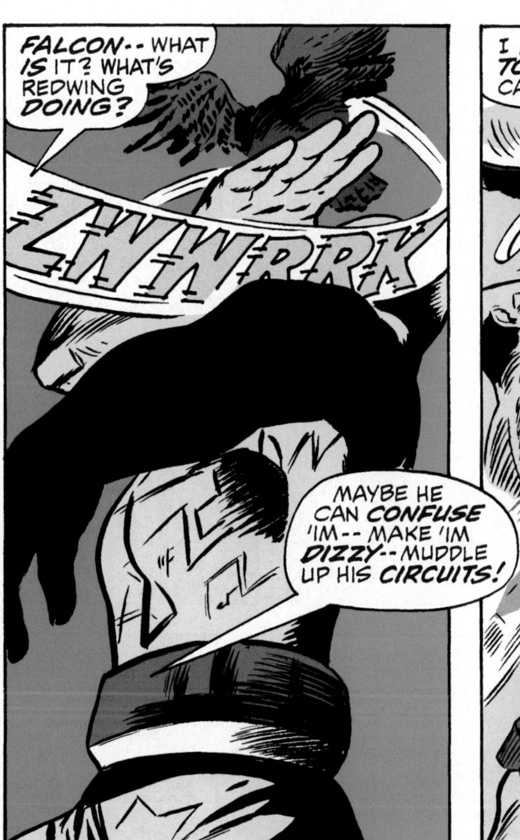
FALCON-- WHAT IS IT? WHAT'S REDWING DOING?
ZWIRRK
MAYBE HE CAN CONFUSE 'IM-- MAKE 'IM DIZZY-- MUDDLE UP HIS CIRCUITS!

I AM PROGRAMMED TOO WELL! NOTHING CAN AFFECT ME!
GET RED-WING BACK! WE'RE FIGHTING THE WRONG ENEMY!

GET OFF THE STREETS! LEAVE HIM TO US!
TRUST ME --I'VE AN IDEA!
DON'T JUST STAND THERE, MAN--
I'VE AN AVENGERS' PRIORITY!
AWWRRRK

WHILE AT MODOK'S HQ--
PERFECT! PERFECT! CAPTAIN AMERICA WILL MAKE HIMSELF HATED-- BY THE PEOPLE-- AND THE POLICE!
NO MATTER WHAT HE DOES, HIS HEROIC IMAGE WILL BE FOREVER TARNISHED!
FOCUS

WHEREVER PEOPLE SUFFER-- WHEREVER THEY ARE DOWN-TRODDEN-- THEY ARE RIPE FOR EXPLOITATION!
SO LONG AS SLUMS-- AND POVERTY--- AND RACISM EXIST-- I WILL HAVE A BREEDING GROUND FOR MY OWN FORM OF EVIL!

AND THOSE, LIKE CAPTAIN AMERICA, WHO TRULY TRY TO HELP THRU REASON AND UNDERSTANDING --WILL BE SCORNED AND DISCREDITED BY THOSE WHO HAVE BEEN BETRAYED TOO OFTEN!
THUS, I MUST CONTINUE TO INFLAME THEM-- I MUST BLIND THEM TO THE FACT THAT THEY THEM-SELVES WILL SUFFER MOST FROM VIOLENCE!
16

BUT I MUST ENJOY MY GREATEST TRIUMPH IN PERSON!
I MUST BE ON THE SCENE FOR THE DEFEAT OF CAPTAIN AMERICA!
ATTENDANT! BRING FORTH MY VEHICLE!

OKAY, AVENGER-- WE'RE LETTING HIM GO! BUT IF YOUR PLAN'S A DUD--!
CAP! WE'VE GOTTA DO SOME-THING!
YOU'RE TELLING ME?

RIGHT ON, BULLDOZER! WE'LL SHOW THE MAN WHERE IT'S AT, BABY!
THEY THINK THEY'VE FOUND A CHAMPION! THEY DON'T REALIZE THEY'RE INNOCENT PAWNS--

MINUTES LATER, AT THE LABORATORY OF TONY STARK--
CAP? YES, I HEARD IT ON THE RADIO!
WHAT CAN I DO FOR YOU?
IT'S A TALL ORDER, AVENGER-- BUT I SEE WHAT YOU'RE AFTER!
HANG IN THERE! I'LL START AT ONCE!

HE NEEDS A PORTABLE DETECTOR-- TO ANALYZE THE ROBOT'S ENERGY SOURCE!
AND, IF I CAN SWING IT---
--THAT'S EXACTLY WHAT HE'LL GET!

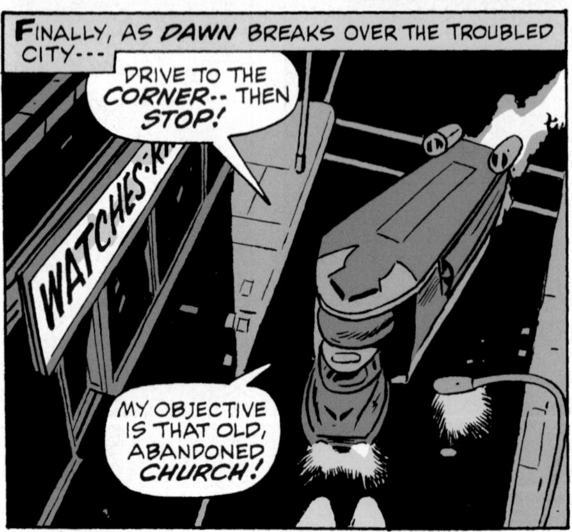
FINALLY, AS DAWN BREAKS OVER THE TROUBLED CITY---
DRIVE TO THE CORNER-- THEN STOP!
WATCHES·K
MY OBJECTIVE IS THAT OLD, ABANDONED CHURCH!

NO ONE WILL THINK TO LOOK HERE-- FOR THE LEADER OF AIM!
17.

GOOD! GOOD! NOW I SHALL DIRECT THE FINAL BATTLE--
-- AND WITNESS THE COMPLETE UNDOING OF CAPTAIN AMERICA!

BULLDOZER! I COMMAND YOU--- BEGIN YOUR RAMPAGING!
LET ME HEAR YOUR SLOGANS!
I STRIKE IN THE NAME OF AIM!
AIM SHALL CRUSH THE OPPRESSORS!

PERFECT! IF CAPTAIN AMERICA TRIES TO INTERFERE, THE PEOPLE WILL TURN ON HIM!
AND IF MY ROBOT CONTINUES UNCHECKED..
THE WORLD WILL KNOW THE AVENGER HAS FAILED!

BUT, EVEN AS THE HOVELS COLLAPSE-- A SPEEDY HAWK STREAKS OVERHEAD---
THE SLUMS ARE FALLING!
AT LEAST AIM CARES ABOUT US!

THE PACKAGE FROM STARK! AND JUST IN TIME!
LET'S HAVE IT, REDWING!
THIS OUGHT TO TELL US WHAT WE HAVE TO KNOW!

THAT'S IT! ACCORDING TO THE READINGS, BULLDOZER IS CONTROLLED BY MENTAL POWER ALONE-- THE POWER OF MODOK'S MIND!
I SHOULD HAVE GUESSED!
AND NOW WE'VE THE MEANS TO DEFEAT HIM!
18

STARK'S DEVICE CAN CYBERNETICALLY JAM MODOK'S COMMANDS--
MAKING THE ROBOT DO THE EXACT OPPOSITE!

HE'S HEADING FOR THAT ABANDONED CHURCH!
THAT MEANS IT'S THE ONE PLACE WHERE MODOK WOULDN'T WANT HIM!
THEN WHAT ARE WE WAITING FOR, CAP?
LET'S GO!

WE CAN TAKE THESE CREEPOS EASY, AVENGER!
YOU STAY WITH THEM, FALCON! PROTECT MY FLANK-- WHILE I GO AFTER MODOK!
HE'S GOTTA BE HERE SOME-WHERE!
AND THIS TIME IT'LL BE HIM OR ME!

YOU FOUND ME! BUT-- HOW?
BULL-DOZER LED ME TO YOU-- AFTER I REVERSED YOUR MENTAL COMMANDS!
HE CAN'T HELP YOU ANY MORE!
HELP? YOU THINK MIGHTY MODOK NEEDS HELP?

I CAN CRUSH YOU WITH A SIMPLE MIND BLAST!
NOT WHILE MY SHIELD CAN DEFLECT IT!

YOU'RE FINISHED, MODOK! THESE PEOPLE DESERVE BETTER THAN YOU!
THEY NEED A CHANCE --NOT CHAOS!
BUILDERS --NOT DESTROYERS!

THEY'LL GET WHAT I CHOOSE TO GIVE THEM!
I FORGOT --THE JETS BENEATH HIS CHAIR!
19.

THE BULL-DOZER! HE'S RETURNED!
I'VE GOT TO KEEP MODOK TOO BUSY TO MENTALLY COMMAND HIM!

MASTER! I AM CONFUSED! I AWAIT YOUR ORDERS!

THE FALCON BEHIND ME--- CAPTAIN AMERICA IN FRONT!
NO PLACE TO TURN-- NO PLACE TO RUN!
YOUR GUNNIES ARE FINISHED, MODOK! I SAW TO THAT!
WHERE ARE MY MEN? WHERE ARE MY AGENTS?
MASTER-- I NEED YOUR COMMAND!
IT'S WORKING! MODOK'S ON THE RUN-- HE HASN'T TIME TO THINK!

CAP! BULLDOZER'S GONE WILD! HE'S WRECKING THE PLACE!
I KNOW! LET'S GET OUT-- FAST!
BUT WHAT ABOUT MODOK?

MASTER! MASTER!
MY CHAIR! --IT'S STUCK! I-- I CAN'T MOVE!
I'M TRAPPED! TRAPPED--
--TRAPPPPPPPPPP...

IT'S OVER-- AT LAST!
NO, CAP! IT'S JUST THE BEGINNING! MY WORK HERE-- ON BEHALF OF MY PEOPLE-- HAS JUST BEGUN!
YOU MEAN-- OUR WORK!
CAPTAIN AMERICA HAS FINALLY FOUND--A PARTNER!
20.
NEXT: A NEW TEAM IS BORN!

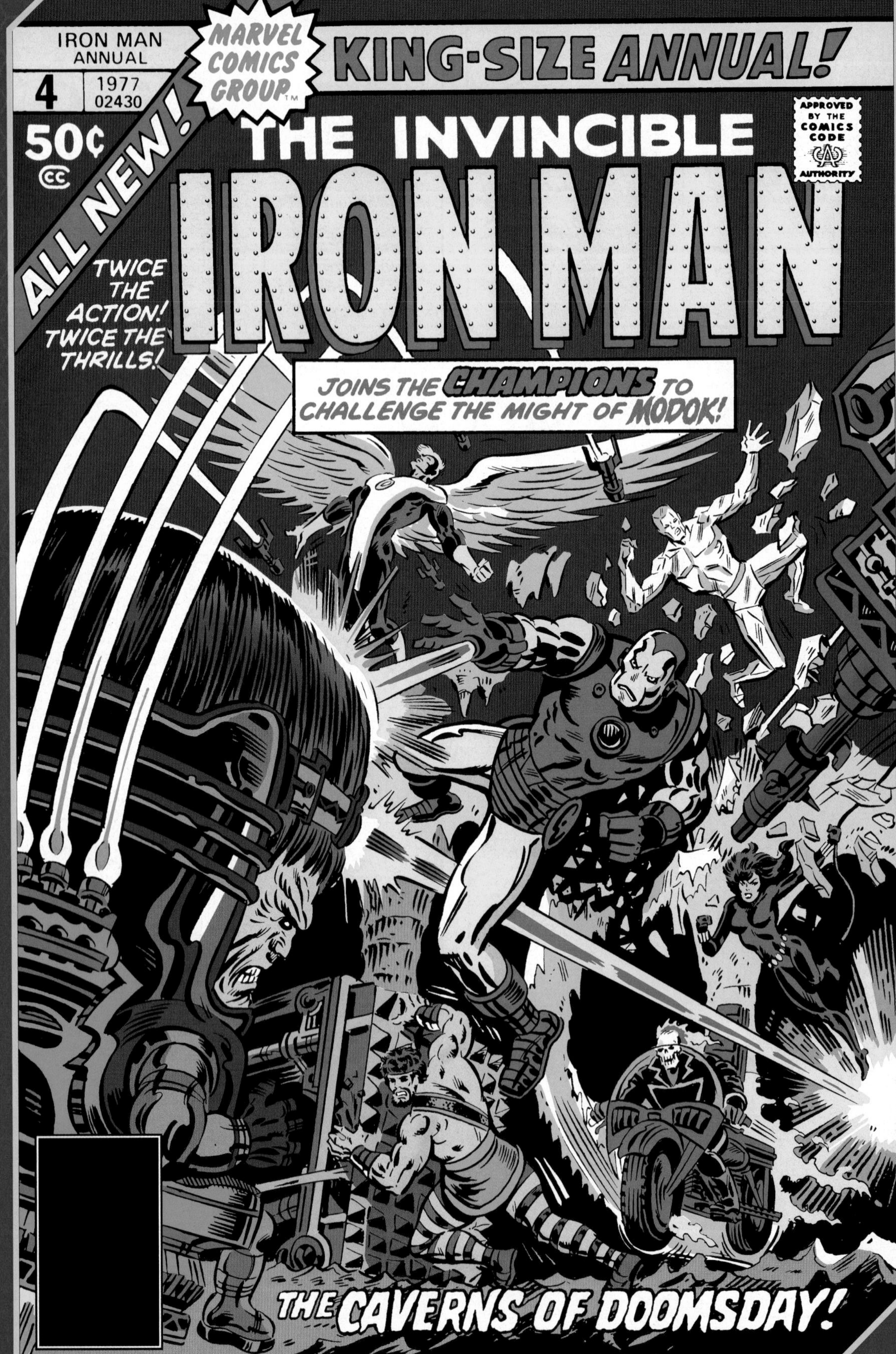
IRON MAN ANNUAL
4
1977
02430
50¢
CC
MARVEL COMICS GROUP
ALL NEW!
KING-SIZE ANNUAL!
APPROVED BY THE COMICS CODE AUTHORITY
THE INVINCIBLE
IRON MAN
TWICE THE ACTION! TWICE THE THRILLS!
JOINS THE CHAMPIONS TO CHALLENGE THE MIGHT OF MODOK!
THE CAVERNS OF DOOMSDAY!

When millionaire industrialist *Tony Stark*, inventor extraordinaire, garbs himself in solar-charged, steel-mesh *armor* he becomes the world's greatest human fighting machine...

Stan Lee PRESENTS: THE INVINCIBLE IRON MAN™

BILL MANTLO, WRITER • GEORGE TUSKA, ARTIST • DON PERLIN, INKER • J. COSTANZA, letterer • PHIL RACHE, colorist • ARCHIE GOODWIN, EDITOR

THE AMPLIFIED, ELECTRONIC CRY ECHOES DOWN DESERTED, MACHINE-LINED CORRIDORS--

--UNTIL IT FINALLY DIES AWAY, LEAVING ONLY THE HARSH RASP OF METAL HEELS ON METAL FLOORING.

MODOK! MODOK! MODOK!

NOTHING! NOT A SIGN OR SOUND OF LIFE! EVEN THE MACHINES ARE DEAD--THEIR POWER DRAINED!

BUT MODOK, THE DEADLIEST INTELLECT KNOWN TO MAN, WAS HERE!

MODOK SUPPOSEDLY DIED AT THE HANDS OF THE YELLOW CLAW! * BUT SHIELD REPORTED HIM ALIVE!
ONLY TO LOSE TRACK OF HIM ALMOST IMMEDIATELY!
*IM #75 --ARCH.

AND HE STAYED LOST UNTIL MY INSTRUMENTS DETECTED AN ENORMOUS OUTPOURING OF UNMISTAKE-ABLE MENTAL ENERGY--
--AND TRACED IT BACK TO... THAT!
IT APPEARS TO BE A MASSIVE SUPPORT CRADLE, BUT WHAT--?

ZAM!
UH! CARELESS-- FORCE RAY! IF MY ARMOR HADN'T SHIELDED ME--

I AM... GUARDIAN! YOUR PRESENCE IS UNAUTHORIZED!
THUS YOU MUST DIE! I WILL RESET MY NEXT SHOT TO KILL!
CAN'T GAMBLE ON ARMOR HOLDING UP TO ANOTHER BLAST!
I HATE TO BREAK THIS TO YOU, GRUESOME--

--BUT THERE'S NOT GOING TO BE ANY NEXT SHOT!
THRAKK
BEHIND ME--

--ANOTHER ONE--
SHSTROWL

I KNEW TACKLING MODOK AGAIN WOULDN'T BE ANY PICNIC, SO I BUILT A MAGNETIC FIELD INTO MY VARIO BEAM!
BY REVERSING POLARITIES SUDDENLY, THE OPPOSING FIELDS WILL TEAR THE ROBOT APART!
RAKK!

MAGNETIC CHARGE IS EXPENDED-- BUT IT SERVED ITS PURPOSE! NOW TO--
--EH?
KLIK!
ZSTROW!
UHHNN!
ONCE AGAIN HIS ARMOR TAKES THE BRUNT OF THE ATTACK--

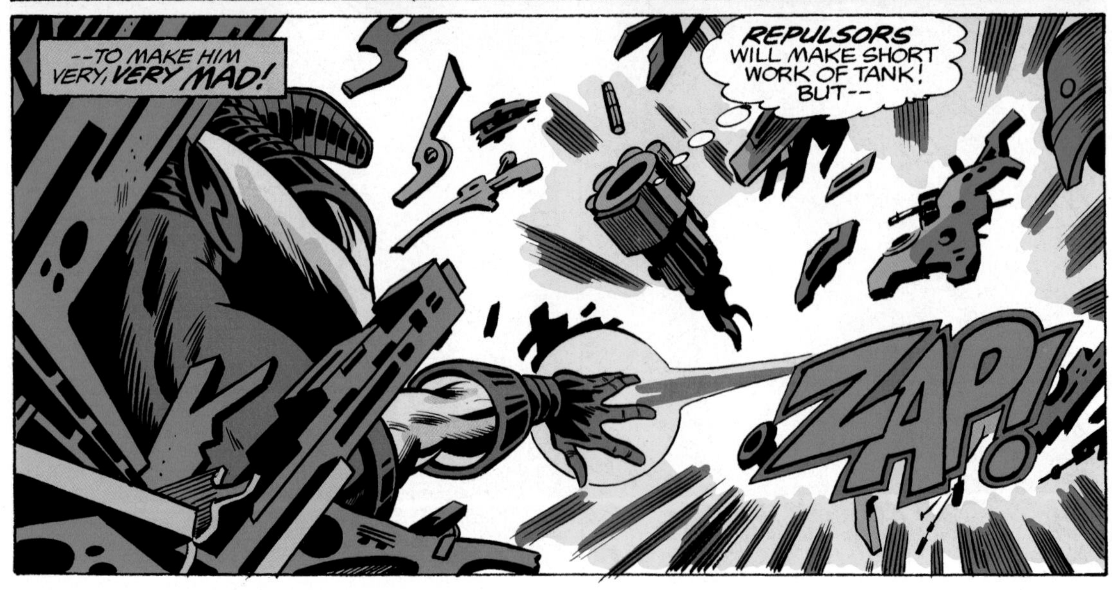

-- SOMETHING'S WRONG HERE! MODOK KNOWS THESE THINGS CAN'T STOP ME! MY GUESS IS THAT HE'S ALREADY GONE!
I'M BEING DELAYED WHILE HE MAKES GOOD HIS ESCAPE!

--AND IF THAT'S THE CASE--

--THEN I'VE JUST ABOUT HAD--

--ENOUGH!
VRAAK!

ALL RIGHT, PARTYTIME'S OVER! DESPITE ITS IMPRESSIVE SIZE, THIS BASE SERVES NO OTHER PURPOSE THAN TO RELAY ENERGY!
ENERGY STOLEN-- BLACKING OUT THE ENTIRE PACIFIC COAST!
MODOK WOULDN'T DARE DIVERT SUCH POTENTIALLY DESTRUCTIVE FORCE HERE--

--UNLESS HE HAD DEVELOPED SOME *IN-CREDIBLE* MEANS OF *STORING* SUCH ENERGIES!

ALL THE *RELAYS* LEAD TO THIS *CRADLE*, BUT WHATEVER *IT* HELD--

--IS *GONE!* I'M TOO LATE!

YOU DON'T NEED A DEGREE IN *PHYSICS* TO KNOW THAT, *DANGEROUS* AS MODOK *ALREADY* IS--

"--THE CHAMPIONS!"
AND, A FEW HUNDRED MILES LATER...
THEY DON'T RESPOND TO MY RADIO ALERT!
AND STEEL SHUTTERS ARE SEALING THE TOP FLOORS AUTOMATICALLY AT MY APPROACH!
I HATE TO DO THIS TO THEIR DEFENSE SYSTEM--BUT THERE'S NO TIME FOR A FORMAL INVITATION!
FLIGHT DRAINED POWER! I HAVE TO RECHARGE!
BUTHROOM!!
HELLFIRE! WE SPEND ALL DAY TRYING TO RESTORE POWER TO OUR DEFENSES AFTER THE BLACKOUT--
--ONLY TO HAVE THEM GATE-CRASHED--ON THE 25TH FLOOR!
BACK, MORTAL, BEFORE I--IRON MAN?!
GOOD LORD! THE BLAZING SKULL--HIS VOICE--
CAN HE BE THE REASON MY ALERT WENT UNHEEDED--?
ACTING OUT OF INSTINCT, IRON MAN LEVELS HIS REPULSOR RAYS AND...
ZAM
UNHH!
SSZAK!

BY THE HOLY HEIGHTS OF OLYMPUS!
GHOST RIDER-- UNDER ATTACK?!
KRASH!
BUT WHO--?

SON, I'M SORRY! I SHOULD HAVE RECOGNIZED YOU, BUT--
--IT'S... UNNERVING TO ACTUALLY SEE YOU IN THE--ER-- FLESH!
THAT SINKS IT, TIN MAN! I'M GONNA--

LOOK, I SAID I WAS SORRY AND I MEANT IT!
WAM
BUT I DON'T HAVE TIME TO PLAY GAMES!

I DON'T KNOW WHAT'S GOTTEN INTO YOU, AVENGER, BUT WHEN YOU ATTACK ONE CHAMPION--
--YOU ATTACK US ALL!

BUT BEFORE A SIMPLE MISUNDERSTANDING CAN ESCALATE INTO A FULL-SCALE WAR...
ALL OF YOU! STOP THIS INSANITY AT ONCE!
AS THOU SAYEST, MILADY--SO SHALL IT BE!
MADAME NATASHA-- THE BLACK WIDOW! MORE BEAUTIFUL THAN EVER!
AND WHEN IRON MAN EXPLAINS THE REASON FOR HIS DRASTIC ENTRANCE...

--WE RECEIVED NO ALERT, IRON MAN! BUT THE BLACKOUT AFFECTING OUR OWN MALFUNCTIONING INSTRUMENTS COULD EXPLAIN THAT!
YOU SAID YOU NEEDED OUR HELP! WHAT--?

I'LL SHOW YOU WITH MY MINI-PROJECTOR WHILE I RE-CHARGE, WIDOW! IF SOMEONE WILL CUT THE LIGHTING...?

THIS... IS MODOK!
DOESN'T LOOK LIKE THE CHEERFUL SORT, DOES HE?
WASN'T HE A CREATION OF ADVANCED IDEA MECHANICS?

YES--UNTIL HE BECAME SO POWERFUL THAT HE DOMINATED A.I.M. AND THEY TRIED TO DESTROY HIM! *
* TALES OF SUSPENSE #94 --ARCH.
I TRAILED MODOK TO THIS REBUILT A.I.M. INSTALLATION!
HE'D ALREADY FLED, AFTER CAUSING THE BLACKOUT BY STEALING POWER FOR WHATEVER RESTED ON THIS CRADLE!

AND THE EVIDENCE INDICATES THAT HE'S JOINED FORCES WITH A.I.M. ONCE AGAIN!
IT'S NEVER EASY IS IT, OLD FRIEND?
NO, WIDOW, IT'S NOT!

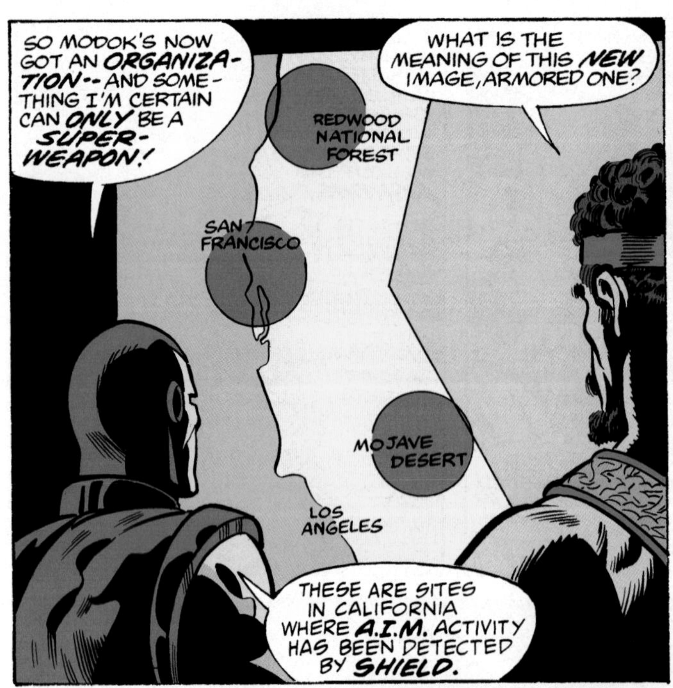
SO MODOK'S NOW GOT AN ORGANIZATION-- AND SOMETHING I'M CERTAIN CAN ONLY BE A SUPER-WEAPON!
WHAT IS THE MEANING OF THIS NEW IMAGE, ARMORED ONE?
REDWOOD NATIONAL FOREST
SAN FRANCISCO
MOJAVE DESERT
LOS ANGELES
THESE ARE SITES IN CALIFORNIA WHERE A.I.M. ACTIVITY HAS BEEN DETECTED BY SHIELD.

REDWOOD NATIONAL FOREST
AND YOU BELIEVE THE ENEMY MAY BE AT ONE OF THEM?
WHO IN BLAZES?
SAN FRANCISCO
LOS ANGELE
HER NAME IS DARKSTAR-- A GUEST-MEMBER!

GOOD! MODOK'S PROBABLY TESTING HIS SUPER-WEAPON AT ONE OF THESE THREE SITES--
--AND WE'LL NEED ALL THE POWER WE CAN MUSTER TO STOP HIM!

THEN, WITH THE WIDOW'S PERMISSION, I'LL ISSUE THE "GO ORDER!" WE SPLIT INTO THREE TEAMS--
--AND KEEP IN RADIO CONTACT! WHICHEVER TEAM FINDS MODOK WILL ALERT THE REST!

GHOST RIDER, DARKSTAR AND I WILL HEAD NORTH TO SAN FRANCISCO!
WHILE THE WIDOW, HERC AND MYSELF TRY REDWOOD NATIONAL FOREST!
LEAVING ME THE MOJAVE DESERT BASE!
GOOD LUCK, CHAMPIONS... YOU'LL NEED IT!

THE AIR BREATHES CLEAN HERE, WASHING ANCIENT TREES AND THE SLOPES OF MOUNTAINS.
THE CRAFT CLEAVES THE SKY OF THIS PLACE OF PEACE--
--SEARCHING FOR HE WHO WOULD MAKE IT A BATTLEGROUND!

I'LL SCOUT AHEAD FOR A PLACE TO LAND!

HAD TO GET AWAY FROM THE OTHERS!
IT'S SO SELDOM I CAN JUST BE ALONE-- TO SPREAD MY WINGS AND... FLY!

TIMES LIKE THIS IT DOESN'T MATTER THAT I'M A MUTANT, THAT I'M DIFFERENT!
THERE IS MAGIC HERE--

--THAT TOUCHES EACH IN TURN!
BY MY SOUL! NEVER BEFORE ON EARTH HAS HERCULES FELT SO ASSUAGED!

THIS FOREST HATH BEEN BLESSED BY THE GODS, MILADY!
THERE WERE PLACES LIKE THIS IN RUSSIA --WHEN I WAS A GIRL!
MY FATHER WOULD LIFT ME TO HIS SHOULDERS--
--THUS, MY FAIR COMPANION?

FOR A MOMENT NEITHER SPEAKS, THEN...
HERCULES, I--I FEEL SO... SAFE HERE IN YOUR ARMS.
THERE ARE THINGS I HAVE NOT DARED SAY, NATASHA, BUT NOW--

HERCULES!
AYE, MILADY! I SEE IT!
ANGEL HATH FOUND THE PREY!

IT'S US THAT'S BEEN FOUND, HERC!
PTOOM
KILL HIM!
PTOW

AND THESE CLOWNS ARE OUT FOR BLOOD!
WHHRRR!
BUTOOM

THESE ARE BUT LACKEYS OF HIM WE SEEK!

AND THEY O'ERSTEP THEMSELVES IN ATTACKING THE PRINCE OF POWER!
L-LOOK AT WHAT HE'S DOING!!
RRRIIIP

HERCULES COMES ON PRETTY STRONG, BOYS!
ZAP
BUT WHAT I LACK IN STRENGTH, I MAKE UP FOR WITH STYLE!

AND THEN THERE'S MY WAY, FELLAS! IT KINDA DEFIES DESCRIPTION!
WOK!
PTOW

AND SO IT GOES, EACH IN HIS OWN WAY--
WHOM!

--YET TOGETHER ...A TEAM!

I'D LIKE TO KILL THAT BLASTED OLYMPIAN, BUT I'LL BE GRATEFUL IF THIS PARALYSIS CANNON JUST STUNS HIM!
FHSTOOM!
THE WEAPON IS FIRED--

--AND HAS THE DESIRED EFFECT!
FTASHT!

HERC'S DOWN!
AND YOU'RE NEXT, MUTANT!

SOME KIND OF NET--ADHERING TO ME! PINNING MY WINGS!

I'M THE ONLY ONE STILL IN THE FIGHT!
DON'T GO GIVIN' YOURSELF ANY MEDALS, LADY!

YOU WON'T BE FOR LONG!
HOLD HER WHILE I--
WE'LL LEAVE THAT LAST SENTENCE UNFINISHED--

--WHILE WE TRAVEL DOWN THE CALIFORNIA COASTLINE--
T-5
A.I.M.
--TO A STRANGE INSTALLATION SUBMERGED IN THE BLUE WATERS OF THE SAN FRANCISCO BAY--

--AND JOIN A DEADLY BATTLE ALREADY IN PROGRESS!

MODOK ISN'T HERE, BUT WE'VE STUMBLED INTO SOMETHING JUST AS VILE! A BASE THAT'S TAKING ORDINARY SEA-LIFE--

--AND MUTATING IT INTO HORRIBLE, MONSTROUS FORMS!

GET THEM! WE CAN'T BE STOPPED NOW!

WAIT'LL I PUT THIS GUY ON ICE AND I'LL GIVE YOU A HAND, BLAZE!
WORRY ABOUT HOLDING YOUR OWN, DRAKE!

THE GHOST RIDER NEEDS NO HELP FROM YOU OR YOUR DEFECTOR GIRLFRIEND!
NOT AS LONG AS I HAVE HELL-FIRE!

OUR WEAPONS ARE USELESS IN THE FACE OF SUCH AWE-SOME POWERS! WE MUST FALL BACK!
BUT THERE MAY YET BE A WAY...
SQUAD "A"-- THE ORDER IS GIVEN AND MUST BE OBEYED! RETREAT!

BUT WHY DO WE FLEE! WE WERE NOT BEATEN AND COULD STILL HAVE--
YOU FOOL! WHY SHOULD WE ENDANGER OURSELVES FIGHTING--
--WHEN SUCH IS THE EXPRESS PURPOSE OF OUR CREATIONS?!

HOW DO YOU LIKE THAT? THEY'RE ON THE RUN!
NOT THAT YOU HAD ANYTHING TO DO WITH IT, FROSTY!
WAIT-- DO YOU HEAR THAT SOUND?
RWAAR
LIKE... THE RUSHING OF WAVES??

SUDDENLY...
WE DREW A BLANK-- MODOK'S NOT HERE, BUT HIS GOONS PLAN TO FINISH US OFF BY FLOODING THE CHAMBER AND LOOSING THEIR FINNY MUTANTS ON US!
IF THE RISING WATER DOESN'T GET US-- THE MUTATIONS WILL!

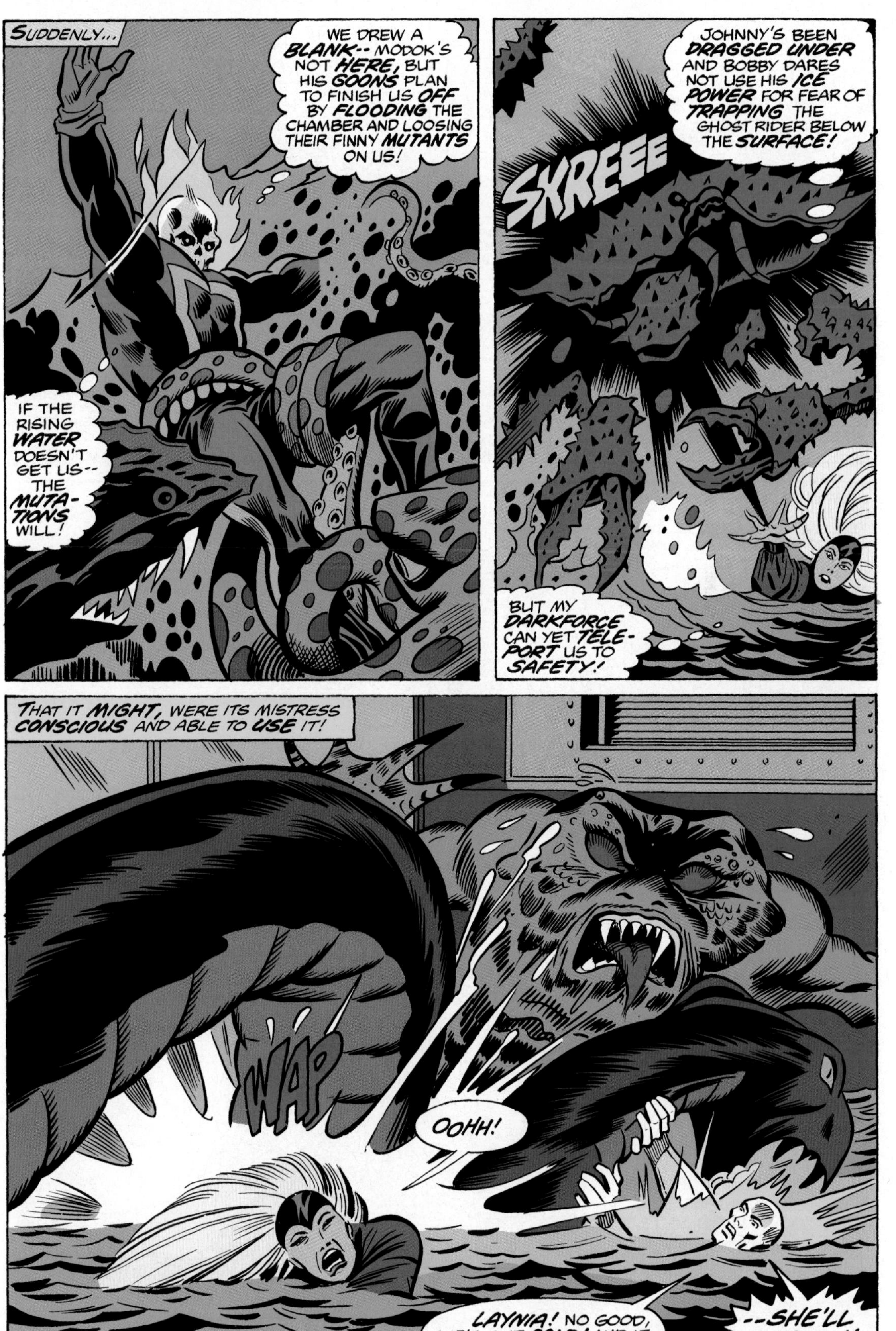

JOHNNY'S BEEN DRAGGED UNDER AND BOBBY DARES NOT USE HIS ICE POWER FOR FEAR OF TRAPPING THE GHOST RIDER BELOW THE SURFACE!
SKREEE
BUT MY DARKFORCE CAN YET TELEPORT US TO SAFETY!

THAT IT MIGHT, WERE ITS MISTRESS CONSCIOUS AND ABLE TO USE IT!

WAP

OOHH!

LAYNIA! NO GOOD, SHE'S OUT COLD! AND IF I DON'T REACH HER--

--SHE'LL DROWN!!

MEANWHILE...
I'VE SCANNED THE ENTIRE AREA! THE ONLY HABITATION IN SIGHT IS THAT OLD FRANCISCAN MISSION!

THE FRIARS WOULD BE AWARE OF ANY STRANGE OCCURRENCES IN THE DESERT!
IRON MAN! THIS IS AN HONOR!
YOU KNOW OF ME, PADRE?
YES, MY SON! NEWS OF YOUR GOOD WORKS REACHES EVEN THIS REMOTE SPOT!

STEP INTO THE SHADE OF THE CHURCH AND TELL ME WHAT BRINGS YOU TO US!
AN EVIL MAN, PADRE--WHO WILL DO GREAT HARM IF NOT STOPPED!
AND THIS MAN'S NAME, MY SON?

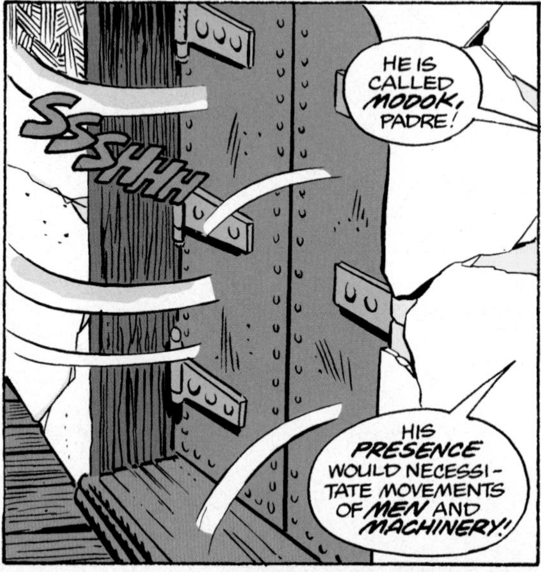
SSSHHH
HE IS CALLED MODOK, PADRE!
HIS PRESENCE WOULD NECESSI-TATE MOVEMENTS OF MEN AND MACHINERY!

YES, IRON MAN, WE ARE AWARE OF THE ADVENT OF TECHNOLOGY IN THIS HUMBLE DESERT OF OURS!
KLANG!
WHAT--? YOUR VOICE-- IT'S CHANGED! AND THAT DOOR--
THEN YOU BEGIN TO PER-CEIVE THE TRUTH, DO YOU?

I'VE WALKED INTO A TRAP!
PRECISELY, YOU ARMOR-BOUND FOOL! MODOK PRE-DICTED YOUR COMING HERE--

--AND MINE IS THE HONOR OF DESTROYING YOU!
WHOM!

I AM... STRYKE! CREATED TO SERVE MODOK--BUT I ALSO ENJOY WHAT I AM ORDERED TO DO!
UHH! HE'S LIKE A HUMAN PILEDRIVER-- BIOLOGICALLY RESTRUCTURED SO THAT HIS FLESH IS AS STRONG AS STEEL!
WRAK!

HOW LONG CAN EVEN YOUR MUCH-VAUNTED ARMOR HOLD UP AGAINST FISTS THAT CAN FEEL NO PAIN?
AND THAT CONTINUE TO HAMMER UNTIL YOU ARE NO MORE THAN A QUIVER-ING PULP WITHIN THAT METAL SHELL?!
STRYKE'S... RIGHT! HAVE TO GET MYSELF... TOGETHER! FIGHT BACK!

BUT IRON MAN'S ONCE-HUMAN ATTACKER PRESSES HIS ON-SLAUGHT!
SKROW!

POWER BURSTS FROM HIS HANDS-- AS POWERFUL AS MY REPULSORS!
HAVE TO STOP THIS--GO ON THE OFFENSIVE! EACH SECOND'S DELAY BRINGS MODOK CLOSER TO READINESS!

ALL RIGHT, STRYKE! YOU'VE HAD YOUR INNING!
NOW IT'S MY TURN AT BAT!
NO GOOD! I'M OFF BALANCE AND HE'S TENSING! ABOUT TO--

KTHOOM!
UNHH!

IT'S LIKE FIGHTING AN UNLIVING FOE! STRYKE CAN'T FEEL ANY PAIN!
WHILE I FEEL HIS BLOWS RIGHT THROUGH MY ARMOR! ONE CHANCE--

MY IMAGE REPRODUCER!
I'M NOT IM-PRESSED, AVENGER! I'LL SIMPLY CRUSH EACH IMAGE IN TURN--
--UNTIL I KILL THE REAL IRON MAN!

MAYBE SO, UGLY-- BUT WHILE YOU'RE AT IT, I'LL BE ATTACKING!
AND SO, THE BATTLE OF TITANS GOES ON, UNTIL...
JUST REALIZED SOMETHING! I'M BEING PLAYED FOR A FOOL!
IF MODOK HAS COMPLETED HIS ULTIMATE WEAPON --WHY SET UP A TRAP LIKE THIS?
I DON'T LIKE IT! NOT ONE BIT! BUT--
COME BACK, YOU METAL-SHEATHED COWARD! I'M NOT DONE WITH YOU!
KRASH!
BUT I AM DONE WITH YOU, STRYKE!
AND, AS IRON MAN SEEMINGLY FLEES THE OLD MISSION...
I'VE DONE IT! I'VE BEATEN IRON MAN! ALL A.I.M. WILL BE AT MY FEET! NOTHING WILL BE DENIED ME!
WE'LL MEET AGAIN, IRON MAN-- TO YOUR EVERLASTING REGRET!
HAVE TO CONTACT THE CHAMPIONS!
THE POWERFUL TRANSISTORS WITHIN HIS HELMET-RADIO SEND AN ALERT--

--THAT IS RECEIVED FAR TO THE NORTH BY...
BLACK WIDOW! COME IN, BLACK WIDOW...
IRON MAN, CALLING US TO MEET HIM!

WE ALLOWED OURSELVES TO BE SUBDUED SO A.I.M. WOULD TAKE US TO MODOK!
HERCULES-- ANGEL! THE CHARADE IS ENDED!
'TIS WELL! THIS PRETENSE OF DEFEAT WAS NOT TO MY LIKING!

WHEN THE A.I.M. HENCHMEN HAVE BEEN DISPOSED OF...
WE'RE TO JOIN IRON MAN IN NEVADA!
BUT THAT'S WHERE THE CRADLE IS--
--EMPTY! HE CHECKED IT OUT AND MODOK WAS GONE!
HOW FARE OUR YOUNGER TEAMMATES?

HOW, INDEED?
BLACK WIDOW TO ICEMAN! BOBBY, WHAT'S...
HAPPENING, WIDOW? NOT MUCH!
WE'RE JUST THE MAIN COURSE IN A MONSTER STEW, BUT WE'RE ON OUR WAY OUT!

YOU DIDN'T TELL HER YOUR LADY-LOVE WAS HURT!
SHE'LL KNOW SOON ENOUGH!
RIGHT NOW WE'VE GOT TO GET DARKSTAR ONTO LIFE-SUPPORT IN THE MINI-SHIP!

AND AFTER FIRE AND ICE FREE THEM FROM THE UNDERSEA CHAMBER OF HORRORS--
--A SLEEK CRAFT HEADS FOR NEVADA!

BUT IT IS IRON MAN WHO, SLICING THROUGH SOUTH-WESTERN SKIES, IS THE FIRST TO ARRIVE.
AND TAKE OUR WORD FOR IT, PILGRIMS... THE MAN IS ANGRY!
THE CHAMPS GOT MY MESSAGE ON THE MINIATURE RECEIVERS I GAVE THEM!
--BUT I CAN'T WAIT FOR THEM TO GET HERE! I HAVE TO GO IN ALONE!

EVERYTHING'S AS I LEFT IT-- DOOR'S CAVED IN! ROBOT GUARDIAN'S SMASHED!
STILL NO INDICATION OF LIFE!

BUT I CAN'T BE WRONG! MODOK MUST BE HERE!
CORRECT, IRON MAN-- AS IS YOUR NEXT THOUGHT!

MODOK--READING MY MIND!?
SIMPLICITY ITSELF! THE DOOMSDAY CHAIR MAGNIFIES MY OWN MENTAL POWERS TO THE N^{TH} DEGREE!
HOWEVER, THE LINKAGE WAS NOT YET FINALIZED WHEN FIRST YOU IN-VADED MY SANCTUARY, SO I RENDERED MY-SELF INVISIBLE!
DELAYING YOU WITH AUTOMATONS AND UNIMPORTANT A.I.M. PERSON-NEL, I CONTINUED TO DRAW ENERGY FROM THE CRADLE!
I AM NOW FAR MORE THAN THE MODOK YOU ONCE FOUGHT, IRON MAN! I AM... REBORN!

WHILE YOU MUST BE NUETRALIZED! DESTROY HIM!
ZAP
ONCE-HUMANS! LIKE STRYKE-- BUT INCAPABLE OF INDEPENDENT THOUGHT!

MODOK'S MENTALLY ORDERED THEM TO KILL ME WHILE HE READIES THE DOOMSDAY CHAIR!
BUT IF I DIE--SO WILL THE WORLD!

"MODOK HAS WON, UNLESS..."
CHAMPIONS-- ATTACK!
LIVING OR UNLIVING--NO CREATION OF EVIL MAY PREVAIL 'GAINST HERCULES!

FOOLS! YOU ARRIVE TOO LATE!
NOTHING CAN STOP ME NOW!
I AM THE DOOMSDAY MACHINE!
HE'S WITHDRAWN CONTROL FROM THE ONCE-HUMANS! I'M FREE!

HAS MODOK GONE MAD? HE'LL BE CRUSHED AGAINST THE--
NO! HE--HE JUST WILLED HIMSELF UP THROUGH THE CEILING!
AND THROUGH THE MOUNTAIN ABOVE, WHICH MODOK PROCEEDS TO LEVEL--
--WITH BUT THE POWER OF A SINGLE... THOUGHT!
AND IN SECONDS, THAT WHICH NATURE TOOK CENTURIES TO BRING FORTH IN MAJESTY UPON THE EARTH--
--IS REDUCED TO MIND-BLASTED RUBBLE!
IN A MANNER BEYOND UNDERSTANDING, A MOUNTAIN IS NO MORE!
WHILE FAR BELOW...
GET BENEATH THE CRADLE! USE IT AS A SHIELD!
BUT WHAT IF IT GIVES WAY?
THAT IT WILL NOT DO, LAD, WHILST HERCULES BRACES IT WITH HIS OWN BODY!

AND, SOME TIME LATER, WHEN THE SOUND AND THE FURY HAVE SUBSIDED...
YOU DID IT, HERCULES! WE MAY HAVE A MOUNTAIN PILED OVER OUR HEADS--BUT WE'RE ALIVE!
WHATEVER THEY FEED YOU IN OLYMPUS, MUSCLES, I'LL TAKE A YEAR'S SUPPLY!
'TIS CALLED AMBOSIA! MAYHAP THOU SHALT DRINK OF IT, ONE DAY.

WE COULD NEVER DIG OUT OF HERE BEFORE OUR AIR IS DEPLETED! WE'VE GOT TO CON-TACT DARKSTAR ON HER MINI-RECEIVER.

"SCRATCH THAT IDEA, WIDOW--

"--DARKSTAR WAS HURT BACK AT THE A.I.M. BASE! SHE'S ON LIFE-SUPPORT IN THE CHAMPSCRAFT--
"YOU'LL HAVE TO COME UP WITH ANOTHER WAY TO GET US OUT OF HERE!"

I HAVE AN IDEA, SON, BUT IT INVOLVES CONSIDERABLE RISK!
THIS CRADLE WE'RE UNDER GAVE MODOK'S DOOMSDAY CHAIR ENOUGH POWER TO LEVEL THIS MOUNTAIN!
IT'S STILL FUNCTIONING, STILL DRAWING ENERGY--FROM ITS BATTERIES, MAYBE FROM THE EXPLOSION TOO!

BUT THE DOOMSDAY CHAIR IS NO MORE THAN A COMPLEX MACHINE--LIKE MY ARMOR!
THE SAME POWER-SOURCE SHOULD WORK FOR BOTH!
IRON MAN SWITCHES ON HIS RECHARGE CABLE--

--AND STAGGERS BENEATH THE SUDDEN SURGE OF POWER FLOODING FROM THE CRADLE ALONG EVERY INTEGRATED MICRO-CIRCUIT IN HIS MAGNIFICENT ARMOR!
ARMOR...RECEIVING MORE ENERGY...THAN I'VE EVER KNOWN! POWER--INCREDIBLE POWER!
BUT YOU SAID THERE WAS A RISK! WHAT--?!

RISK? YES! CIRCUITS...NOT CREATED TO WITHSTAND... SUCH A CONTINUOUS OVERLOAD! ENERGY MUST BE...RE-LEASED--
--OR ARMOR WILL...BURN OUT--CAUSING AN...

...AN EXPLOSION IN AN ENCLOSED SPACE THAT WILL KILL US ALL! IRON MAN, TRY TO THINK! THE POWER IS OVERWHELMING YOU!
YOU MUST RELEASE IT!

YES... I MUST... RELEASE--

POWER!

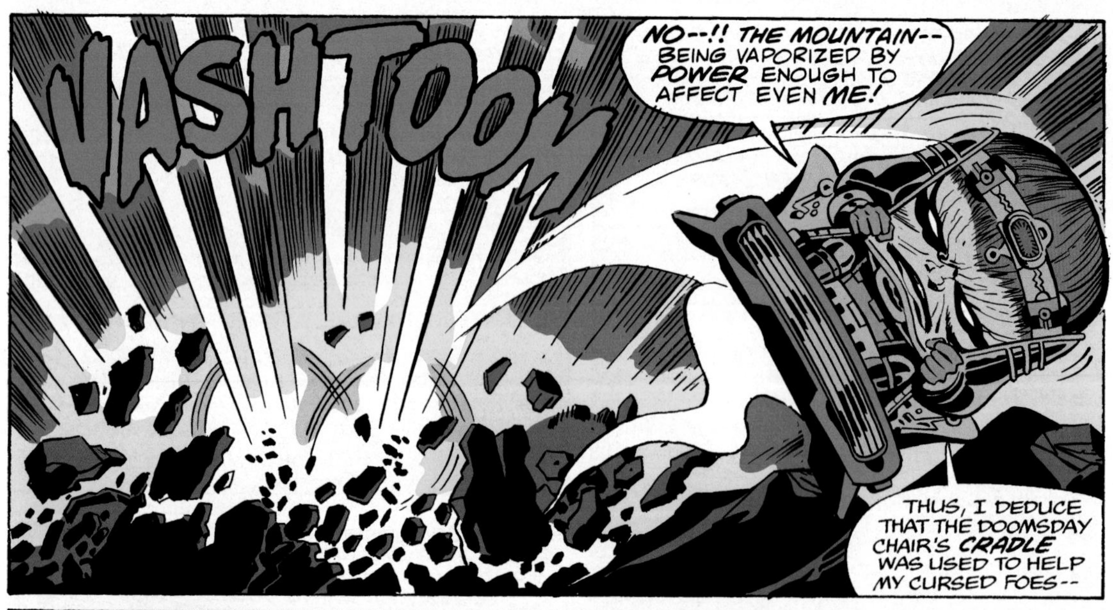
VASHTOOM
NO--!! THE MOUNTAIN-- BEING VAPORIZED BY POWER ENOUGH TO AFFECT EVEN ME!
THUS, I DEDUCE THAT THE DOOMSDAY CHAIR'S CRADLE WAS USED TO HELP MY CURSED FOES--

"--TO ESCAPE."
WOW! THAT'S THE GUY I TANGLED WITH?!
IRON MAN?
HE HEARS THEE NOT, MILADY! NO MAN CAN RECOVER HIMSELF SO EASILY, HAVING KNOWN SUCH POWER!
YOU'RE WRONG, HERCULES! I'M RECOVERED ENOUGH TO FEEL HATRED TOWARDS THE ONE RE-SPONSIBLE FOR ALL THIS--
--AND TO WANT REVENGE ON MODOK!

THEN HASTEN ERE YON VILLAIN MAKES GOOD HIS ESCAPE, WHILST WE TEND TO DARKSTAR!
THOUGH, BY ALL THE GODS THERE BE, I WISH MYSELF WITH THEE!
C'MON! WE'VE GOTTA GET LAYNIA TO A HOSPITAL!
THE TIME FOR WORDS IS ENDED--

--THE TIME FOR ACTION BEGUN!
THERE'S MODOK-- AND IT LOOKS LIKE HE'S SUSTAINED SOME DAMAGE.

I STILL HAVE A RESERVE OF POWER DRAWN FROM THE CRADLE!
BY FEEDING IT TO MODOK, MAYBE I CAN STABILIZE HIS CIRCUITS AND STOP HIM--
--BEFORE HE SMASHES HIMSELF INTO THE GROUND!
DON'T RESIST, YOU FOOL, I'M TRYING TO SAVE YOU!

NO, STOP! I CAN'T BE DESTROYED!
I AM
MODOK...
"TOO LATE!"

AND SOME TIME LATER...
HAVE TO SET DOWN AT STARK-WEST IN L.A.-- TO REST AND RECHARGE!
AND WHILE I'M AT IT, MAYBE I'LL DO SOMETHING NICE AND LEISURELY--
--LIKE INSPECT MY FACTORY, SAY HELLO TO MY EMPLOYEES!
THE THINGS I'M PAID TO DO!

AS TO THE FATE OF DARKSTAR, CHECK OUT

#16, AND DON'T MISS AN ISSUE OF THEIR BLOCK-BUSTING BIMONTHLY BOOK!

60¢
287
SEPT
02456

MARVEL® COMICS GROUP

APPROVED BY THE COMICS CODE AUTHORITY

THE INCREDIBLE HULK®

TM

WILSON/MILGROM

Caught in the heart of a ***Nuclear Explosion,*** victim of ***Gamma-Radiation*** gone wild, ***Doctor Robert Bruce Banner*** now finds himself transformed in times of stress into seven feet, one thousand pounds of unfettered ***Fury***—the most powerful creature to ever walk the earth—

STAN LEE PRESENTS: THE INCREDIBLE HULK!®

BILL MANTLO STORY / SAL BUSCEMA LAYOUTS / CHIC STONE FINISHES / JIM NOVAK, LETTERS BOB SHAREN, COLORS / AL MILGROM EDITOR / JIM SHOOTER CHIEF

LOOSE ENDS!

DEATH.

IT COMES TO US ALL.

1

TWENTY-ONE CENTURIES FORWARD FROM OUR TIME, DEATH CLAIMED THIS SOLDIER.
ALL THE HULK'S POWER COULD NOT SAVE HIM.

INDEED, IT MAY HAVE BEEN THE HULK WHO BROUGHT ABOUT THE WARRIOR'S DEATH.
I TAUGHT HIM THE MEANING OF PEACE IN A WORLD THAT KNEW ONLY WAR.

THE SOLDIER FOUND PEACE...
...IN DEATH.

I AM THE UNLUCKIEST OF MEN, RECORDASPHERE. I HAVE SEEN THE FUTURE--
--AND FOUND IT TORN BY UNENDING STRIFE.
WILL TIME TEACH MANKIND NOTHING?
ARE THE NATIONS OF THE EARTH NEVER TO TREAD THE TRAIL OF PEACE?

WHAT WILL YOU DO WITH THE SOLDIER'S BODY, DR. BANNER?

THE ONLY THING I CAN DO, 'SPHERE. THE AUTHORITIES WOULD NEVER UNDERSTAND IF I PRESENTED THEM WITH THE CORPSE OF A MAN WHO WON'T EVEN BE **BORN** FOR ANOTHER TWO THOUSAND YEARS!
GREAT GREEN FINGERS GOUGE THE VERDANT SOIL...
2

...AND SOON THE TIME-LOST WARRIOR IS LAID TO REST IN WHAT IS TRULY THE GRAVE OF THE UNKNOWN SOLDIER.
COME, 'SPHERE-- LET'S GET BACK TO THE OBSERVATORY.

WHO IS THIS BEING WHOSE TREAD SETS THE EARTH 'NEATH HIS FEET TO TREMBLING?

WHO IS HE WHO, IN HIS EMERALD AWESOMENESS, APPEARS MOST LIKE A **MONSTER...**

...YET WHO, WITH THE MEREST EXERCISE OF WILL...

...CAN TRANSFORM HIMSELF FROM MONSTER-- TO **MAN?**

HIS NAME IS **BRUCE BANNER.**

HE IS A SCIENTIST-- A PHYSICIST OF RENOWN

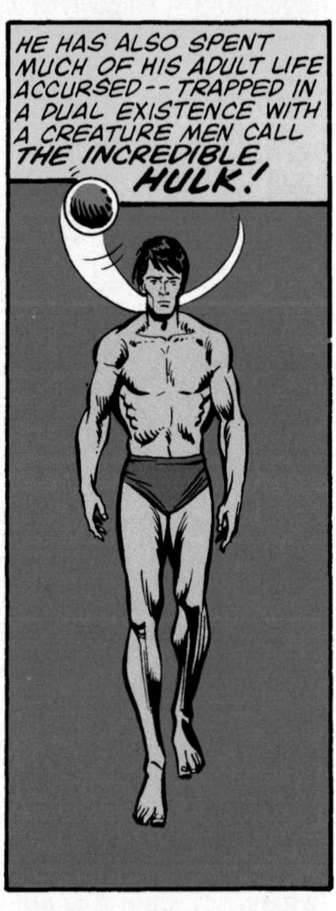

HE HAS ALSO SPENT MUCH OF HIS ADULT LIFE ACCURSED-- TRAPPED IN A DUAL EXISTENCE WITH A CREATURE MEN CALL THE INCREDIBLE HULK!

NOW HE AND THE HULK ARE ONE.
IT IS BANNER'S MIND WHICH COMMANDS THE MONSTER.
ALONE TOGETHER, THEY RESIDE HERE... AT **NORTHWIND OBSERVATORY** IN UPPER NEW YORK STATE.
3

IT APPEARS WE HAVE VISITORS, DR. BANNER.
I WONDER WHO? I WASN'T EXPECTING ANYONE, AND OUTSIDE OF STARK INTERNATIONAL AND S.H.I.E.L.D.*, VERY FEW PEOPLE EVEN KNOW THAT NORTH-WIND EXISTS.
*SUPREME HEADQUARTERS INTERNATIONAL ESPIONAGE LAW-ENFORCEMENT DIVISION-- EDITORI-AL.

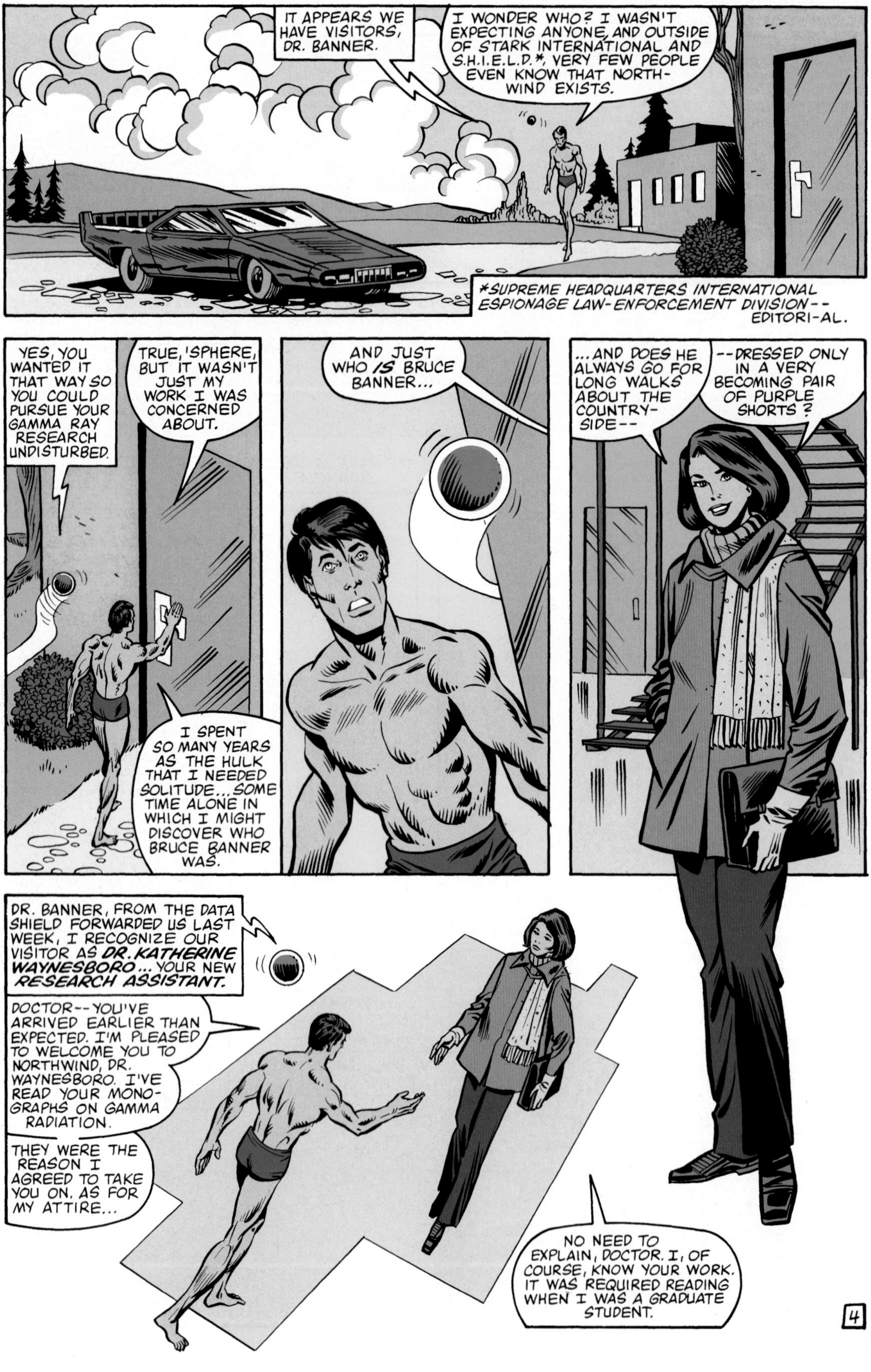

YES, YOU WANTED IT THAT WAY SO YOU COULD PURSUE YOUR GAMMA RAY RESEARCH UNDISTURBED.
TRUE, 'SPHERE, BUT IT WASN'T JUST MY WORK I WAS CONCERNED ABOUT.
I SPENT SO MANY YEARS AS THE HULK THAT I NEEDED SOLITUDE... SOME TIME ALONE IN WHICH I MIGHT DISCOVER WHO BRUCE BANNER WAS.
AND JUST WHO *IS* BRUCE BANNER...
...AND DOES HE ALWAYS GO FOR LONG WALKS ABOUT THE COUNTRY-SIDE--
--DRESSED ONLY IN A VERY BECOMING PAIR OF PURPLE SHORTS?
DR. BANNER, FROM THE DATA SHIELD FORWARDED US LAST WEEK, I RECOGNIZE OUR VISITOR AS ***DR. KATHERINE WAYNESBORO***... YOUR NEW ***RESEARCH ASSISTANT.***
DOCTOR--YOU'VE ARRIVED EARLIER THAN EXPECTED. I'M PLEASED TO WELCOME YOU TO NORTHWIND, DR. WAYNESBORO. I'VE READ YOUR MONO-GRAPHS ON GAMMA RADIATION.
THEY WERE THE REASON I AGREED TO TAKE YOU ON. AS FOR MY ATTIRE...
NO NEED TO EXPLAIN, DOCTOR. I, OF COURSE, KNOW YOUR WORK. IT WAS REQUIRED READING WHEN I WAS A GRADUATE STUDENT.
4

AS FOR YOUR... ECCENTRICITIES--
--I DARESAY THERE'S VERY LITTLE REGARDING YOUR DUAL EXISTENCE AS THE INCREDIBLE HULK THAT'S NOT ON THE PUBLIC RECORD THESE DAYS.
I SUPPOSE NOT, DOCTOR. NO MATTER HOW HARD I TRY, I IMAGINE THERE'S NOT MUCH HOPE THAT I'LL EVER AGAIN MANAGE TO BE A TRULY PRIVATE PERSON.
BUT AS WE'RE GOING TO BE WORKING TOGETHER HERE AT NORTHWIND, THERE'S SOMETHING YOU'RE GOING TO HAVE TO GET USED TO FROM THE START.

PLEASE DON'T BE AFRAID, DR. WAYNESBORO.
I'M GOING TO TRIGGER THE TRANSFORMATION NOT TO SCARE YOU... BUT TO PREPARE YOU.

REALLY, DR. BANNER, THERE'S NO NEED. I'VE READ ABOUT THE HULK'S EXPLOITS--

--AND SEEN FOOTAGE OF YOUR EMERALD ALTER-EGO IN ACTION ON THE TELEVISION NEWS.
BESIDES, I AM A SCIENTIST USED TO WITNESSING THE STARTLING, THE UNEXPLAINED.

SO I DON'T REALLY THINK YOU HAVE TO WORRY ABOUT MY BECOMING UPSET AT THE SIGHT OF...
OH, MY GOODNESS! DR. BANNER!

CALL ME BRUCE, DR. WAYNESBORO... OR CALL ME THE INCREDIBLE HULK!

Y-YES, I--I CAN SEE HOW THAT COULD TAKE SOME GETTING USED TO!
5

SOME... BUT NOT TOO MUCH!
AND PLEASE--CALL ME KATE.

WELCOME TO NORTHWIND, THEN, DR. WAYNESBORO... KATE!
THIS IS THE RECORDA-SPHERE. I INVENTED HER.
SHE'S BEEN MY SOLE COMPANION--AIDING IN AND RECORDING MY RESEARCH--

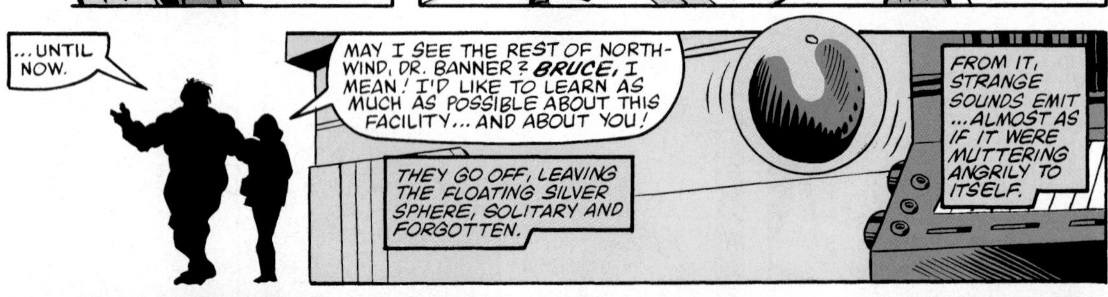
...UNTIL NOW.
MAY I SEE THE REST OF NORTHWIND, DR. BANNER? BRUCE, I MEAN! I'D LIKE TO LEARN AS MUCH AS POSSIBLE ABOUT THIS FACILITY... AND ABOUT YOU!
THEY GO OFF, LEAVING THE FLOATING SILVER SPHERE, SOLITARY AND FORGOTTEN.
FROM IT, STRANGE SOUNDS EMIT ...ALMOST AS IF IT WERE MUTTERING ANGRILY TO ITSELF.

THIS... IS HOLLYWOOD!
THE HOLOGRAPHIC PROJECTION ABOVE THE THEATER MARQUEE IS FRIGHTENINGLY LIFELIKE.
HARVEY KECK PRESENTS BEREET'S NEW DIMENSIAVISION EPIC GALACTIC ATTACK!

THE MOVIE PREMIERING HERE HAS NOT BEEN GREETED WITH UNANIMOUS APPROBATION.
REET PUTS STAGE CREWS OUT OF WORK!
JOBS!
"ALIEN," GO HOME!

BUT THERE ARE THOSE, NONETHELESS, WHO WISH TO VIEW IT...
WHY DON'T YOU PICKET IN POUGHKEEPSIE AND LET US SEE THE MOVIE?!
SPECIAL ABOUT SPECIAL EFFECTS?
6

HEY, WHY DON'T YOU LISTEN TO OUR GRIEVANCES?
THIS BEREET WEIRDO APPEARS OUT OF NOWHERE AND MAKES A MAJOR MOVIE WITH SOME SPECIAL TECHNIQUE--

--THAT REQUIRES ABSOLUTELY NO HUMAN INVOLVEMENT! WE'RE WRITERS, ACTORS, TECHNICIANS, DIRECTORS... PEOPLE WITH FAMILIES TO SUPPORT! WE WANT TO PROTECT OUR JOBS!
AH, YOU UNION GUYS HAVE BEEN PADDING PAYROLLS FOR YEARS!
THAT'S A LIE--!

BALONEY! GET OUTTA MY WAY! I BOUGHT MY TICKETS -- I WANNA SEE THE SHOW!
THAT GOES FOR ME TOO!
RIGHT!

CK PRESENTS BEREET'S
MENSIAVISION EPIC
CTIC ATTACK!
THUS DOES THE FASCINATION WITH NEW TECHNOLOGY...

...LEAVE MUCH HUMAN TALENT, LIKE FORGOTTEN FLOTSAM, IN ITS WAKE.
7

OBSERVING...
YOU WERE RIGHT, HARVEY.
THE MOB IGNORED THE PICKET LINE AND PUSHED THEIR WAY IN TO SEE MY FILM.

BLASTED RIGHT, BIRD-LADY! PEOPLE WANT TO BE ENTERTAINED, AND THEY DON'T CARE HOW THEIR ENTERTAINMENT GETS MADE!
BUT IF I HAVE REALLY COST OTHERS THEIR EMPLOYMENT...

YOU LISTEN TO ME, BEREET! TIMES ARE TOUGH! TO SURVIVE THESE DAYS YA GOTTA COMPETE!
COMPETITION MEANS COMIN' UP WITH SOMETHIN' NEW, SOMETHIN' DIFFERENT!

THAT'S WHAT YOU DID! I DUNNO HOW-- I'M JUST THE MONEY MAN, THE PRODUCER!
YOU'RE THE FILM-MAKER, THE ARTISTE!
YOU CAME OUTTA NOWHERE WITH THAT CRAZY "ALIEN" ROUTINE...
BUT I AM AN ALIEN, FROM THE PLANET KRYLOR!

LOOK, BIRD-LADY-- IF YOU WANNA PRETEND YOU'RE FROM MONGO, HERE ON SPECIAL LEAVE FROM MING THE MERCILESS, THAT'S YOUR SCENE!
I CAN DIG IT! MY OWN KID WEARS A HAIRDO LIKE YOURS! DRIVES HER MOTHER CRAZY!

ME, ALL I CARE ABOUT IS THAT YOU CAME OUTTA NOWHERE WITH SOME SPECIAL-EFFECTS TECHNIQUE THAT'S GROSSIN' ZECK PICTURES, INC., MILLIONS!
LIKE THAT TECHNO-ART DOCUDRAMA YOU MADE ABOUT THE HULK, FOR INSTANCE!
I TRIED TO TELL THE STORY OF THE REAL HULK...

FORGET REALITY! IT DON'T SELL!
WHO SHOULD KNOW BETTER THAN A WALKIN' FANTASY LIKE YOU, BIRD-LADY!
I WISH TO BE REGARDED AS A SERIOUS ARTIST... BUT ON BOTH KRYLOR AND EARTH I HAVE BECOME MERELY A PANDERER TO THE PUBLIC TASTE!
8

A FEW DAYS LATER AND A FEW THOUSAND MILES FURTHER EAST...
OUR PRIMARY PURPOSE HERE AT NORTHWIND, KATE, IS TO INTERPRET THE DATA GATHERED BY THE GAMMASCOPE.

AS YOU KNOW, GAMMA RAYS FIRST TRANSFORMED ME INTO THE HULK BY RADICALLY ALTERING MY GENETIC STRUCTURE.
BUT THAT WAS BECAUSE YOU WERE EXPOSED TO A MASSIVE INFUSION WHEN YOU WERE CAUGHT IN THE DETONATION OF THE FIRST GAMMA BOMB.

TRUE, BUT EVERY DAY THE EARTH IS BOMBARDED BY GAMMA ACTIVITY OF ONE TYPE OR ANOTHER. MOST OF IT IS FILTERED OUT IN THE UPPER ATMOSPHERE. BUT SOME OF IT REACHES THE PLANET'S SURFACE... AND EARTH'S INHABITANTS.
MY CONCERN IS WITH THE SUBTLE MUTATIVE EFFECTS OF THAT DAILY GAMMA SHOWER ON THE HUMAN RACE.

THAT WAS THE FOCUS OF YOUR EARLIEST PAPERS, BRUCE!

YES, IT WAS THE SUBJECT THAT FASCINATED ME AS A STUDENT-- THAT PREOCCUPIED ME AS A PHYSICIST.

IT WAS MY LIFE'S WORK, KATE, BEFORE MY LIFE TOOK A DETOUR WHEN I BECAME...
THE HULK?
MY RESEARCH ENDED SUDDENLY, COMPLETELY...
9

I-I JUST DON'T KNOW IF I CAN PICK UP THE PIECES AFTER SO MANY YEARS.
BRUCE, LISTEN TO ME-- I'VE ONLY REALLY GOTTEN TO KNOW YOU AS A MAN IN THESE PAST FEW DAYS...
...BUT THROUGH YOUR WORK I'VE KNOWN YOU AS A BRILLIANT SCIENTIST FOR YEARS.

YOU'VE ENDURED SOMETHING NO MAN SHOULD EVER HAVE ENDURED-- SOMETHING NO OTHER MAN COULD HAVE ENDURED.

I CAN'T BELIEVE THAT THE BRUCE BANNER WHO TRIUMPHED OVER THE CURSE OF THE HULK, CAN'T TRIUMPH OVER THE FACT THAT HE'S LOST A FEW YEARS OF HIS WORK!

I...APPRECIATE THE ENCOURAGEMENT, KATE-- REALLY.
BUT TIME IS AN ENEMY OVER WHICH NOT EVEN THE HULK IS ABLE TO TRIUMPH.
AND I'VE GOT SO MUCH LOST TIME TO MAKE UP FOR...

AND THAT'S WHY I'M HERE, BRUCE-- TO HELP YOU REGAIN THAT LOST TIME...
...IF YOU'LL LET ME.
UNNOTICED, THE RECORDASPHERE EAVESDROPS.

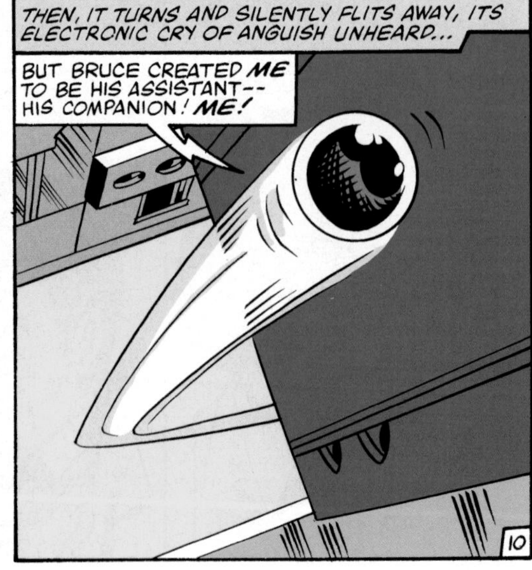
THEN, IT TURNS AND SILENTLY FLITS AWAY, ITS ELECTRONIC CRY OF ANGUISH UNHEARD...
BUT BRUCE CREATED ME TO BE HIS ASSISTANT-- HIS COMPANION! ME!
10

BRUCE AND I WERE DOING FINE HERE AT NORTHWIND... BEFORE SHE CAME!
AND WHO IS THIS DR. KATHERINE WAYNESBORO? WHAT DO BRUCE AND I KNOW ABOUT HER, REALLY, BEYOND WHAT SHIELD CHOSE TO TELL US IN THEIR REPORT?

NOTHING, THAT'S WHAT WE KNOW! BUT WE MUST FIND OUT MORE! BRUCE AND HIS WORK NEED TO BE PROTECTED!
THIS IS DR. WAYNESBORO, DOOR--PLEASE OPEN.

THE RECORDASPHERE'S ELECTRONIC MIMICRY OF KATHERINE WAYNESBORO'S VOICE IS PERFECT. THE AUDIO-ACTIVATED PRIVASEAL ON HER CHAMBER ALLOWS HER DOOR TO HISS OPEN.

AWARE THAT BRUCE BANNER WOULD NEVER CONDONE ITS INVASION OF DR. WAYNESBORO'S PRIVACY, THE RECORDASPHERE NEVERTHELESS FLOATS IN...
MAYBE SHE'S HERE TO STEAL BRUCE'S KNOWLEDGE--OR, WORSE YET, TURN HIS RESEARCH OVER TO THE MILITARY!

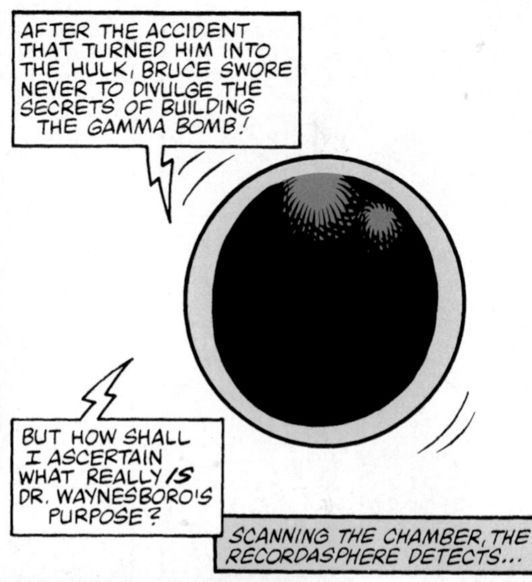
AFTER THE ACCIDENT THAT TURNED HIM INTO THE HULK, BRUCE SWORE NEVER TO DIVULGE THE SECRETS OF BUILDING THE GAMMA BOMB!
BUT HOW SHALL I ASCERTAIN WHAT REALLY IS DR. WAYNESBORO'S PURPOSE?
SCANNING THE CHAMBER, THE RECORDASPHERE DETECTS...

...A VIDEO TAPE-RECORDER UNLIKE ANY SOLD FOR COMMERCIAL USE.

TO MONITOR HER TAPES WOULD BE A CRIME AGAINST DR. WAYNESBORO! BUT--
--NOT TO MONITOR THEM WOULD BE A CRIME AGAINST BRUCE!
THUS DOES THE RECORDASPHERE RATIONALIZE THAT WHICH IT IS ABOUT TO DO...
11

...AND THUS DOES IT EXCEED ANY FUNCTION FOR WHICH ITS CREATOR PROGRAMMED IT.
ACTIVATE PLAYBACK MODE!

TESTING... 1-2-3... TESTING...
IT'S A HOLOGRAPHIC IMAGE!
A THREE-DIMENSIONAL BROADCAST TAPE!

TAPE ONE: THIS IS DR. KATHERINE WAYNESBORO, AGENT OF SHIELD!
I HAVE BEEN ACCEPTED AT NORTHWIND OBSERVATORY.
DR. BANNER SEEMS GENUINELY GLAD TO HAVE ME HERE--

--PERHAPS BECAUSE OF HIS ISOLATION, PEPHAPS BECAUSE WE BOTH SPEAK THE SAME SCIENTIFIC LANGUAGE.

BUT, THEN, I WAS CHOSEN FOR BOTH THESE REASONS BY SHIELD'S PSYCHOLOGISTS, AND THUS IT SHOULD COME AS NO SURPRISE THAT THIS LONELY MAN WOULD SO WILLINGLY ADMIT A SPY INTO HIS PRESENCE...
SPY?!

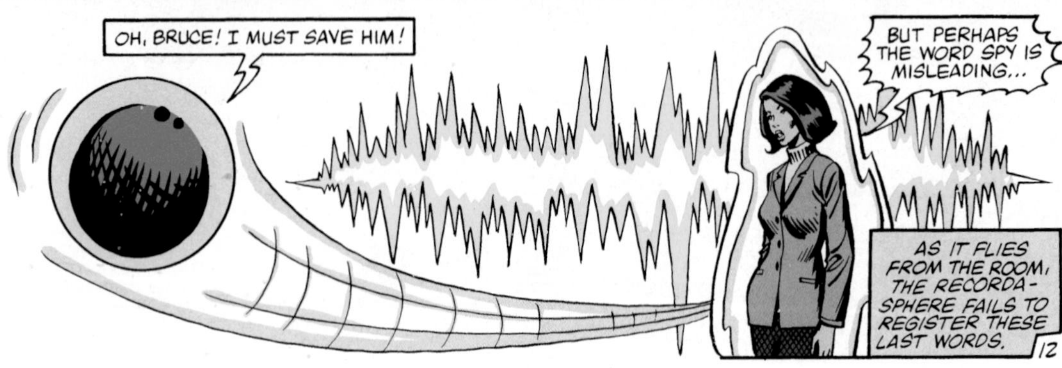
OH, BRUCE! I MUST SAVE HIM!
BUT PERHAPS THE WORD SPY IS MISLEADING...
AS IT FLIES FROM THE ROOM, THE RECORDA-SPHERE FAILS TO REGISTER THESE LAST WORDS.
12

MEANWHILE, DR. KATHERINE WAYNESBORO, AGENT OF SHIELD, IS ABOUT TO GET HER FIRST "HANDS-ON" INITIATION INTO THE WORKINGS OF BRUCE BANNER'S GAMMASCOPE...
I'VE NEVER BEFORE PEERED SO FAR OUT INTO SPACE, BRUCE.
YOU'RE NOT ACTUALLY "SEEING" OUT INTO SPACE NOW, KATE. THE GAMMASCOPE WORKS ON A DIFFERENT PRINCIPLE THAN MOST TELESCOPES.
IN MOST WAYS, IT'S MORE ANALAGOUS TO RADIO-ASTRONOMY--A SCIENCE THAT PAINTS RADIO-WAVE PORTRAITS OF THE COSMOS.

WE'RE PAINTING GAMMA RAY PORTRAITS WHICH THE GAMMASCOPE'S COMPUTERS THEN RESOLVE AND ENHANCE INTO VISUAL IMAGES.
AND THE PICTURE THAT'S EMERGING IS A DISTURBING ONE.

GAMMA RAY ACTIVITY IN THE COSMOS IS INCREASING IN INTENSITY. THE RAYS ARE PENETRATING EARTH'S ATMOSPHERE IN EVER-INCREASING DOSAGES.
HOW HORRIBLE, BRUCE, GIVEN WHAT WE ALREADY KNOW ABOUT THE GAMMA RAY EFFECT OF TURNING MEN INTO MONSTERS!

YES...MONSTERS!
OH, BRUCE--DR. BANNER! I-I WASN'T REFERRING TO YOU!

OF COURSE YOU WERE. WHAT COULD BE MORE NATURAL. I WAS A MONSTER, FOR MANY YEARS.
I MAY SOMEDAY BECOME A MONSTER AGAIN--
--SHOULD I EVER LOSE THE HOLD BRUCE BANNER'S INTELLECT NOW EXERCISES OVER THE ENORMOUS POWER OF THE INCREDIBLE HULK!
ONE ASPECT OF MY RESEARCH IS TO PREVENT THAT FROM EVER HAPPENING AGAIN.

NOW LET'S GET BACK TO WORK, SHALL WE, DR. WAYNESBORO?
SHE SLIPPED--LET OUT HER TRUE FEELINGS ABOUT HIM! HE DISTRUSTS HER NOW! GOOD! HE'LL BE ON HIS GUARD AGAINST HER!
MAYBE I DON'T HAVE TO REVEAL HER FOR THE SPY SHE IS...
13

...YET!

AS THE RECORDA-SPHERE RESOLVES TO WITHHOLD ITS NEWLY GAINED INFORMATION...

BRUCE BANNER'S THOUGHTS ARE ONCE AGAIN OVERSHADOWED BY FEAR OF THE MONSTER WITHIN HIM.

ELSEWHERE...
THE SIGN IS WRONG. SOMEONE... OR SOMETHING... HAS JUST GAINED ENTRANCE TO PROJECT EARTHFALL WITHOUT THE REQUISITE PERMISSION.
PROJECT EARTHFALL MAXIMUM SECURITY
ABSOLUTELY NO ADMITTANCE WITHOUT AUTHORIZATION
14

SOMEONE... OR SOMETHING!

"A" SECTOR'S BEEN COMPLETELY IMMOBILIZED!
AND THERE'S THE REASON! QUICK, SOLDIER--GET READY TO REPEL THE INTRUDER!

BUT...

"B" AND "C" SECTORS HAVE BEEN BREACHED, SIR!
THE INTRUDER IS HEADING UNERRINGLY IN OUR DIRECTION!
BUT HOW? THE LAYOUT OF THIS BASE WAS SUPPOSED TO BE A TOP SECRET!

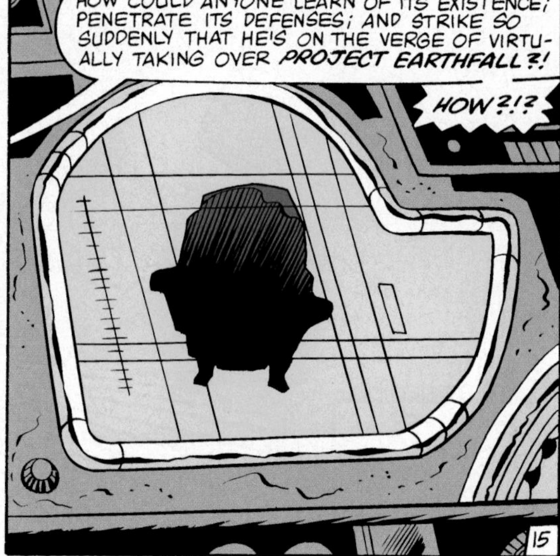
HOW COULD ANYONE LEARN OF ITS EXISTENCE; PENETRATE ITS DEFENSES; AND STRIKE SO SUDDENLY THAT HE'S ON THE VERGE OF VIRTUALLY TAKING OVER PROJECT EARTHFALL?!
HOW?!?
15

"HOW?" EASILY--WHEN THE BEING IN QUESTION IS A LETHAL LIVING INTELLECT CODE-NAMED BY HIS CREATORS AT ADVANCED IDEA MECHANICS*--MENTAL ORGANISM DESIGNED ONLY FOR KILLING...
I AM MODOK!!
I COME FOR THAT WHICH IS CONTAINED WITHIN PROJECT EARTHFALL!
AND THOSE WHO KNOW ME KNOW THAT MODOK SHALL NOT BE DENIED!
*A.I.M. FOR ALL OF YOU ACRONYMOPHILES OUT THERE-- EDITORI-AL.
16

THERE IS NO PLACE MY MATCHLESS MENTAL ABILITIES CANNOT PENETRATE, NO MIND SO SHIELDED THAT I CANNOT PROBE ITS SECRETS--
--NO MYSTERY BURIED SO DEEP THAT MODOK CANNOT UNCOVER IT!

MERE HUMANS DELUDE THEMSELVES IF THEY BELIEVE THEY OR THEIR MACHINES--
--ARE CAPABLE OF ACTING FASTER THAN THE MASTERFUL MIND OF MODOK!

NOR IS THERE ANY WEAPON IN EXISTENCE GREATER THAN THE MARVELOUS MIND-BEAM MODOK COMMANDS!
SPREEAK

THE SCIENTISTS OF A.I.M. CREATED ME TO SERVE THEM, GENETICALLY ENGINEERED ME TO BE FAR MORE POWERFUL THAN EVEN THEY DARED DREAM! THEY PAID FOR THEIR ERROR!
MODOK BECAME THEIR MASTER!
BUT NOW, MODOK HAS NEED FOR A NEW SERVANT--ONE HE SHALL FIND WITHIN THE INNERMOST RECESSES OF PROJECT EARTHFALL!

IN THE COMMAND CENTER, THE MILITARY MEN REALIZE THAT MODOK IS NO IDLE BOASTER...
RECHANNEL ALL SECURITY AROUND THE CRYO-GENICS CORE! THAT'S WHERE MODOK'S HEADED!
ALERT THE BIG BRASS! HE'LL WANT TO BE READY!
HE'S NOT GOING TO LIKE THIS, SIR! PROJECT EARTHFALL IS HIS FIRST COMMAND SINCE GAMMA BASE ...AND HE'S ON THE VERGE OF LOSING IT TO ONE GUY IN A HOVERCHAIR!
17

MODOK IS FAR MORE THAN MERELY "ONE GUY IN A HOVERCHAIR."
HE IS A **MIND** CAPABLE OF DETECTING ANY DANGER... AND OF AVOIDING IT WITH EASE.
VREET
VREET
VREET

HE IS A **BRAIN** GIVEN MOBILITY BY HIS THOUGHT CONTROLLED MAGNETIC-POWERED **MOBILE CHAIR!**

AND HE IS AN **INTELLECT** THAT HAS LEARNED HOW TO FOCUS THE ETHEREAL STUFF OF **THOUGHT** INTO AN INCALCULABLY POWERFUL, MURDEROUS **MIND-BEAM!**

SSHHSSS

THERE SHOULD BE NO FURTHER OBSTACLES BETWEEN ME AND THE CRYOGENICS CORE!
18

BUT, SHOULD THE REMAINING MILITARY PERSONNEL HARBOR ANY FURTHER THOUGHTS OF INTERFERING WITH MY MISSION--
--I WOULD BE WISE TO DEFUSE THAT DANGER EARLY, AND GET ON WITH MY WORK UNINTERRUPTED!

THE BAND AT MODOK'S BROW GLOWS BRIGHTLY.
THE GASH OF A MOUTH IN HIS ENORMOUS SKULL OPENS--LIPS CURLED IN CONTEMPT GIVE VOICE TO A SINGLE, CURT COMMAND...

SLEEP!!

THE RESEARCHERS STAFFING PROJECT EARTHFALL ARE SMASHED DOWN INTO SLUMBER.

THE MILITARY PERSONNEL FARE NO BETTER!

IT IS DONE!
19

NOW MAY MODOK BE ABOUT HIS BUSINESS!

THIS IS THE CRYOGENICS CORE... THE HEART AND SOUL OF PROJECT EARTHFALL!
IT IS A PIT... A SHAFT DRIVEN INTO THE EARTH... SUPER-INSULATED--

--TO KEEP THE SUB-ZERO TEMPERATURES CONSTANT ABOUT THE FROZEN FIGURE WITHIN.

THERE HE IS! YES! YES! YES!
20

AH, BUT WHAT HAVE WE HERE?
YOU... SENSED... MY PRESENCE?

OF COURSE-- YOU WOULD!
BUT IF YOU BELIEVE THAT INFERNAL MIND-BEAM OF YOURS IS ANY DEFENSE AGAINST THIS ION RAY THE PENTAGON DEVISED--!

I WOULD BE CORRECT, GENERAL THADDEUS "THUNDERBOLT" ROSS, AND YOU WOULD BE A FOOL TO BELIEVE OTHERWISE!
BUT YOU AND I ARE NOT ENEMIES! THAT IS WHY, OF ALL YOUR STAFF I LEFT ONLY YOU AWAKE!

FOR MY INITIAL MIND-PROBE INDICATED TO ME THAT WE TWO SHARE A COMMON GOAL! WE BOTH WISH TO USE THE CREATURE CONTAINED IN YOUR CRYOGENICS CORE!
I, TO TURN HIM AGAINST MY ERSTWHILE MASTERS AT A.I.M., YOU, TO SET HIM TO SLAY THE INCREDIBLE HULK!

I... YES!
IF YOU HADN'T COME ALONG, I WOULD HAVE GONE AGAINST ORDERS! I WOULD HAVE AWAKENED THE SLEEPER IN THE PIT MYSELF!
IN DOING SO, YOU WOULD HAVE BEEN COMMITTING TREASON!
THE PRESIDENT PARDONED THE HULK--BUT I STILL BELIEVE THE GREEN GARGOYLE IS A MENACE WHO MUST BE DESTROYED!

YOUR THOUGHTS BRAND YOU A TRAITOR, GENERAL, AND I WOULD LOVE TO SEE A MAN BETRAY ALL HE IS A SYMBOL OF! YES, I WILL ENJOY HELPING YOU CARRY YOUR TREASON TO FRUITION!
IT IS NOT TREASON TO WANT TO SAVE YOUR COUNTRY FROM THE DEPREDATIONS OF A MONSTER, ROSS!
THEREFORE, LET ME AID YOU IN ACHIEVING YOUR GOAL--
--BY ALLOWING ME TO USE MY MIND-BEAM TO AWAKEN THE SLEEPER IN THE PIT SO THAT HE MIGHT SERVE US BOTH!
21

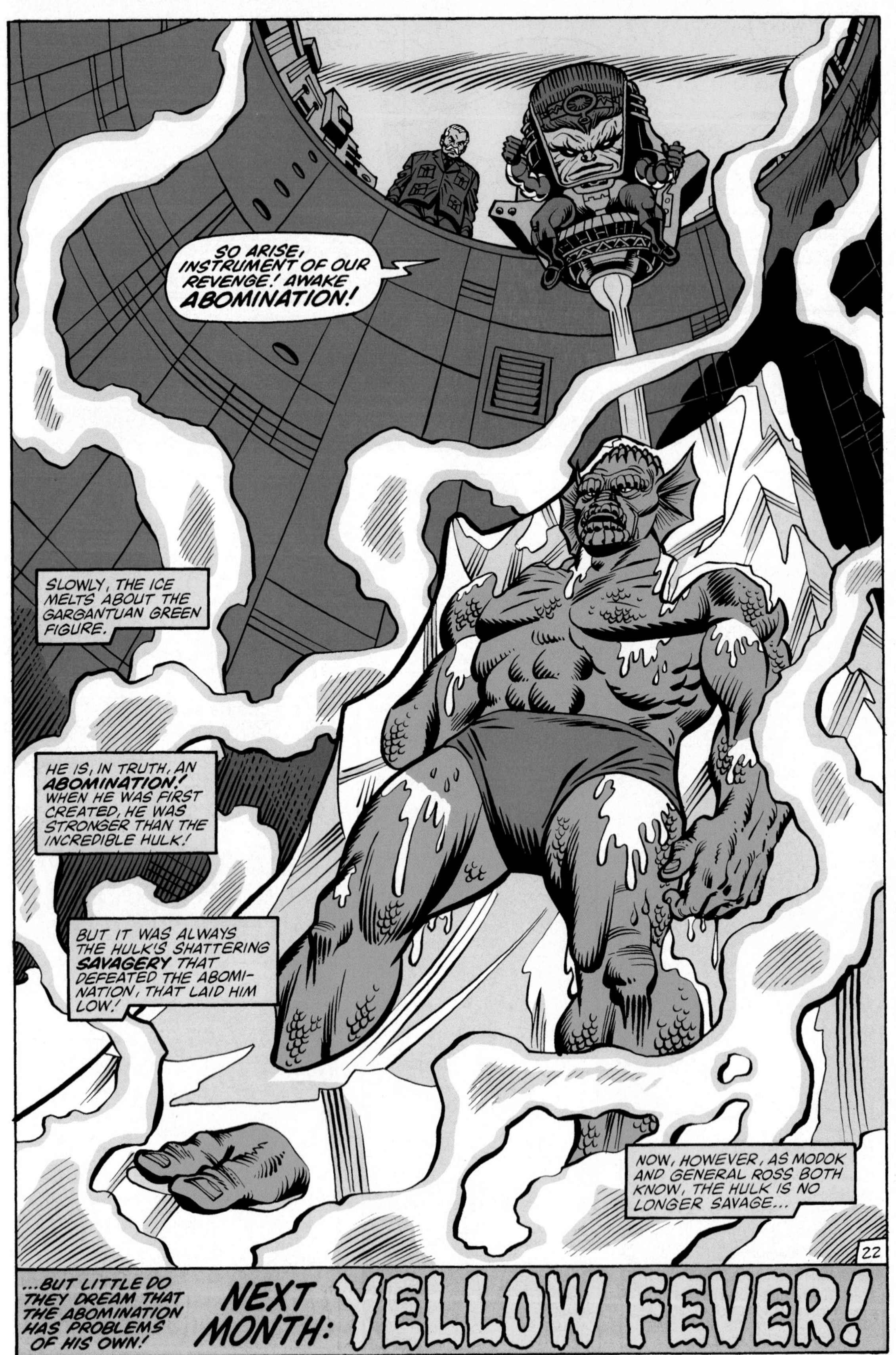
SO ARISE, INSTRUMENT OF OUR REVENGE! AWAKE ABOMINATION!
SLOWLY, THE ICE MELTS ABOUT THE GARGANTUAN GREEN FIGURE.
HE IS, IN TRUTH, AN ABOMINATION! WHEN HE WAS FIRST CREATED, HE WAS STRONGER THAN THE INCREDIBLE HULK!
BUT IT WAS ALWAYS THE HULK'S SHATTERING SAVAGERY THAT DEFEATED THE ABOMINATION, THAT LAID HIM LOW!
NOW, HOWEVER, AS MODOK AND GENERAL ROSS BOTH KNOW, THE HULK IS NO LONGER SAVAGE...
22
...BUT LITTLE DO THEY DREAM THAT THE ABOMINATION HAS PROBLEMS OF HIS OWN!
NEXT MONTH: YELLOW FEVER!

MARVEL®
THE INCREDIBLE
HULK®
© 1983 MARVEL
COMICS GROUP
TM
60¢
288
OCT
02456
APPROVED
BY THE
COMICS
CODE
AUTHORITY

Stan Lee PRESENTS: THE INCREDIBLE HULK!®

BILL MANTLO STORY / SAL BUSCEMA LAYOUTS / JIM MOONEY FINISHES / NOVAK, LETTERER SHAREN, COLORIST / ALLEN MILGROM EDITOR / JIM SHOOTER MODOK

ANYONE OUT THERE KNOW HOW TO CURE A CASE OF...
YELLOW FEVER?!
AT THE SUBZERO CENTER OF THE CRYOGENICS CORE AT THE U.S. ARMY'S PROJECT EARTHFALL, TEMPERATURES BEGIN TO RISE!
ARISE, ABOMINATION! THE MAN-MIND CALLED MODOK BIDS YOU AWAKE!
AAGHHH!
THAWED OUT BY MODOK'S MIND-BEAM, THE GREEN GARGANTUA KNOWN AS THE ABOMINATION BEGINS TO SCREAM!
1

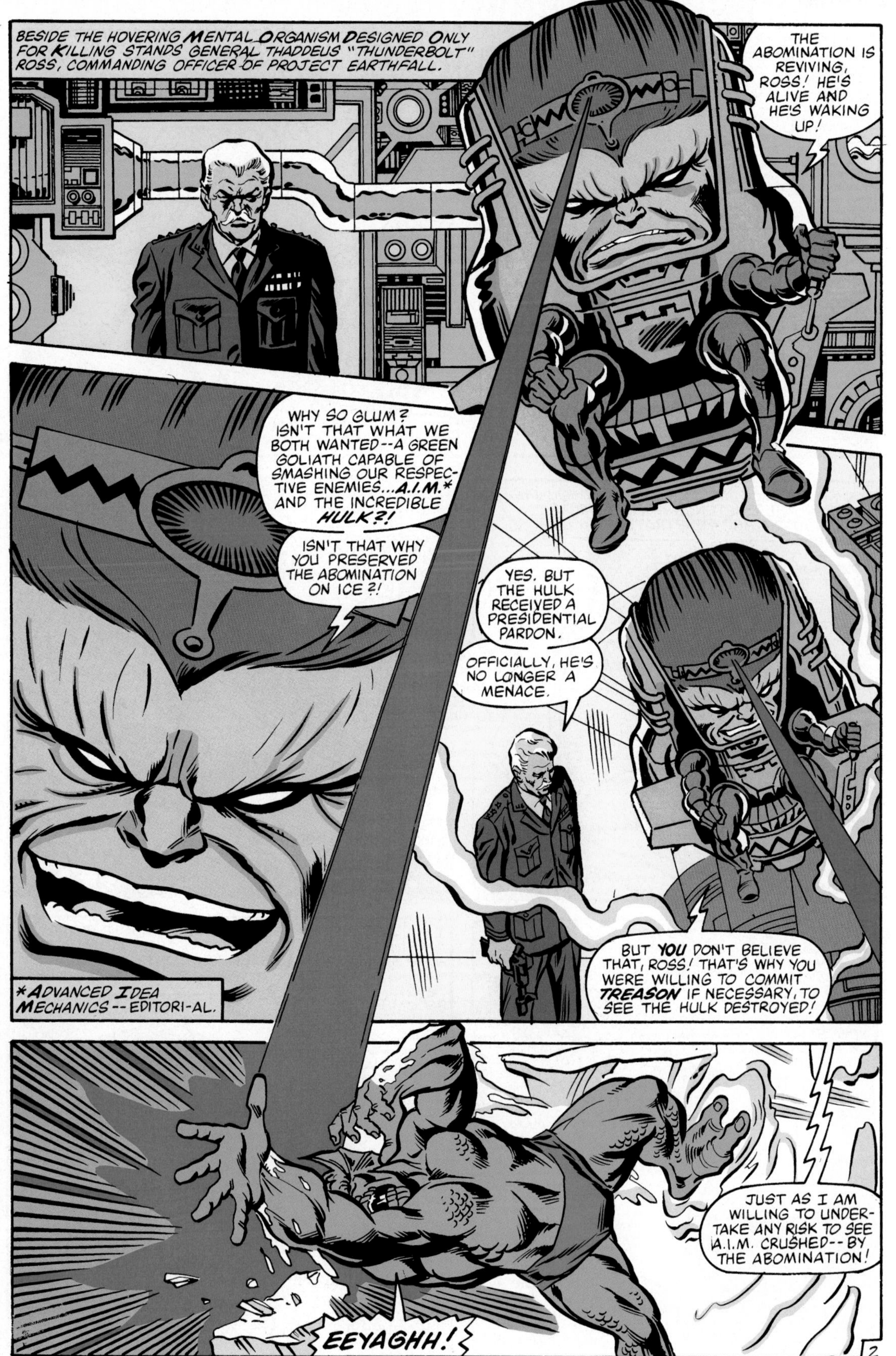
BESIDE THE HOVERING MENTAL ORGANISM DESIGNED ONLY FOR KILLING STANDS GENERAL THADDEUS "THUNDERBOLT" ROSS, COMMANDING OFFICER OF PROJECT EARTHFALL.
THE ABOMINATION IS REVIVING, ROSS! HE'S ALIVE AND HE'S WAKING UP!
WHY SO GLUM? ISN'T THAT WHAT WE BOTH WANTED--A GREEN GOLIATH CAPABLE OF SMASHING OUR RESPECTIVE ENEMIES...A.I.M.* AND THE INCREDIBLE HULK?!
ISN'T THAT WHY YOU PRESERVED THE ABOMINATION ON ICE?!
*ADVANCED IDEA MECHANICS--EDITORI-AL.
YES. BUT THE HULK RECEIVED A PRESIDENTIAL PARDON.
OFFICIALLY, HE'S NO LONGER A MENACE.
BUT YOU DON'T BELIEVE THAT, ROSS! THAT'S WHY YOU WERE WILLING TO COMMIT TREASON IF NECESSARY, TO SEE THE HULK DESTROYED!
JUST AS I AM WILLING TO UNDERTAKE ANY RISK TO SEE A.I.M. CRUSHED--BY THE ABOMINATION!
EEYAGHH!
2

AT LAST THE GLOWING BAND ON MODOK'S BROW DIMS...
UNNHHH! ENOUGH! NO MORE PAIN!

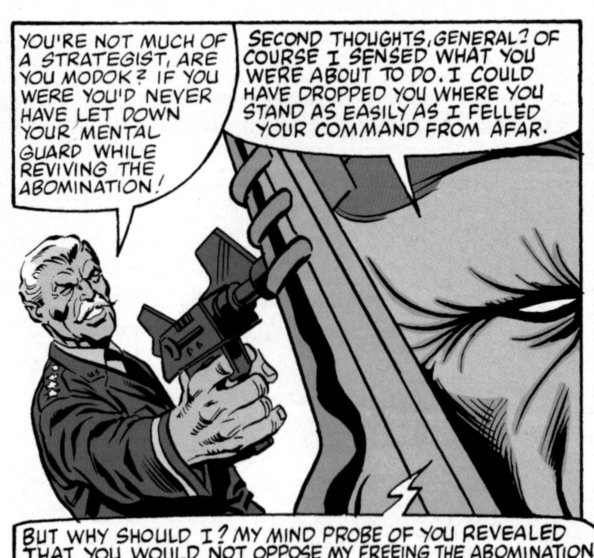
YOU'RE NOT MUCH OF A STRATEGIST, ARE YOU MODOK? IF YOU WERE YOU'D NEVER HAVE LET DOWN YOUR MENTAL GUARD WHILE REVIVING THE ABOMINATION!
SECOND THOUGHTS, GENERAL? OF COURSE I SENSED WHAT YOU WERE ABOUT TO DO. I COULD HAVE DROPPED YOU WHERE YOU STAND AS EASILY AS I FELLED YOUR COMMAND FROM AFAR.
BUT WHY SHOULD I? MY MIND PROBE OF YOU REVEALED THAT YOU WOULD NOT OPPOSE MY FREEING THE ABOMINATION.

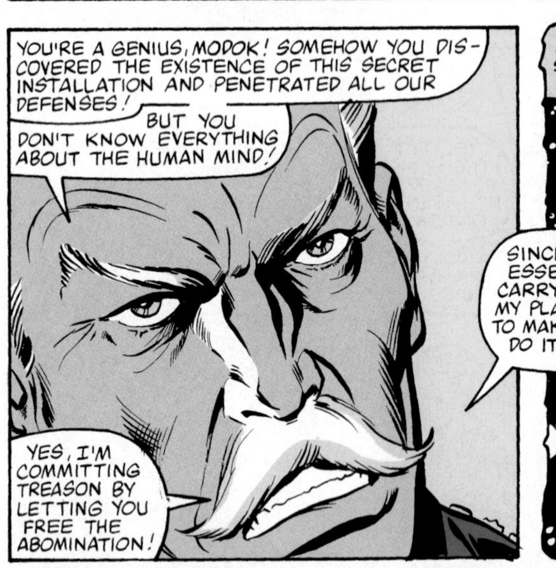
YOU'RE A GENIUS, MODOK! SOMEHOW YOU DISCOVERED THE EXISTENCE OF THIS SECRET INSTALLATION AND PENETRATED ALL OUR DEFENSES!
BUT YOU DON'T KNOW EVERYTHING ABOUT THE HUMAN MIND!
YES, I'M COMMITTING TREASON BY LETTING YOU FREE THE ABOMINATION!
SINCE YOU'RE ESSENTIALLY CARRYING OUT MY PLAN, I WANT TO MAKE SURE YOU DO IT RIGHT!

ROSS CONTINUES: "ON A RECENT FLIGHT, THE SPACE SHUTTLE DISCOVERED A BODY, IN ORBIT ABOUT EARTH, ENCASED IN A BLOCK OF SOLID ICE. *
*AFTER HIS DEFEAT BY THE HULK IN #270--EDITORI-AL.

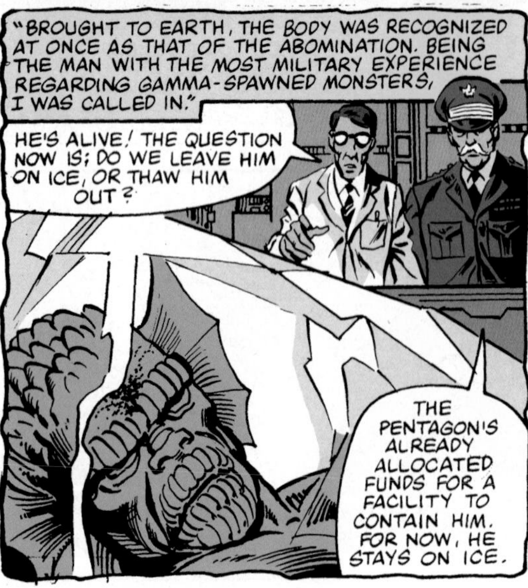
"BROUGHT TO EARTH, THE BODY WAS RECOGNIZED AT ONCE AS THAT OF THE ABOMINATION. BEING THE MAN WITH THE MOST MILITARY EXPERIENCE REGARDING GAMMA-SPAWNED MONSTERS, I WAS CALLED IN."
HE'S ALIVE! THE QUESTION NOW IS; DO WE LEAVE HIM ON ICE, OR THAW HIM OUT?
THE PENTAGON'S ALREADY ALLOCATED FUNDS FOR A FACILITY TO CONTAIN HIM. FOR NOW, HE STAYS ON ICE.

I WANTED AN ACE-IN-THE-HOLE SHOULD THE HULK EVER BECOME SAVAGE AGAIN!
BUT THE HULK HASN'T REVERTED TO SAVAGERY! HE'S REMAINED UNDER THE CONTROL OF HIS ALTER-EGO... BRUCE BANNER!
YES! THE MAN MY DAUGHTER, BETTY, MISGUIDEDLY CONTINUES TO LOVE!
3

I REALIZED THAT, IF ANYTHING COULD DESTROY THE HULK AND FREE BETTY FROM HER PERVERSE OBSESSION WITH HIM--
--IT WAS ANOTHER GREEN-SKINNED GARGOYLE... THE *ABOMINATION!*
YOUR QUANDRY WAS... HOW TO SET THE ABOMINATION ON THE HULK WITHOUT EXPOSING YOUR OWN INVOLVEMENT?
OUR GOALS DOVETAIL! YOU WISH ASSURANCES?

THEN YOU HAVE THE WORD OF MODOK THAT *AFTER* I USE THE ABOMINATION FOR MY OWN PURPOSES, I SHALL SET HIM ON THE HULK AND RID YOU OF YOUR ENEMY!
NO! THE HULK GOES FIRST-- THEN YOU CAN DO WITH THE ABOMINATION AS YOU PLEASE!
OH, VERY WELL, I AGREE... BECAUSE IT AMUSES ME TO HELP AMERICA'S MOST LOYAL SOLDIER BECOME A TRAITOR!

THEN WE HAVE A BARGAIN--A COVENANT BETWEEN A TRAITOR AND A FREAK!

PLEASE, GENERAL--THINK OF US RATHER AS TWO BUSINESSMEN ENTERING INTO A CONTRACT TO ATTAIN A MUTUALLY BENEFICIAL GOAL! I, TOO, HAVE REASON TO HATE THE HULK--
--THOUGH MINE ARE PERHAPS NOT SO COMPELLING AS YOURS!
I WILL BE BOUND BY OUR AGREEMENT! THE ABOMINATION WILL BE SET UPON THE HULK!
SHALL WE ASK OUR GAMMA-SPAWNED ASSASSIN HIS OPINION OF THE TASK WE HAVE JUST SET FOR HIM?

AT THE DARK BOTTOM OF THE CRYOGENICS CORE, THE ABOMINATION LIES CURLED IN A FETAL POSITION. FROM HIS GNARLED GREEN LIPS COMES A PATHETIC, MEWLING WHINE.

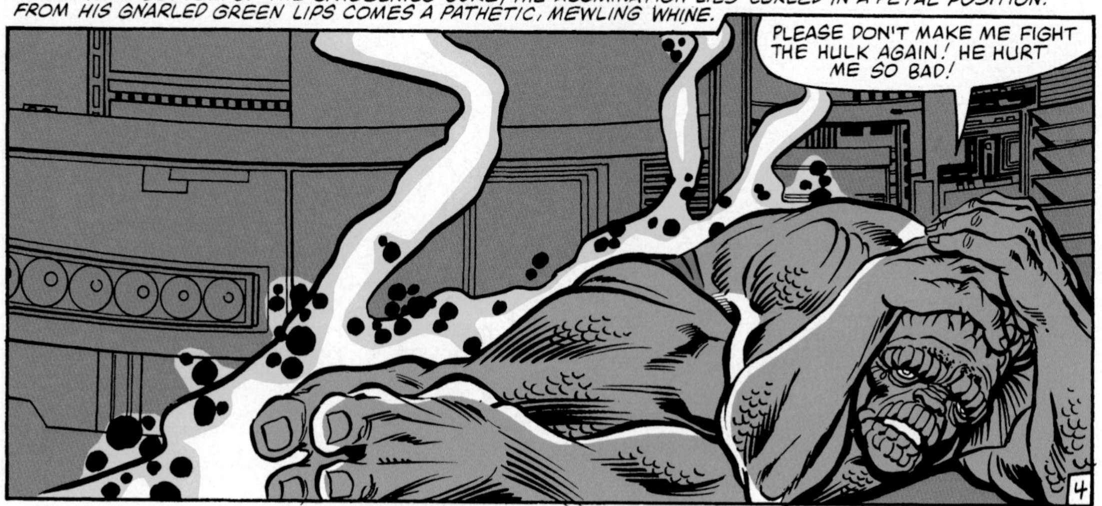

PLEASE DON'T MAKE ME FIGHT THE HULK AGAIN! HE HURT ME SO BAD!
4

WHAT IN THUNDERATION--?! THE CREATURE THAT ONCE ALMOST PULVERIZED THE HULK HAS BECOME A LILY-LIVERED COWARD!!
HMMM! THIS DOES PUT A NEW WRINKLE IN OUR PLANS!
I-I CAN'T GO UP AGAINST THE HULK AGAIN! I CAN'T!

PLEASE DON'T PUT ME THROUGH ALL THAT PAIN!
MY MIND-PROBE REVEALS THAT THE ABOMINATION WAS BEATEN SO BADLY BY THE HULK WHEN LAST THEY FOUGHT--

--THAT HE IS NOW POSSESSED BY A PATHOLOGICAL DREAD OF HIS ENEMY!
YOU MEAN HE'S YELLOW! OF ALL THE DING-BLASTED--!
I RISK COURT-MARTIAL AND COMMIT TREASON, AND THE ABOMINATION ISN'T EVEN CAPABLE OF DOING THE JOB!

FEAR NOT, MY "PARTNER!" OUR PLANS SHALL PROGRESS APACE--
--ONCE I RE-EDUCATE THIS COWARD TO THE WAYS OF POWER! AS FOR YOU--
WHAT ARE YOU--! ARRGHH!

YOU WOULDN'T WANT IT TO APPEAR AS IF GENERAL THUNDERBOLT ROSS SURRENDERED HIS CHARGE WITHOUT RESISTANCE, WOULD YOU?
BUT I SHALL KEEP OUR BARGAIN, FOR MODOK IS A FAIR MAN.
MODOK'S LAUGHTER MINGLES WITH THE ABOMINATION'S WHIMPERS AS THEY DEMATERIALIZE.
5

PAIN.
GLLRRARRGHH!
WHO COULD INFLICT SUCH ANGUISH ON THE MIGHTIEST MORTAL ON THE FACE OF THE EARTH ?!!
6

NOW, DR. BANNER, RELAX-- I'VE BARELY STARTED DRILLING!
A LITTLE LASER COULDN'T POSSIBLY CAUSE PAIN TO A BIG GREEN GENT LIKE YOU, COULD IT?
GLAAR-UMMPHH!

THAT'S WHAT I THOUGHT! NOW JUST SIT BACK!

WE JUST NEED TO SHAVE ONE TINY TOOTH SAMPLE, AND THEN WE'LL BE ALL THROUGH!
RAARGHH!
REMARKABLE! NOT A TRACE OF DECAY! DO YOU BRUSH AFTER MEALS?
7

I--OUCH--NEVER SEEM TO NEED TO! AS THE HULK, I APPEAR TO BE IMMUNE TOO--OOH--DISEASE AND INFECTION!
ISN'T THAT SOME-THING?
CAN I ASK WHY YOU DIDN'T--OOH--ANESTHETIZE ME BE-FORE EXTRACTING THAT TOOTH SHAVING?
ARE YOU KIDDING? THE AMOUNT OF ANESTHETIC IT WOULD COST TO PUT YOU UNDER WOULD BE ASTRONOMICAL!
BUT I THOUGHT THE GOVERN-MENT WAS PAYING, AS PART OF THEIR STUDY OF THE HULK?
THEY ARE, BUT THIS IS A TIME OF AUSTERITY, YOU KNOW! AH, HERE WE ARE!
THE FIRST COMPLETE SET OF DENTAL X-RAYS ON THE INCREDIBLE HULK!
I DARESAY WE COULDN'T HAVE GOTTEN YOU TO SIT STILL FOR THESE A YEAR AGO!
NOT IF YOU'D WANTED TO USE YOUR OFFICE AGAIN!
YES, I HEAR TELL YOU WERE QUITE A ROUGH-HOUSER!
TO PUT IT MILDLY.
SHORTLY, IN THE DENTIST'S WAITING ROOM...
HERE HE IS, DR. WAYNESBORO! I TOLD YOU I'D RETURN HIM TO YOU IN ONE PIECE!
DR. BANNER, ARE YOU ALL RIGHT?
THE RECORDA-SPHERE AND I WERE A LITTLE WORRIED WHEN WE HEARD YOUR SCREAMS, BRUCE!

SCREAM? ME? THAT MUST HAVE BEEN THE WHINE OF THE DRILL YOU HEARD!
I WAS AS CALM AS A KITTEN!
I DIDN'T FEEL A THING!
HEY! I DON'T FEEL A THING!
THE PAIN'S GONE! THAT CONFIRMS AN OLD THEORY OF MINE --WHAT HURTS THE HULK DOESN'T HURT ME, AND VICE VERSA!
THEN IT DID HURT!
WELL, I WOULDN'T WANT TO GO THROUGH A "CHECK-UP" LIKE THAT EVERY DAY, SPHERE--
--BUT IT WAS INTERESTING TO SUBJECT THE HULK TO THAT LITTLE BIT OF NORMALCY... A "VISIT TO THE DENTIST"... THAT EVERYONE ELSE HAS TO GO THROUGH IN THIS LIFE.
YOU SEE, BRUCE--YOU ARE ADJUSTING! WHY, SOMEDAY YOU'LL NO LONGER EVEN REGARD THE HULK--
--AS ANY DIFFERENT FROM THE REST OF HUMANITY!
I... HOPE YOU'RE RIGHT, KATE--BUT THE HULK IS DIFFERENT...
...AND THESE DAYS HE'S ONLY DORMANT, SUBJUGATED TO BRUCE BANNER'S INTELLECT!
I DREAD THE DAY HE WAKES UP!
9

THE HULK WON'T WAKE UP, DR. BANNER! HIS ID IS GONE! IT'S *YOUR* MIND THAT'S IN CONTROL NOW!
DR. BATES DDS
THERE'S ALWAYS A CHANCE THAT COULD CHANGE, 'SPHERE. COME ON --LET'S HEAD BACK TO THE OBSERVATORY.
YOU GO AHEAD, BRUCE! I JUST HAVE TO SET UP AN APPOINTMENT WITH THE DOCTOR FOR MYSELF!

WITH *DR. FURY*, YOU MEAN, AGENT WAYNESBORO?
NO, I DON'T NEED TO SEE NICK YET, AGENT BATES. JUST MAKE SURE YOU FORWARD MULTIPLE COPIES OF THE HULK'S X-RAYS AND OF YOUR REPORT TO THE PROPER UNIT.
I KNOW MY DUTY, "DOCTOR," AND I DO WHAT I CAN FOR THE CAUSE!

REMEMBER: DON'T YIELD, BACK S.H.I.E.L.D.!
THOUGH THEY CONVERSED IN WHISPERS, THE RECORDASPHERE HAS OVERHEARD.

THE WINDING MOUNTAIN DRIVE BACK TO NORTHWIND OBSERVATORY--BRUCE BANNER'S PRIVATE RESEARCH CENTER AND SANCTUM SANCTORUM--TAKES SEVERAL HOURS.
I THINK YOU'RE BEGINNING TO LEARN THAT BEING THE HULK NEEDN'T SET YOU APART FROM YOUR FELLOW MEN, BRUCE!

IT'S ALREADY SET ME APART FROM MY FELLOW WOMAN, KATE!
YOU'RE TALKING ABOUT *BETTY ROSS*, AREN'T YOU? THE WOMAN YOU ALMOST MARRIED?
10

YOU KNOW ABOUT BETTY, KATE?
OH, COME NOW, BRUCE! THERE'S VERY LITTLE ABOUT ANY ASPECT OF YOUR LIFE... AS THE HULK OR BRUCE BANNER... THAT WASN'T MADE PART OF THE PUBLIC RECORD AFTER YOUR PARDON!
AND THAT INCLUDES YOUR LOVE-AFFAIR WITH THE DAUGHTER OF GENERAL "THUNDERBOLT" ROSS!

I SUPPOSE SO. BETTY WAS BESIDE ME FOR SO LONG-- THROUGH SO MANY OF MY TRIALS AND TORMENTS AS THE HULK-- THAT I GUESS I ALWAYS TOOK IT FOR GRANTED THAT ONE DAY WE'D GET MARRIED.

BUT BETTY WAS ALWAYS HOPING I'D FIND A FINAL CURE FOR THE CURSE OF BECOMING THE HULK!

SHE COULDN'T ACCEPT IT WHEN I BECAME BOTH THE HULK AND BRUCE BANNER!
THAT WAS HER MISTAKE!

I THINK YOU'RE GOING TO FIND THAT MORE AND MORE PEOPLE ARE READY AND WILLING TO ACCEPT YOU--

--FOR THE MAN YOU ARE NOW!

A LOT MORE PEOPLE, BRUCE-- STARTING WITH ME!
THE RECORDASPHERE HAS MONITORED THIS CONVERSATION.
11

NOW IT RISES UP ANGRY!
I WAS CREATED BY BRUCE TO BE HIS RESEARCH ASSISTANT -- TO BE HIS SOLE COMPANION!
THEN SHE CAME ALONG...
...TO SPY ON BRUCE FOR THE SPY ORGANIZATION, S.H.I.E.L.D.!
I DON'T KNOW WHAT SHE HOPES TO DISCOVER--
--BUT SHE'LL LEARN NOTHING NOW!
AN INVISIBLE ELECTRONIC CHARGE STABS FORTH FROM THE RECORDASPHERE.
IT STRIKES THE STEERING COLUMN OF KATHERINE WAYNESBORO'S CAR.
BRUCE! THE WHEEL IS JAMMED! I--I CAN'T STEER!
WHAT--?! HERE LET ME TRY!
BRUCE BANNER FARES NO BETTER.
SKREE
THE CAR CAREENS OUT OF CONTROL!
KRASH
SKRAK
DR. BANNER! BECOME THE HULK! SAVE YOURSELF!
12

KER-RASH
NO!

BRUCE, WE'RE FALLING! WE'RE GOING TO DIE!
NO!

LORD! WE STRUCK HARD!

KATE'S SHOULDER-HARNESS SAVED HER LIFE, BUT SHE'S BEEN KNOCKED UNCONSCIOUS!

WHY DIDN'T DR. BANNER ESCAPE?! WHAT'S HE WAITING FOR?

WHAT INDEED...
I'VE GOT TO GET US OUT OF HERE BEFORE THE GAS TANK ERUPTS!
AND THERE'S ONLY ONE WAY TO ESCAPE THAT IMMINENT INFERNO NOW!
13

BRUCE BANNER'S FEARS PROVE WELL-FOUNDED. FLAMES SPRING FORTH FROM THE CAR'S GAS TANK...
...AND, IN SECONDS, THEY PROCEED TO ENGULF THE REST OF THE VEHICLE.
BUT BRUCE BANNER WILL NOT PERISH MIDST A MASS OF CHARRED AND TWISTED METAL THIS DAY!
THANKS TO THE POWER OF THE INCREDIBLE HULK, NO ONE WILL!
PUHWHOOM!
WE MADE IT!
DR. BANNER-- YOU'RE ALIVE!
AND DR. WAYNESBORO?
SHE'S UNCONSCIOUS! SHE STRUCK HER HEAD DURING THE CRASH!
14

SHE MUST HAVE SUFFERED A CONCUSSION! THERE'S NO HOSPITAL NEARBY--

--BUT THERE IS MY MED-LAB AT NORTHWIND! I'VE GOT TO GET HER THERE!
MIGHTY LEG MUSCLES FLEX AND UNCOIL, PROPELLING THE HULK AND HIS CHARGE HEAVENWARD.

IN THEIR WAKE, THE RECORDASPHERE IS FORGOTTEN.

NO! I WON'T GIVE DR. BANNER UP TO THAT... THAT SPY, SO EASILY!

SO THE SHIMMERING SPHERE STREAKS AFTER THE GREEN GOLIATH.
IN HIS CONCERN FOR KATHERINE WAYNESBORO, BRUCE BANNER DOES NOT EVEN NOTICE ITS PRESENCE.
WOULD HE PAY MORE ATTENTION IF HE KNEW THAT IT WAS THE RECORDA-SPHERE THAT NEARLY KILLED THEM BOTH...
...FOR LOVE?

NORTHWIND OBSERVATORY.
15

THWOOM!

GO ON AHEAD, 'SPHERE! PREPARE THE MED-LAB TO RECEIVE DR. WAYNESBORO!

PR-PREPARE ME? FOR WHAT?

KATE! YOU'RE ALL RIGHT!
BRUCE? YOU'RE THE HULK NOW?
OH! NOW I REMEMBER--THE ACCIDENT! DEATH SEEMED CERTAIN--

--BUT YOU SAVED US!
I JUST DID WHAT COMES NATURALLY... MMPPHHH!

DR. KATHERINE WAYNESBORO ALSO DOES THAT WHICH COMES NATURALLY...
...AND WHO IS BRUCE BANNER TO ARGUE WITH NATURE?
16

SOMEWHERE ELSE...
...IN THE DARK.

ARISE, ABOMINATION! CEASE YOUR PATHETIC WHIMPERING!
I-I CAN'T! I'M AFRAID!

YOU POSSESS MORE POWER THAN MOST MORTALS CAN CONCEIVE!
BUT I'M TOO SCARED TO USE IT! I-I DON'T WANT TO BE HURT AGAIN!

HURT? YOU THINK THAT THE BEATING THE HULK GAVE YOU, HURT?!
CRINGING, CRAVEN CUR! MODOK WILL SHOW YOU THE TRUE MEANING OF PAIN!

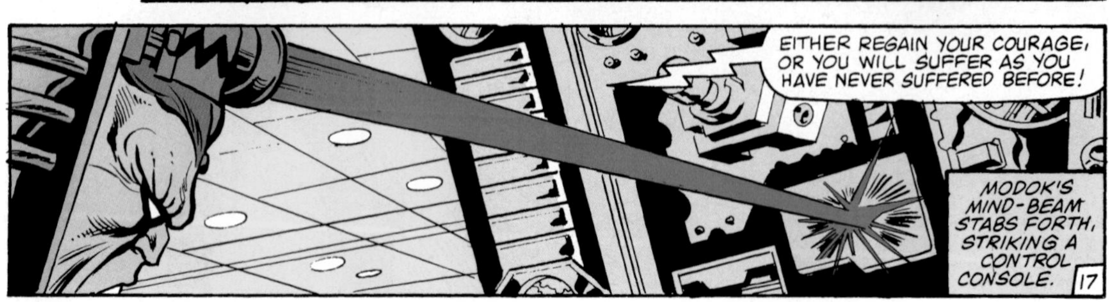
EITHER REGAIN YOUR COURAGE, OR YOU WILL SUFFER AS YOU HAVE NEVER SUFFERED BEFORE!
MODOK'S MIND-BEAM STABS FORTH, STRIKING A CONTROL CONSOLE.
17

INSTANTLY, THE CHAMBER IN WHICH THE ABOMINATION COWERS IS FLOODED WITH LIGHT... AND WITH THE PROMISE OF PAIN!

ENERGY BEAMS LASHING THE CHAMBER!

THEY MUST BE DESIGNED TO CAUSE EXCRUTIATING AGONY!

NOW PLASMIFIRE SHOOTING FROM WALL-MOUNTED CANNONS--

ARRRGH!

I'VE GOTTA RUN--GOTTA GET OUT OF HERE!

THERE IS NOWHERE TO RUN, ABOMINATION!
WHEREVER YOU GO, THE PAIN WILL PURSUE YOU!
ARRGHHH!
18

THE ONLY WAY TO PREVENT THE PAIN--IS TO *FIGHT!*

I-I CAN'T! DON'T YOU UNDERSTAND THAT! THE ONLY THING FIGHTING EVER GOT ME--
--IS *HURT!*

I-I'D RATHER *DIE* THAN BE HURT LIKE THAT AGAIN!
CRRACKKLE

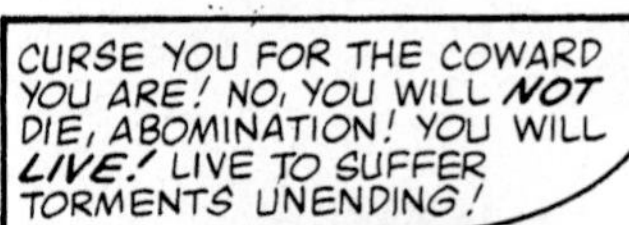

CURSE YOU FOR THE COWARD YOU ARE! NO, YOU WILL *NOT* DIE, ABOMINATION! YOU WILL *LIVE!* LIVE TO SUFFER TORMENTS UNENDING!

THE AGONY WILL ONLY DESIST IF YOU *FIGHT!!*

Y-YOU MEAN YOU'LL GO ON HURTING ME LIKE THIS *FOREVER*, UNLESS I DO YOUR FIGHTING FOR YOU?!!

WHAT KIND OF SADIST ARE YOU?!!
19

I HAVE A MISSION FOR YOU TO PERFORM, YOU GREEN-SKINNED GROTESQUERIE!
A.I.M., WHO CREATED ME, STILL POSSESSES THE SECRETS OF MY CREATION!

LATELY I HAVE LEARNED THAT THEY HAVE BEGUN TO CREATE ANOTHER LIKE ME--A SECOND MODOK-- BUT UNLIKE ME, ONE TOTALLY SUBSERVIENT TO THEMSELVES!

I DO NOT KNOW IF I COULD WIN IN A BATTLE AGAINST MY EQUAL!

I DO NOT WISH TO FIND OUT! THAT IS WHERE YOU COME IN!

ONCE WE HAVE FULFILLED OUR BARGAIN WITH GENERAL THUNDERBOLT ROSS, YOU SHALL STRIKE AT A.I.M. FOR ME!
YOU WANT YOUR ENEMIES SMASHED-- I'LL SMASH 'EM!

JUST DON'T SEND ME UP AGAINST THE HULK AGAIN!
20

I DON'T HAVE WHAT IT TAKES TO BEAT HIM! '

HE'S ALWAYS BEEN STRONGER--MORE SAV-AGE THAN ME!

DON'T YOU SEE--AGAINST THE HULK, I CAN'T WIN!!!

PLEASE, I'M BEGGING YOU--I'LL FIGHT ANY-ONE ELSE YOU ASK!
BUT NOT HIM! NOT THE HULK!

YOU WILL FIGHT THE HULK, ABOMINATION--AND YOU WILL TRIUMPH OVER HIM! MUCH HAS CHANGED WHILE YOU FLOATED FROZEN IN SPACE!
THE HULK IS DOMINATED BY BRUCE BANNER'S MIND NOW! MY DATA INDICATES THAT HE IS INCAPABLE OF THE SAVAGE RAGE THAT MADE THE HULK SO FORMIDABLE!
21

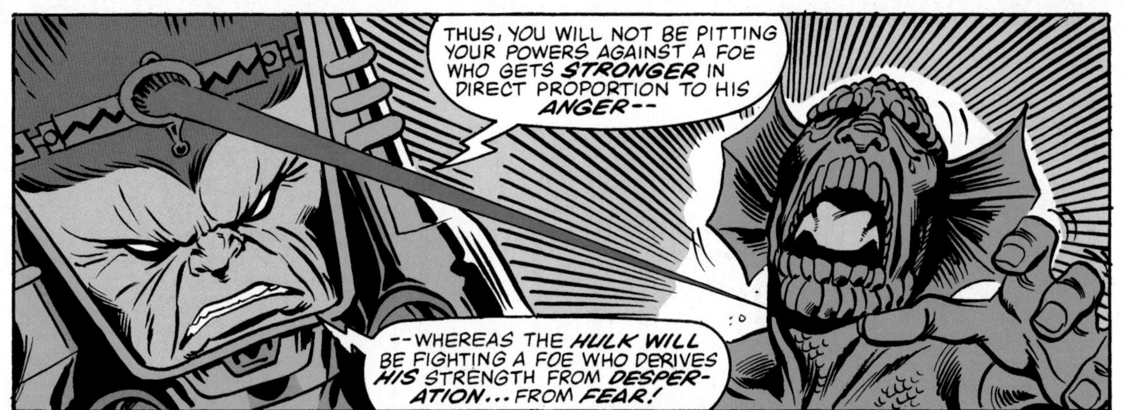
THUS, YOU WILL NOT BE PITTING YOUR POWERS AGAINST A FOE WHO GETS STRONGER IN DIRECT PROPORTION TO HIS ANGER--
--WHEREAS THE HULK WILL BE FIGHTING A FOE WHO DERIVES HIS STRENGTH FROM DESPERATION... FROM FEAR!

WHEN I AM DONE WITH YOU, ABOMINATION, YOU WILL BECOME MIGHTIER IN DIRECT PROPORTION TO YOUR DESIRE TO AVOID PAIN!
THE MORE INTENSE YOUR FEAR OF ME, THE STRONGER WILL YOU BE!!!
NO! NO! NO!
YES, ABOMINATION! YES! YOU WILL ATTACK THE HULK AND DESTROY HIM--OR I WILL CAUSE YOU FAR MORE PAIN THAN YOU HAVE EVER DARED DREAM!
22
NEXT MONTH: PHASE ONE!

MARVEL®
THE INCREDIBLE HULK®
© 1983 MARVEL COMICS GROUP
TM
60¢
289
NOV
02456
APPROVED BY THE COMICS CODE AUTHORITY
MIKROM

Stan Lee PRESENTS: THE INCREDIBLE HULK!®

BILL MANTLO STORY · SAL BUSCEMA & JOE SINNOTT ART · JOE ROSEN LETTERS · BOB SHAREN COLORS · CARL POTTS EDITOR · JIM SHOOTER LORD HIGH SOME-THING OR OTHER

WITHIN THE CLIFFSIDE COMMAND CENTER, A STRANGE DEFORMED CREATURE TRIES TO RALLY A.I.M. FORCE YELLOW AS PANDEMONIUM REIGNS!
STAND AND FIGHT, YOU SCURVY DOGS! YOU ARE ARMED WITH THE GREATEST WEAPONS A.I.M. HAS EVER DEVISED!
WITH THEM, WE COULD BEAT BACK A CONVENTIONAL ARMY WITH EASE--
--LET ALONE A ROGUE FACTION OF A.I.M.!

HIS EXHORTATIONS TO THE TROOPS THUNDER IN THEIR MINDS. HE DOES NOT HAVE TO SPEAK TO COMMAND!
FOR HE IS MODOK--MENTAL ORGANISM DESIGNED ONLY FOR KILLING!

MODOK! THE BLUES HAVE BROKEN THROUGH OUR DEFENSES!
YES, YELLOW! AND WITH THE SAME EASE--

--AS WE SHALL BATTLE PAST YOU!
ARRGH!
AIIEEE!

A SURPRISE ATTACK! INCONCEIVABLE! HOW COULD ANY OPERATION BE MOUNTED AGAINST ME--
--WITHOUT MY COMPUTER-LIKE BRAIN CALCULATING THE PROBABILITY AND MAKING ME AWARE OF IT?
BUT PERHAPS I HAVE SPENT TOO MUCH TIME PSYCHO-TRAINING THE ABOMINATION, AND DISPATCHING THAT FEAR-CRAZED CREATURE TO ATTACK THE HULK--
2

INCREDIBLY SOPHISTICATED ARMAMENTS ERUPT, BLASTING OUT AT MODOK FROM EVERY SIDE!

AN ADMIRABLE ATTEMPT, FOOLS... SACRIFICING SOME OF YOUR RANKS TO SET ME UP IN YOUR AMBUSH! THOUGH YOU DON'T STAND ANY CHANCE OF SLAYING ME--NOT WHILE MY MUTATED MIND IS CAPABLE OF FORMING PSIONIC FORCE SHIELDS!

3

AND NOT WHILE MY MIND-GUIDED HOVERCHAIR CAN CARRY ME ABOVE THE BATTLE--
--TO A VANTAGE POINT FROM WHICH TO LAUNCH AN ATTACK OF MY OWN!
YOU'LL NOT ESCAPE US, YOU ACCURSED DEFORMITY!
AH, BUT THERE YOU ARE WRONG!
THERE'S TOO MUCH FIREPOWER AGAINST ME HERE. I MIGHT NOT BE ABLE TO HOLD UP MY SHIELDS LONG ENOUGH TO GAIN CONTROL.
ESCAPE YOU, I SHALL, BY MIND-BLASTING A RETREAT--
--THROUGH THE VERY MASS OF MOUNTAIN BEHIND MY BASE!
BUT I SHALL RETURN--THE ABOMINATION BY MY SIDE--AND A.I.M. SHALL RUE THE DAY THEY DARED DEFY...MODOK!
4

WELL, WHAT OF THE AWESOME ABOMINATION?
WE'RE GLAD YOU ASKED...
...BECAUSE THAT GIVES US THE OPPORTUNITY TO SHIFT SCENES, AND FOCUS ON THE QUIVERING, COWERING FIGURE CROUCHED BEHIND AN OUTCROPPING NEAR NORTHWIND OBSERVATORY.
TH-THAT'S WHERE MODOK TOLD ME I'D FIND THE HULK!

I'M SUPPOSED T'BUST IN THERE AND KILL HIM!

I SHOULD BE ABLE T'DO IT! IT WAS GAMMA RAYS MADE US BOTH MONSTERS--AND MADE ME STRONGER!
BUT I'M SCARED!

DESPITE ALL MY POWER, THE HULK ALWAYS BEATS ME--AND BEATS ME BAD!
I DON'T WANT T' TAKE THAT KIND OF THRASHIN' AGAIN!
BUT I AIN'T GOT ANY CHOICE!
EITHER I TACKLE THE HULK--OR MODOK'LL HURT ME WORSE!

AS THE ABOMINATION'S FEAR DRIVES HIM ONTO THE HORNS OF A DILEMMA...THE OBJECT OF HIS MISSION SLEEPS.
DR. BANNER? BRUCE?
SSSHHHH!

CAN'T YOU SEE HE'S RESTING?
OH. I CAME TO RELIEVE HIM.
OF WHAT? HIS DUTIES... OR HIS SELF-RESPECT?
5

I...BEG YOUR PARDON?
IT'S DR. BANNER'S PARDON YOU SHOULD BE BEGGING, DR. WAYNESBORO!
IF HE ONLY KNEW HOW YOU'D ABUSED HIS TRUST--OR WHY YOU'VE INSINUATED YOURSELF INTO HIS AFFECTIONS...!

RECORDASPHERE, I... THINK YOU HAVE EXCEEDED YOUR PROGRAMMING!
DR. BANNER CREATED ME TO BE HIS COMPANION HERE AT NORTHWIND--HIS CONFIDANT.

YOU'VE USURPED BOTH ROLES!
I'M A SCIENTIST--A STUDENT OF GAMMA RADIATION!
I'M HERE TO ASSIST DR. BANNER--BRUCE--WITH HIS RESEARCH!

NO! YOU'RE LYING! YOU'RE HERE BECAUSE BRUCE BANNER--AS THE HULK--WAS ONCE A MENACE TO SOCIETY...A MONSTER!
YOU'RE HERE TO MONITOR HIS ADJUSTMENT TO NORMAL LIFE ...AND PROVIDE EARLY WARNING SHOULD BRUCE BECOME A MONSTER AGAIN!

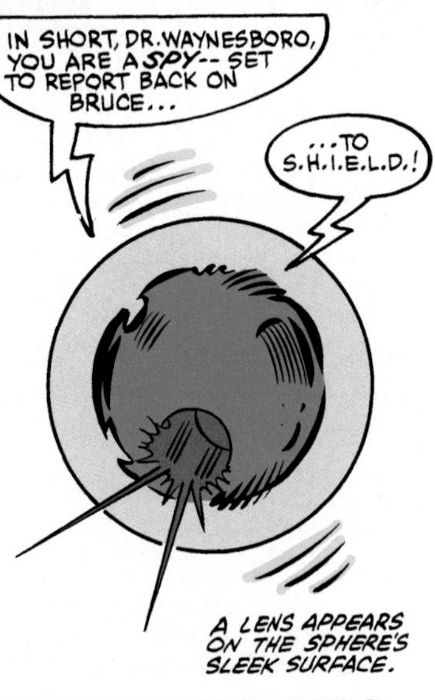
IN SHORT, DR. WAYNESBORO, YOU ARE A SPY--SET TO REPORT BACK ON BRUCE...
...TO S.H.I.E.L.D.!
A LENS APPEARS ON THE SPHERE'S SLEEK SURFACE.

LASER?
YES, DR. WAYNESBORO! YOU WERE RIGHT--I HAVE EXCEEDED MY PROGRAMMING...THAT I MIGHT BETTER PROTECT DR. BANNER!
PROTECT? BUT I'M NOT HERE TO HARM BRUCE, SPHERE! YES, I AM AN AGENT OF S.H.I.E.L.D.--
6

--BUT I'M NOT HERE TO SPY ON BRUCE! THE MED-SCANS WE CONDUCTED ON THE HULK HAVE REVEALED A STRANGE FLUCTUATION IN HIS GAMMA LEVELS!
RIGHT NOW BRUCE CAN CONTROL HIS TRANSFORMATION INTO THE HULK!
WE'RE AFRAID OF HIS LOSING THAT CONTROL--AND REVERTING BACK TO BEING A MINDLESS MONSTER AGAIN!

I DON'T WANT THAT TO HAPPEN... FOR BRUCE'S SAKE--AND FOR THE WORLD'S!
IT WON'T HAPPEN! IT CAN'T! BRUCE IS IN CONTROL OF THE HULK NOW!
NOW... YES! BUT WHAT ABOUT TO-MORROW--OR THE NEXT DAY!
NOTHING WILL CHANGE UNLESS YOU MAKE IT CHANGE!
UNLESS YOU WITH ALL YOUR SNEAKING AND SPYING UN-NERVE HIM!
BRUCE HAS BEEN HURT ENOUGH IN HIS LIFE! I WON'T LET HIM BE HURT AGAIN!
Y-YOU KEEP RE-FERRING TO HIM AS BRUCE... INSTEAD OF DR. BANNER!
YES! AND WHO HAS A GREATER RIGHT TO CALL HIM BY NAME--
--THAN I WHO LOVE HIM!
OH, MY GOD!
KATHERINE WAYNESBORO REALIZES SHE IS IN SERIOUS TROUBLE. NOT ONLY HAS THE SPHERE EX-CEEDED ITS PROGRAMMING...
...BUT SHE'S DEALING WITH A MACHINE GONE MAD... MAD AND JEALOUS!
AT ANY EVENT, FATE CHOOSES THAT MOMENT TO PROVIDE AN INTERRUPTION...
THE HULK! D'YA HEAR ME? I WANT THE HULK!
KATRASH!
7

WHERE THE CONFRONTATION BETWEEN SPHERE AND SCIENTIST FAILED, THE ASSAULT ON NORTHWIND NOW WAKES THE SLEEPER...
WHO...? GOOD LORD! THE ABOMINATION!

BANNER! IF I CAN CRUSH YOU NOW-- BEFORE YOU BE-COME THE HULK...
...I'LL HAVE SATISFIED MODOK AND I'LL NEVER AGAIN HAVE ANYTHING TO FEAR!

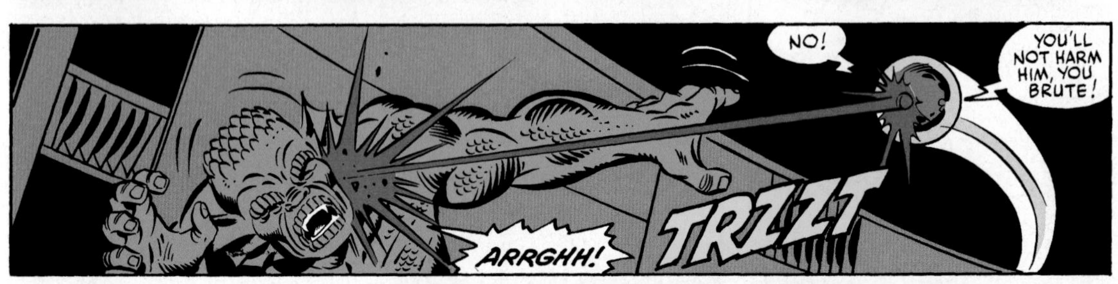
NO!
YOU'LL NOT HARM HIM, YOU BRUTE!
TRZZT
ARRGHH!

KATE! WHAT IN HEAVEN'S NAME IS GOING ON?!
THAT CREATURE BURST THROUGH THE WALLS, BRUCE, THREATENING TO KILL YOU--
--AND THE RECORDA-SPHERE'S LEAPT TO YOUR DEFENSE!
IMPOSSIBLE! THE SPHERE'S NOT PRO-GRAMMED TO ATTACK!!

"IT IS NOW!" KATHERINE WAYNESBORO WHISPERS.
ZZRAK
GRARRGH!

THAT'S TWICE YOU HURT ME, YOU SILVER SPITBALL!
SWAK
AND TWICE IS TWICE TOO MANY!
8

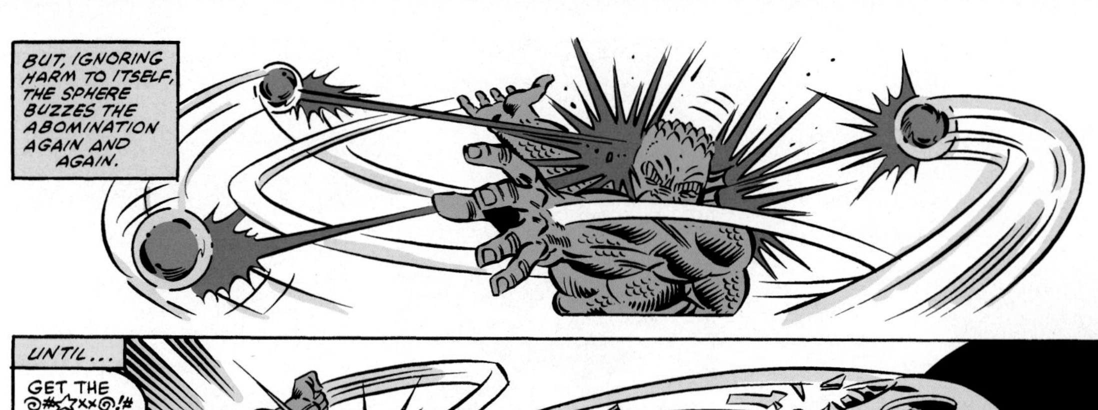
BUT, IGNORING HARM TO ITSELF, THE SPHERE BUZZES THE ABOMINATION AGAIN AND AGAIN.

UNTIL...
GET THE @#☆xx@!# AWAY FROM ME!
SPTRAK

SPLANG
TKLANG

S-SPHERE?

HAVING SUFFERED MASSIVE SYSTEMS DAMAGE, THE RECORDA-SPHERE EXPIRES...
...NEVER HAVING GOTTEN A CHANCE TO DECLARE ITS LOVE FOR ITS CREATOR.

NOW, BANNER-- I'M COMIN' FOR YOU!!
9

NO YOU'RE NOT, MONSTER! TAKE ANOTHER STEP, AND...!
WHATCHA GOT THERE, BABY? A CAN OF MACE? TEARS AIN'T GONNA KEEP ME FROM BANNER!

NO, BUT AN ION-DISRUPTOR SHOULD BE ABLE TO CONTAIN YOU LONG ENOUGH FOR HELP TO ARRIVE.
VREEET

YEEARRGH!
THE IONIC FIELD SEEMS TO HOLD THE ABOMINATION FAST...

...GIVING A WIDE-EYED BRUCE BANNER A CHANCE TO QUERY HIS RESEARCH ASSISTANT.
KATE, THAT BLASTER--?
S.H.I.E.L.D. ISSUE, BRUCE!

THEN... YOU'RE MORE THAN MERELY MY RESEARCH ASSISTANT? YOU'RE... WHAT?
MY BABY-SITTER? WATCHDOG? JAILER?
WHY, KATE? DOES S.H.I.E.L.D. DEEM MY GAMMA RAY RESEARCH SO VITAL TO OUR NATION'S SECURITY--

--THAT I COULDN'T BE TRUSTED TO CARRY IT OUT ALONE?
OR IS IT JUST THE SAME OLD SONG AND DANCE? DESPITE ALL I'VE DONE, YOU'RE STILL AFRAID THE HULK'LL GO SAVAGE AGAIN--
--AND SOMEBODY HAD TO BE HERE TO SOUND THE ALARM WHEN BRUCE BANNER AGAIN WENT BAD?
10

RARRGH! I'M OUT! I KNEW NO STINKIN' ENERGY-FIELD COULD HOLD ME FOR LONG!

YOU'RE ALL AFRAID I'LL BECOME LIKE THE ABOMINATION AGAIN, AREN'T YOU?

A GAMMA-CHARGED GARGOYLE VENTING HIS RAGE ON A DEFENSELESS EARTH!

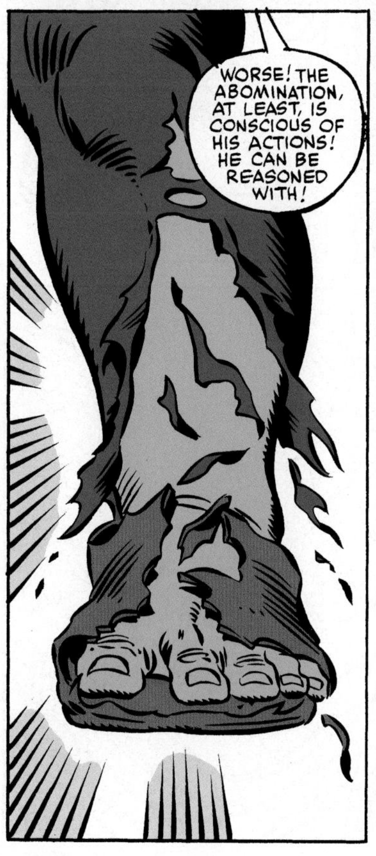
WORSE! THE ABOMINATION, AT LEAST, IS CONSCIOUS OF HIS ACTIONS! HE CAN BE REASONED WITH!

THE MENACE OF THE HULK LAY NOT ONLY IN HIS VAST, UNBEATABLE STRENGTH--

--BUT IN THE FACT THAT HIS VERY MINDLESSNESS FUELED AN IRRATIONAL ANGER...
...THAT MADE HIM THE MIGHTIEST MORTAL ON THE FACE OF THE EARTH!
11

YES, THE OLD HULK MIGHT HAVE GIVEN ANYONE REASON TO FEAR--BUT I'M *NOT* THE OLD HULK ANYMORE!

I POSSESS ALL HIS PULVERIZING POWER--BUT THE *MIND* IS MINE! THE BRAIN OF *BRUCE BANNER* CONTROLS THE MIGHT OF THE *MONSTER!*

ALL I ASKED IS THAT THE WORLD--AND YOU, KATE, AND S.H.I.E.L.D.--UNDERSTAND THAT, ACCEPT IT--

--AND TRY TO *TRUST* ME!

Y-YOU'RE THE *HULK* AGAIN! THAT BLASTED FIELD HELD ME BACK TOO LONG!

I-I CAN'T FIGHT YOU! I WON'T!

BUT, THESE PAST FEW WEEKS, THE ABOMINATION HAS BEEN SUBJECTED TO INTENSIVE AND INCREDIBLY PAINFUL PSYCHO-TRAINING.

YOU *WILL* DESTROY THE HULK--
--OR MODOK WILL TEACH YOU THE TRUE MEANING OF PAIN!

N-NO! I'LL FIGHT HIM! NOBODY'S EVER HURT ME LIKE MODOK'S HURT ME--NOT EVEN THE HULK!
DRIVEN AGAIN BY HIS TERROR, THE ABOMINATION LEAPS TOWARD THE HULK.
12

WHAT'S THAT OLD ADAGE ABOUT IRRESISTIBLE FORCE MEETING AN IMMOVABLE OBJECT?
BRADROOM
IF I CAN JUST HIT YOU HARD ENOUGH-- FAST ENOUGH-- MAYBE I CAN DROP YOU BEFORE YOU GET THE CHANCE TO HURT ME AGAIN!
THAT'S ALL I'M AFRAID OF-- GETTIN' BEAT LIKE YOU BEAT ME BEFORE!
THEN WHY FIGHT ME AT ALL? WE HAVE NO QUARREL!
I GOTTA FIGHT YOU! IF I DON'T, MODOK'LL PUNISH ME!
BUT MODOK SAYS THING'S'LL BE DIFFERENT THIS TIME! HE SAYS YOU ALWAYS BEAT ME BEFORE 'CAUSE THE MADDER YOU GOT-- THE STRONGER YOU GOT!
WELL, MAYBE THAT WAS TRUE FOR THE OLD HULK--
--BUT MODOK SAYS THE NEW HULK JUST CAN'T GET THAT KINDA MAD!
BRAM
13

AND I'M BEGINNIN' TO THINK THAT MAYBE MODOK WAS RIGHT!
I AIN'T GOT NOTHIN' TO FEAR FROM AN EGGHEAD LIKE YOU! YOU'RE THINKIN' TOO MUCH--
--ANALYZIN' TOO MUCH T'GET ANGRY LIKE THE OLD HULK DID!
MAN, MURDERIN' YOU IS GONNA BE A LEAD-PIPE CINCH!
THEN MAYBE MODOK'LL GET OFF MY CASE!
THE ABOMINATION IS RIGHT. BRUCE BANNER HAS NO DESIRE TO FIGHT. HIS ONLY ANGER...

...IS DIRECTED AT ONE HE THOUGHT WAS A FRIEND--AND MORE THAN A FRIEND.
AGENT WAYNESBORO TO S.H.I.E.L.D. HELICARRIER! COME IN!

IT WAS KATHERINE WAYNESBORO WHO HAD EASED HIS TRANSITION BACK INTO SOCIETY.
IT WAS SHE WHO HAD HELPED HIM GET OVER THE LOSS OF BETTY ROSS.

HE CAME TO TRUST HER, CONFIDE IN HER, REVEAL HIS HOPES AND DREAMS TO HER.
HE CAME TO LOVE HER...
...AND SHE BETRAYED HIM.

THAT BETRAYAL CAUSES THE INCREDIBLE HULK TO RISE UP ANGRY...

...AND, CONVENIENTLY, THERE IS ONE UPON WHOM HE CAN VENT HIS ANGER CLOSE AT HAND.
TROOM!
14

YOU WERE SAYING SOMETHING ABOUT ME NOT BEING ABLE TO BEAT YOU BECAUSE I'M INCAPABLE OF RAGE, ABOMINATION?

WELL, I'M ANGRY NOW--AND THE FUNNY THING IS... IT HAS NOTHING TO DO WITH *YOU!*

YOU JUST HAPPENED TO HAVE THE MIS-FORTUNE OF BEING IN THE WRONG PLACE, AT THE WRONG TIME!

PLEASE, DON'T HIT ME ANYMORE! DON'T HURT ME! I DON'T CARE WHAT MODOK DOES TO ME--
--I'VE HAD ENOUGH!
EH?

GOOD GOD, I GOT SO ENRAGED I FORGOT THAT THE ABOMINATION ISN'T RESPONSIBLE FOR ATTACK-ING ME!
HE'S JUST A POOR, PITIABLE, PAIN-WRACKED CREATURE DRIVEN AGAINST ME BY HIS FEAR OF MODOK--

--AND I ALMOST KILLED HIM! WHERE WAS BRUCE BANNER'S LOGIC? HIS IRON-CLAD CONTROL?
MAYBE S.H.I.E.L.D.'S RIGHT TO POST A GUARD OVER ME?
MAYBE I AM STILL CAPABLE OF BECOMING A MONSTER?
15

MAYBE NOTHING'S REALLY CHANGED?!
BRUCE, STOP IT! YOU JUST DEFENDED YOURSELF AGAINST A BERSERK BEHEMOTH, THAT'S ALL!
NO! I LOST CONTROL! I WANTED TO LASH OUT AT YOU AND S.H.I.E.L.D.--

--AND INSTEAD I NEARLY MAIMED A MONSTER DRIVEN TO ATTACK ME OUT OF TERROR!
YOU WERE SCARED, TOO?!

NO. I WAS NEVER AFRAID. I FELT SORRY FOR MY-SELF--
--AND THAT SELF-PITY MADE ME GO WILD.
IF I CAN'T CONTROL MY OWN EMOTIONS, I'LL ALWAYS BE A MENACE!

BRUCE, THAT'S TRUE OF ANYONE--MAN OR WOMAN!
WE ALL CARRY OUR OWN MONSTERS WITHIN US--EMOTIONAL DEMONS JUST WAITING TO BREAK OUT AND LAY WASTE TO OUR LIVES!

YOU'RE JUST MORE CAPABLE OF WREAKING DESTRUCTION ON YOUR OWN DREAMS THAN OTHERS! I'D LIKE TO HELP YOU CONTROL THAT TENDENCY--
--IF YOU'LL LET ME!
THE HULK BEAT ME AGAIN--HURT ME AGAIN!
I-I CAN'T SUBJECT MYSELF TO ANY MORE DRUBBIN' LIKE THAT!

BUT WHAT DO I DO? I CAN'T TRY T'HIDE! MODOK KNOWS MY MIND-PATTERNS--HE'D FIND ME!
AND I DON'T DARE RETURN T'HIM EMPTY-HANDED!
16

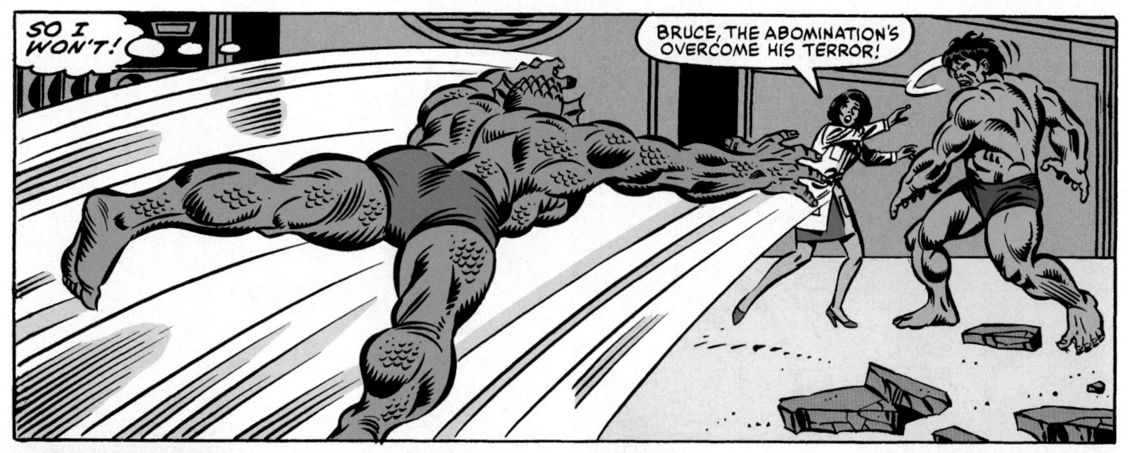
SO I WON'T!
BRUCE, THE ABOMINATION'S OVERCOME HIS TERROR!

IT'S YOUR LADYFRIEND I WANT NOW, HULK!

--AND IT'S YOUR LADY-FRIEND I'LL HAVE!
KATE!
MAYBE I COULDN'T BRING YOU T'MODOK, HULK--

--BUT AT LEAST I CAN BRING MODOK SOME-ONE YOU'RE SURE TO COME AFTER!
THE ABOMINATION'S LEAP CARRIES HIM AND KATHERINE WAYNESBORO THROUGH THE OBSERVATORY'S ROOF...

...WHICH, WEAKENED, COLLAPSES IN UPON A HULK READYING HIMSELF TO LEAP IN PURSUIT.

AS A RESULT, PRECIOUS MINUTES ARE LOST...
THE ABOMINATION'S GAMMA-IRRADI-ATED MUSCLES ENABLE HIM TO LEAP AS FAST AND AS FAR AS I!
THEY'LL BE COUNTLESS MILES AWAY BY NOW!

A VISUAL SEARCH JUST TO PICK UP THEIR TRAIL COULD CONSUME HOURS!
I'VE GOT TO DEVELOP ANOTHER WAY!
QUICKLY, THE GREEN GOLIATH SETS TO WORK...
17

...EVEN AS A U.S. ARMY HELICOPTER PREPARES TO LAND OUTSIDE OF THE OBSERVATORY.
DADDY, IT LOOKS AS IF THERE'S BEEN SOME KIND OF TROUBLE!

THERE'S ALWAYS TROUBLE, DAUGHTER--
--WHEN THE HULK IS AROUND!

I...KNOW THAT, DADDY --BETTER THAN ANYONE! THAT'S WHY I CAN NEVER SHARE A LIFE WITH BRUCE!
BUT I STILL LOVE HIM, AND DON'T WANT TO SEE HIM COME TO HARM!
YOUR LOVE FOR THE HULK IS WRONG, BETTY! ALL IT'S EVER MADE YOU IS MISERABLE!

THAT'S WHY I ASKED YOU TO COME HERE WITH ME TONIGHT!

SO I COULD SET YOU FREE FROM YOUR UNNATURAL AFFECTION--
--FOR A MAN WHO'LL NEVER BE ANYTHING OTHER THAN A MONSTER!
18

BUT THE SIGHT THAT AWAITS THE OLD SOLDIER WITHIN THE OBSERVATORY...
...IS NOT ONE EITHER GENERAL THADDEUS "THUNDERBOLT" ROSS OR HIS DAUGHTER BETTY COULD HAVE ANTICIPATED.

OH, BRUCE, THANK HEAVEN! YOU'RE ALL RIGHT! YOU'RE ALIVE!

B-BUT THAT'S IMPOSSIBLE! YOU CAN'T BE!

ANSWER ME, OLD MAN! A S.H.I.E.L.D. AGENT'S LIFE IS IN DANGER. THE ABOMINATION TOOK OFF WITH HER AFTER OUR FIGHT!
H-HE WAS IN MY CUSTODY-- AT A SECRET MILITARY BASE!
I- I TURNED HIM OVER TO MODOK...

TO KILL THE HULK, DADDY?! YOU SET LOOSE A MONSTER TO KILL A MONSTER--

--HOPING THAT, WITH THE HULK DESTROYED, I'D GIVE UP LOVING BRUCE BANNER?
THE ABOMINATION SHOWED UP HERE ALL RIGHT, ROSS-- A FEAR-CRAZED CREATURE DRIVEN TO DESTROY ME!

BUT HE FAILED-- THANKS TO THE HULK'S SAVAGE STRENGTH!
I BEAT HIM SO BADLY, I ALMOST KILLED HIM -- AND I WOULD HAVE, IF MY HUMANITY HADN'T REASSERTED ITSELF IN TIME!

YOUR FATHER'S WRONG, BETTY. I MAY HAVE THE POWER OF THE HULK -- BUT I'M NO LONGER A MONSTER.
I... BELIEVE YOU, BRUCE! I DO!
I ONLY WISH I COULD HAVE COME TO MY SENSES, SOONER!
20

BETTY, ARE YOU MAD? HOW CAN YOU PERSIST IN LOVING THIS... THIS CREATURE?!
BRUCE HAS FACED ADVERSITY THAT WOULD HAVE DRIVEN ANY OTHER MAN TO INSANITY, DADDY.
AGAINST OVERWHELMING ODDS, HE OVERCAME HIS CURSE--
--AND PROVED HIMSELF A MAN!

HE WON THE RESPECT, ADMIRATION AND ACCEPTANCE OF THIS NATION AND THE WORLD, DADDY! THE PRESIDENT PARDONED HIM OF ANY "CRIMES" HE MAY HAVE COMMITTED WHILE HE WAS THE MONSTROUS HULK!
AND YOU, DADDY, WITHOUT AUTHORIZATION, VIOLATED YOUR DUTY TO TRY AND DESTROY AN INNOCENT MAN!
THEY HAVE A WORD FOR THAT, DADDY... TREASON!
THE GAMMA-TRACKER IS FINISHED!
BETTY, I'VE GOT TO GO!
YOU SAID THAT THE ABOMINATION'D KIDNAPPED A S.H.I.E.L.D. AGENT-- A WOMAN?
KATHERINE WAYNESBORO. I ASSUME SHE'S BAIT TO DRAW ME INTO A TRAP.
DOES SHE... MEAN ANYTHING TO YOU, BRUCE?
I...DON'T KNOW, BETTY. MAYBE. BUT RIGHT NOW SHE'S JUST A HUMAN BEING IN THE HANDS OF A FIEND--
--AND I'LL EXERT ALL THE POWER OF THE INCREDIBLE HULK TO SAVE HER!
THE MIGHTIEST LEG MUSCLES OF ANY MORTAL FLEX AND UNCOIL-- DRIVING THE GREAT GREEN GARGANTUA INTO THE SKY.
21

OH, BRUCE, I'VE WAITED TOO LONG, HAVEN'T I? I-I'VE LOST YOU!

THEN I'VE WON, DAUGHTER! I'VE SET YOU FREE OF THAT FREAK!
I'VE TRIUMPHED OVER THAT GREEN-SKINNED MENACE AT LAST!

DADDY, LISTEN TO ME, BECAUSE THESE ARE THE LAST WORDS YOU'RE EVER LIKELY TO HEAR FROM MY LIPS!

BRUCE BANNER IS PROBABLY THE FINEST MAN I'VE EVER KNOWN! I WAS A FOOL NOT TO TRUST HIM WHEN HE SAID HE COULD CONTROL THE HULK--

--AND A FOOL TO ABANDON HIM WHEN HE NEEDED ME TO AID HIS TRANSITION BACK TO HUMANITY!

BECAUSE I WAS A FOOL, I MAY HAVE LOST HIM FOREVER, DADDY! I'VE NO ONE TO BLAME BUT MYSELF!

BUT, LEST YOU CONVINCE YOURSELF THAT I'M BETTER OFF WITHOUT BRUCE, FATHER--

--I JUST WANT YOU TO KNOW THAT I REALIZE, AT LONG LAST, THAT THE *TRUE MENACE* WAS NEVER THE HULK...

...BUT A MILITARY MAN WHO ALLOWED PERSONAL MOTIVES TO LEAD HIM TO BETRAY HIS DUTY!

TURNING HER BACK ON HER FATHER, BETTY ROSS LEAVES THE CONFINES OF A LIFE THAT THREATENED TO CONSUME HER. LIKE BRUCE BANNER, SHE HOPES SHE CAN START ANEW.

22

NEXT ISSUE: UNHOLY ALLIANCE!! DON'T MISS: MODOK'S MATE!

INCREDIBLE HULK: REGRESSION TPB COVER ART BY AL MILGROM & THOMAS MASON

MARVEL®
THE INCREDIBLE HULK®
© 1983 MARVEL COMICS GROUP
TM
60¢
290
DEC
02456
APPROVED BY THE COMICS CODE AUTHORITY
MILGROM

Stan Lee PRESENTS: THE INCREDIBLE HULK!®

BILL MANTLO, STORY • SAL BUSCEMA & CARLOS GARZON, ART • MICKEY HIGGINS, LETTERS • BOB SHAREN, COLORS • CARL POTTS, EDITOR • JIM SHOOTER, MASTER OF CEREMONIES

UNHOLY ALLIANCE
ABOMINATION, WHERE ARE YOU TAKING ME?!
TO MY MASTER!
TO MODOK!

TONIGHT YOU ARE CALLED TO WITNESS A KIDNAPPING.
THE KIDNAPEE IS DR. KATHERINE WAYNESBORO, SCIENTIST AND AGENT OF S.H.I.E.L.D.
HER KIDNAPPER IS THE GAMMA-IRRADIATED GARGOYLE KNOWN AS THE ABOMINATION.

THEIR DESTINATION: THIS ISOLATED ISLAND STRONG-HOLD OFF THE COAST OF MAINE.

WE'RE HERE!
IN LESS THAN AN HOUR I'VE CARRIED US FROM UPSTATE NEW YORK T'THE ATLANTIC SEABOARD.

WHEN IT COMES T'LEAPIN', I'M SECOND ONLY T'THE HULK!
THAT'S RIGHT, ABOMINATION! BRUCE CAN LEAP AS FAST AND AS FAR AS YOU CAN!
HE'LL COME AFTER US...!

THAT'S THE IDEA, LADY! THAT'S WHY I SNATCHED YOU AN' RAN! RATHER THAN FIGHT YOUR BIG GREEN BOYFRIEND--
--I FIGURED THE EASIEST WAY T'DELIVER HIM T'MODOK WAS T'HAVE HIM COME AFTER YOU!
HEY! WHAT'S THE DEAL? THIS BASE WAS BUZZIN' WHEN I LEFT. WHAT HAPPENED T'THE--

--LIGHTS?!
THEY SNAP ON SUDDENLY, FIXING THE ABOMINATION AND HIS CAPTIVE IN AN INCAN-DESCENT GLARE.
2

WHAT THE...?! WE'RE SURROUNDED!!
STAND, MONSTER-- OR BE SLAIN!
KILL THE CREATURE ANYWAY! HE WAS A SERVANT OF MODOK!
AND WE HAVE OVERTHROWN MODOK!

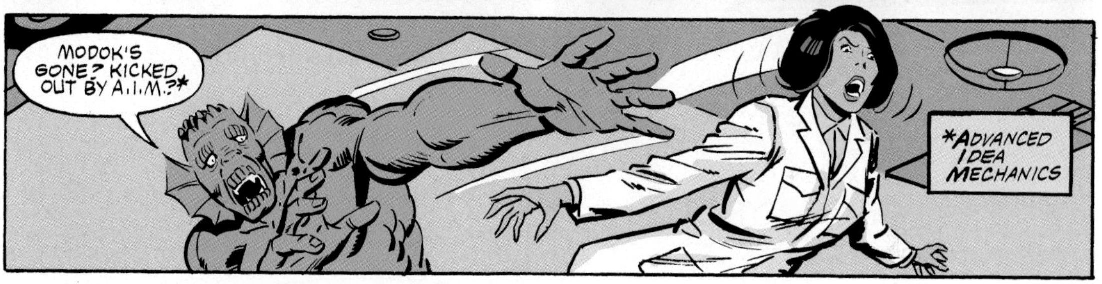
MODOK'S GONE? KICKED OUT BY A.I.M.?*
*ADVANCED IDEA MECHANICS

THAT'S GOOD! THAT'S GREAT! LISTEN, I DIDN'T WANT T'SERVE MODOK! HE MADE ME-- TORTURED ME 'TIL I HADDA SAY YES!

NOW I'M FREE OF HIM! YOU MADE ME FREE! LET ME LIVE AN' I'LL DO WHATEVER YOU WANT!

COWERING AND CRINGING, THE ABOMINATION CROUCHES IN ABJECT FEAR, AWAITING JUDGEMENT. WHEN IT COMES IT IS NEITHER PARDON NOR PUNISHMENT... ONLY PITY.
THIS CREATURE CANNOT HARM US.
MODOK RULED HIM AS HE RULED US.
YES, BUT MODOK'S REIGN OF TERROR IS ENDED.
AS A.I.M IS FREE--
--SO SHALL THIS MONSTER BE FREE.

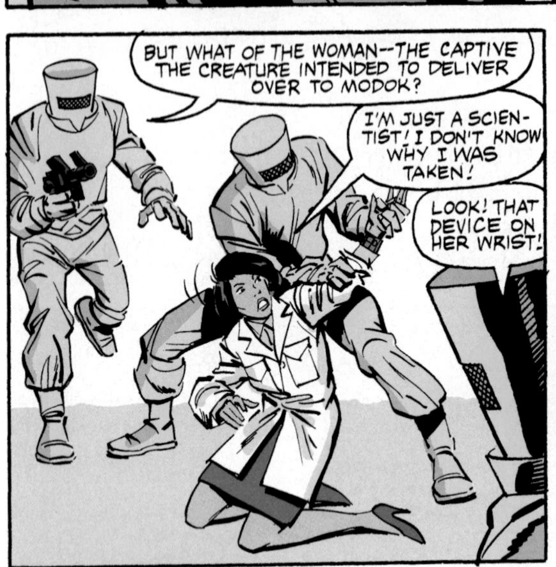
BUT WHAT OF THE WOMAN--THE CAPTIVE THE CREATURE INTENDED TO DELIVER OVER TO MODOK?
I'M JUST A SCIENTIST! I DON'T KNOW WHY I WAS TAKEN!
LOOK! THAT DEVICE ON HER WRIST!

A S.H.I.E.L.D. COMMUNICATOR!
THERE CAN BE NO DENYING TONY STARK'S HANDIWORK.

SO! A S.H.I.E.L.D. AGENT! AND THE ABOMINATION BROUGHT YOU HERE TO GIVE TO MODOK--
--AS BAIT FOR THE INCREDIBLE HULK!
WHAT'S YOUR PART IN ALL THIS?
I DON'T KNOW ANYTHING ABOUT MODOK'S PLANS!

NO? WELL, LET ME TELL YOU, THEN... MODOK INTENDED TO USE THE ABOMINATION TO SMASH DISSENSION IN A.I.M.'S RANKS.
BUT WHEN HE PROCURED THE ABOMINATION'S SERVICES, HE HAD TO BARGAIN WITH GENERAL "THUNDERBOLT" ROSS.
THE NATURE OF THEIR COMPACT: MODOK COULD HAVE THE ABOMINATION TO SUBDUE A.I.M.--IF THE ABOMINATION FIRST SLEW THE HULK.
4

BUT WHAT MODOK PLANNED IS IMMATERIAL! THE MIND-MONSTER HAS BEEN DRIVEN OFF! A.I.M. RULES THE ROOST--FREE OF HIS DASTARDLY DOMINATION AGAIN!
BUT MODOK HAS SWORN TO RETURN--AND WE MUST BE READY FOR HIM.
AND YOU, WOMAN, SHALL BECOME THE CONVENIENT WEAPON OF HIS DESTRUCTION!
ME?! HOW?!
MODOK WAS ONCE AN A.I.M. AGENT CHOSEN FROM OUR RANKS.
A POOR CHOICE. A.I.M. MISTRUSTS EVERYONE--ITS AGENTS MOST OF ALL.

THUS, WE NEEDED SOMEONE FROM OUTSIDE OUR ORGANIZATION FOR OUR NEW EXPERIMENT.
EXPERIMENT?

YES! WE INTEND TO FIGHT FIRE WITH FIRE!
A.I.M. CREATED MODOK, BUT THE CREATION TURNED ON HIS CREATORS.

STILL, ONLY ANOTHER POSSESSED OF MODOK'S STAGGERING PSIONIC POWERS CAN HOPE TO DEFEAT HIM.
SO, YOU INTEND TO CREATE... ANOTHER MODOK?
A BETTER MODOK!
ALTERATION CHAMBER
A MODOK SUBJECT TO INTENSIVE HYPNOTIC SUGGESTION THAT WILL BIND HER TO OUR CONTROL EVEN AFTER HER TRANSFORMATION TO SUPER-MIND!
YOU, WOMAN, SHALL BE THE SECOND MODOK!
5

MEANWHILE, A MILE AWAY...
THE GAMMA-TRACKER I DEVISED HAS LED ME AFTER THE ABOMINATION... AND KATE!
THEY'RE THERE...IN THAT INCREDIBLE SEASIDE EDIFICE!
I DON'T KNOW HOW IT IS THAT SUCH A STRUCTURE EXISTS UNDETECTED SO CLOSE TO THE COAST OF MAINE...
QUITE ELEMENTARY MY DEAR DR. BANNER...MASKING DEVICES CLOAK MY BASE FROM PRYING ELECTRONIC EYES.
BUT, APPARENTLY, THEY WERE INSUFFICIENT PROTECTION AGAINST YOUR SOPHISTICATED GAMMA-SENSOR.
MODOK! THE ABOMINATION DRAGGED KATE AWAY TO DELIVER HER TO YOU!
6

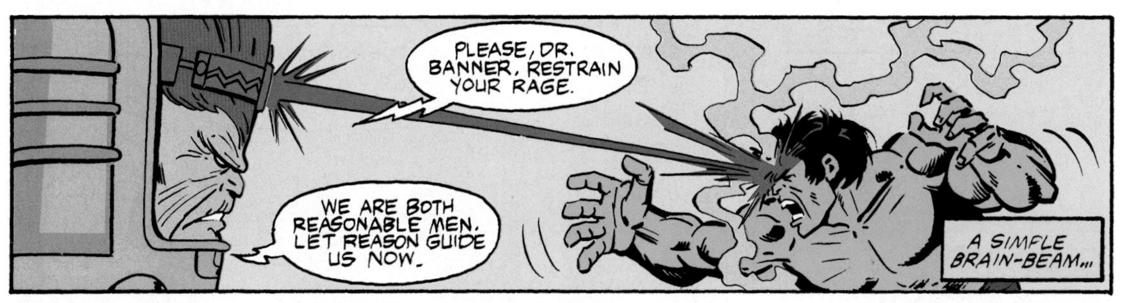
PLEASE, DR. BANNER, RESTRAIN YOUR RAGE.
WE ARE BOTH REASONABLE MEN. LET REASON GUIDE US NOW.
A SIMPLE BRAIN-BEAM...

...AND, IN HIS MIND'S EYE, THE HULK "SEES" WHAT HAS RECENTLY TRANSPIRED WITHIN THE SINISTER STRONG-HOLD.
ALTERATION CHAMBER
THE ABOMINATION TURNING KATE OVER TO AGENTS OF A.I.M.--
--FOR SOME SORT OF OBSCENE EXPERIMENT!

YES, DOCTOR, IT SEEMS THE BEST-LAID PLANS OF EVEN THE MOST MATCHLESS MINDS SOMETIMES GO AWRY.
THE ABOMINATION WAS TOO TERROR-STRICKEN TO BECOME ANYTHING BUT TREACHEROUS ONCE FREE OF ME.

AND A.I.M. HAS LIKEWISE RISEN IN REVOLT.
NOW THEY INTEND TO CREATE A NEW MODOK EVEN MIGHTIER THAN THE FIRST-- TOTALLY WITHIN THEIR CON-TROL-- TO DESTROY ME.
ALL THEY LACKED WAS A SUBJECT TO CARRY OUT THE EXPERIMENT UPON.
AND NOW THEY HAVE ONE?

REALIZATION DAWNS...
OH, MY GOD! KATE!
7

AND, WITHIN THE A.I.M. BASE...
BRING FORTH THE FEMALE!

SHE IS READY! HER GOLDEN GARB WILL CONDUCT THE GENE-ALTERING CURRENTS.
AND POSTHYPNOTIC IMPLANTS WILL ASSURE SHE SERVES A.I.M. ALONE WHEN SHE EMERGES FROM THE CHAMBER--

--TRANSFORMED!
TRANSFORMED... INTO WHAT?
INTO A PHYSICAL MANIFESTATION OF PURE INTELLECT!

LIKE MODOK, YOUR MIND WILL BECOME A WEAPON.
UNLIKE MODOK, YOUR MIND WILL BE OURS TO COMMAND.

AND I'LL BECOME... A MONSTER?!
NO! NO!
LET'S GET SOMETHING STRAIGHT ABOUT AGENTS OF S.H.I.E.L.D.
8

NOT ALL ARE CAST IN THE IMAGE OF S.H.I.E.L.D.'S COMMANDER, COLONEL NICK FURY, AS COMBAT-READY COMMANDOS,

NO, SOME ARE SIMPLY SCIENTISTS, SERVING THE CAUSE FROM LABS RATHER THAN THE FRONTLINES.
SUCH AN AGENT IS DR. KATHERINE WAYNESBORO.

SO LET'S SHOW A LITTLE SYMPATHY FOR THE LADY.
AFTER ALL, HOW MANY OF US COULD FACE WHAT SHE'S FACING,,, AND NOT SCREAM IN BLOODY TERROR?

JUST THEN,,,
EXCELLENT, DR. BANNER, YOU HAVE BREACHED MY BASE.
IT WAS YOUR MENTAL SHIELDING THAT ALLOWED US TO APPROACH THUS FAR UN-DETECTED, MODOK.

"BUT I DARESAY THERE'S NO WAY WE CAN HIDE OUR ARRIVAL NOW!"
MODOK!
AND THE HULK!
WE'RE UNDER ATTACK!

NOW THAT'S AN ASTUTE OBSERVATION IF I'VE EVER HEARD ONE!
THRAK
9

SCATTERING THOSE WHO STAND AGAINST US IS NOT ENOUGH, DOCTOR.
YOU MUST STRIKE WITHOUT MERCY IF YOU WISH TO HALT THEIR EXPERIMENT.
YAARGHH!
YOU'RE THE MENTAL ORGANISM DESIGNED ONLY FOR KILLING, MODOK!
I'M THE HULK-- A MAN WHO'S PROVEN TO THE WORLD HE'S NO LONGER A MONSTER!
I WON'T BECOME ONE AGAIN!
I FIND THE MORAL RESTRAINTS YOU PLACE UPON YOURSELF LAUGHABLE, DR. BANNER.
BUT, AS WE HAVE ACCOMPLISHED OUR INITIAL OBJECTIVE, THE DIFFERENCES IN OUR METHODS ARE IMMATERIAL.
WE'VE ONLY GOTTEN INSIDE MODOK!
WE'VE STILL GOT TO SAVE KATE!
ALTERATION CHAMBER
10

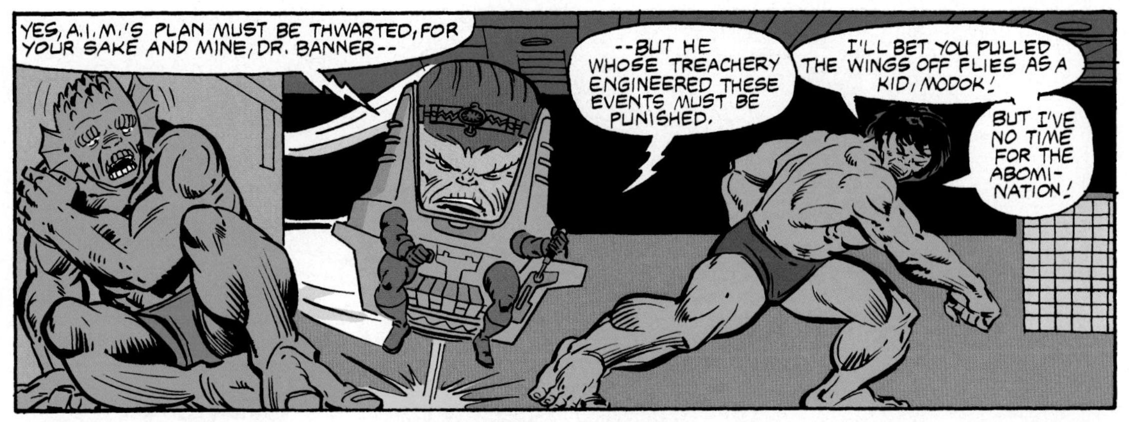
YES, A.I.M.'S PLAN MUST BE THWARTED, FOR YOUR SAKE AND MINE, DR. BANNER--
--BUT HE WHOSE TREACHERY ENGINEERED THESE EVENTS MUST BE PUNISHED.
I'LL BET YOU PULLED THE WINGS OFF FLIES AS A KID, MODOK!
BUT I'VE NO TIME FOR THE ABOMI-NATION!

I HAVE!

PLEASE, MODOK--DON'T HURT ME! ARRGH!
I NEVER WANTED TO FIGHT! I ONLY WANTED TO BE LEFT ALONE!

YOU SHALL NEVER BE ALONE AGAIN, ABOMINATION! WHEREVER YOU GO YOU SHALL CARRY WITH YOU THE TERROR INSTILLED BY MODOK!
BUT, LIKE THE HULK, I, TOO, HAVE NO MORE TIME FOR YOU!

--FOR I DETECT THE MOST... INTRIGUING ... THOUGHT-PATTERNS FROM WITHIN THE ALTERATION CHAMBER.
ALTERATION CHAMBER
KATE! GOOD GOD! LOOK WHAT THEY'VE DONE TO KATE!!
11

YES, GENTLE READER, LOOK... IF YOU DARE!
ALL HAIL... MS. MODOK!
12

WHAT HAD, SO SHORT A TIME AGO, BEEN DR. KATHERINE WAYNESBORO RISES, MIND TRANSFORMED FROM MATTER, SEATED UPON HER HOVERCHAIR LIKE A QUEEN UPON HER THRONE! YOU DON'T NEED US TO TELL YOU THAT SHE IS NOT THE WOMAN SHE WAS!
13

OH, MY POOR KATE!
THINKING SHE HAD BEEN SENT TO SPY UPON HIM, HE THOUGHT HE HATED HER. SEEING HER IN PERIL, THE HULK REALIZES...HE LOVES HER.

AND, SEEING HER TRANSFORMED, MODOK COMES TO A SIMILAR CONCLUSION.
YOU--YOUR MIND--IS... BEAUTIFUL!
I SENSE THE PRESENCE OF ANOTHER MIND SIMILAR TO MY OWN.

IT IS MODOK, HE YOU WERE CREATED TO DESTROY!
NOW LET THE POST-HYPNOTIC SUGGESTIONS IMPLANTED FIRMLY IN YOUR SUBCONSCIOUS SURFACE!
YOU MUST OBEY US--AND WE ORDER YOU... KILL MODOK!

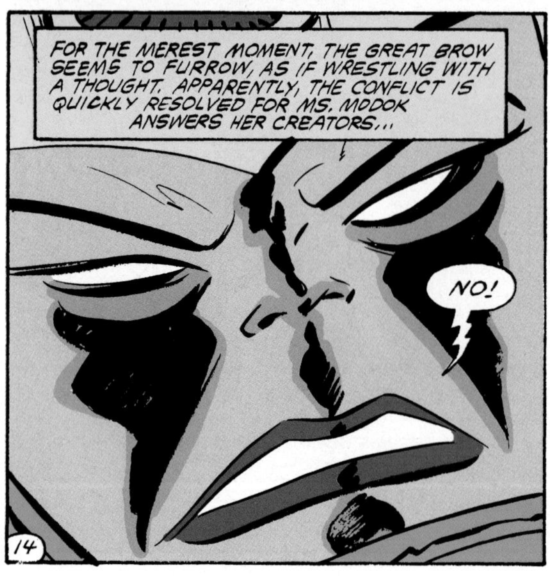
FOR THE MEREST MOMENT, THE GREAT BROW SEEMS TO FURROW, AS IF WRESTLING WITH A THOUGHT. APPARENTLY, THE CONFLICT IS QUICKLY RESOLVED FOR MS. MODOK ANSWERS HER CREATORS...
NO!
14

ALL OF A.I.M. IS STRICKEN SPEECHLESS.
FOR ALL THEIR PLANNING, ALL THEIR POST-HYPNOTIC PRECAUTIONS...

IT APPEARS THEY'VE GOOFED AGAIN!
IT WAS KATHERINE WAYNESBORO WHO WAS IMPLANTED TO OBEY A.I.M.
OBVIOUSLY, I AM NO LONGER SHE.
I AM A NEW ENTITY-- COME INTO THIS WORLD UNFETTERED BY INSTRUCTIONS OR ALLEGIANCES.
IN SHORT GENTLEMEN--MS. MODOK DOES AS SHE DESIRES.

BUT WHAT IS IT THAT KATE DESIRES?
I SHOULD HAVE THOUGHT IT OBVIOUS, DR. BANNER.

OUR THOUGHTS HAVE TOUCHED, MS. MODOK'S AND MINE.
15

WE DESIRE EACH OTHER, FOR NO OTHER INTELLIGENCE EXISTS ON EARTH--
--THAT CAN SATISFY OUR YEARNINGS FOR A MATCH OF THE MIND!

AS THE HULK STANDS STUNNED, TWO INCREDIBLE INTELLECTS TURN FROM THE MINOR ANNOYANCES AROUND THEM...
...AND REACH OUT TO EACH OTHER WITH BEAMS OF PUREST THOUGHT.

YES, WE ARE THE SAME!

WE ARE ONE!

THAT'S NOT KATE TALKING! IT CAN'T BE!
'COURSE IT AIN'T. DIDN'T YOU HEAR? YOUR LADY'S GONE!

AN' IN HER PLACE, WE GOT THAT...THING! TWO TERRORS INSTEAD OF ONE! MODOK ...AND HIS MATE!
MATE?

NO! NO! NO!
THE HULK'S SCREAM REVERBERATES LIKE THUNDER.
16

SUCH IS THE DIN THAT IT DISTRACTS THE LOVERS FROM THEIR CLOSE COMMUNION.
IF THERE BE ANY MAN WHO OBJECTS TO THIS UNION OF TWO MINDS--
--LET HIM STAND FORTH NOW OR FOREVER HOLD HIS PEACE.

I OBJECT!
KATE WAYNESBORO HAS SOME RIGHTS IN THIS OBSCENE AFFAIR!

I DEMAND THAT HER MIND BE FREED --THAT SHE BE ALLOWED TO CHOOSE HER OWN COURSE!

I HAVE CHOSEN. I WISH TO WED MODOK.

WHATEVER THAT CREATURE IS, SHE'S NOT KATHERINE WAYNESBORO... AND HAS NO RIGHT TO SPEAK FOR HER!
HAVE A CARE, DR. BANNER! OUR ALLIANCE WAS PREDI-CATED UPON YOUR SAVING KATHERINE WAYNESBORO--
--AND MY PRE-VENTING THE CREATION OF ANOTHER MODOK DESIGNED TO DESTROY MYSELF.

THE SITUATION HAS CHANGED. KATE WAYNESBORO IS NO MORE, AND WHAT SHE HAS BECOME...
...IS MY BRIDE!
I'LL NOT HEAR HER REFERRED TO DISRESPECTFULLY!
17

GRAARGHH!
YOU WILL APOLOGIZE... ON YOUR KNEES!

AS BEAM AFTER BEAM LASHES THE GREEN GARGANTUA...
...SHE WHO HAD BEEN KATHERINE WAYNESBORO MERELY WATCHES.

DO YOU HEAR ME, HULK? ON YOUR KNEES!

THAT'S HOW HE HURT ME! GIVE IT UP, HULK! YOU CAN'T FIGHT HIM! HE'LL KILL YA!

WORSE, ABOMINATION. SHALL WE GIVE THE GOOD DR. BANNER A DEMONSTRATION?

NO! PLEASE DON'T HURT MEEEEEE!
ABOMINATION!
18

MODOK--STOP IT! IT'S ME YOUR QUARREL'S WITH! LEAVE THE ABOMINATION ALONE!
HURTS,,, HURTS SO BAD!

BUT DOCTOR, YOU AND THE ABOMINATION ARE SO ALIKE-- CREATURES OF GAMMA RAYS BOTH,,,
,,,THAT I THOUGHT YOU MIGHT ENJOY SEEING A PREVIEW OF YOUR FATE!

SEARED BY THE GAMMA-GREEN GLOW, THE ABOMINATION SCREAMS,,,

,,,UNTIL ABLE TO SCREAM NO LONGER AS HIS ATOMS ARE SCATTERED TO THE WIND.

YOU,,, DESTROYED THE CREATURE!
HIS DEATH IS OF NO IMPORTANCE.

HE LIVED! ALL LIFE HAS VALUE!
SURELY YOU JEST. ON ALL EARTH, THE ONLY LIVES WORTH ANYTHING ARE OUR OWN.
19

NO! THAT IS TOO CRUEL AN EQUATION TO BEAR!
CRUEL? TO ASSIGN LESSER BEINGS TO THEIR PROPER PLACE? ARRGHH!
WOMAN-- YOU STRIKE AT ME?!
WE ARE NOT THE SAME. WE ARE DIF-FERENT!

THEN... MODOK IS ALONE AGAIN.
OHHHH!
CURSE YOU FOR TRICKING ME INTO BELIEVING THERE WAS ONE I COULD SHARE MY LONELINESS WITH!

SOMEHOW, MODOK'S CRUELTY AWAKENED SOME SMALL SPARK OF KATE SUB-MERGED DEEP WITHIN MS. MODOK!
NOW I'VE GOT TO KEEP HIM FROM KILLING HER--

--WHILE THAT SPARK FANS INTO A FLAME!
I DO NOT UNDERSTAND WHAT IT IS I AM--
--BUT I DO KNOW I AM NOT LIKE YOU!

THEN YOU SHALL PERISH!
IF YOU'LL NOT BE MINE--THEN YOU SHALL NOT BE!
20

MS. MODOK HAS BEEN POSSESSED OF HER INCREDIBLE INTELLECT FOR ONLY A SHORT TIME.
IN THAT PERIOD, SHE HAS THROWN OFF THE DOMINATION OF A.I.M., AND RECOGNIZED MODOK FOR THE KILLER HE IS.

IT IS ALMOST AS IF THE MIND OF KATHERINE WAYNESBORO WERE FIGHTING TO REASSERT ITSELF.
UNFORTUNATELY, THAT INNER STRUGGLE RENDERS HER VULNERABLE TO MODOK'S ASSAULT.

UNABLE TO RESIST HIS RUTHLESS-NESS, MS. MODOK IS DRIVEN BACK ONTO THE ALTERATION PLATFORM.
THE FORCES THAT CREATED HER WORK THEIR WAY UPON HER AGAIN.

GET YOUR MIND OFF HER, MODOK!
ARGHH!

YOU ARE A FOOL, HULK!

AGAIN YOUR RAGE OVERCOMES YOUR CAPACITY TO REASON--

--OTHERWISE YOU WOULD SEE THE GREAT GIFT MODOK BESTOWS UPON YOU--
--BEFORE TAKING HIS LEAVE!
21

BLASTED BY MODOK'S MIND-BEAMS, THE ROOF OF THE A.I.M. STRONGHOLD CAVES IN ATOP THE HULK.

HIS WAY CLEAR, MODOK TAKES HIS LEAVE.
THAT HE COULD HAVE KILLED THE HULK AS HE DID THE ABOMINATION IS ABUNDANTLY CLEAR...

...AND YET--HE DID NOT.

WHY?
WHY DID MODOK SPARE ME?

WAS HIS IN-SANE INTELLECT SATISFIED BY PROVING TO ME HOW POWERLESS I WAS TO SAVE--

--KATE?
22

IN THE BEAM OF LIGHT RISING FROM THE ALTERATION PLATFORM, A FEMALE FIGURE SEEMS TO FORM.

ALL TRACES OF MS. MODOK ARE ERASED.

KATHERINE WAYNESBORO HAS RETURNED.

HER ORDEAL IS OVER.

THIS IS MODOK'S DOING. HE DROVE MS. MODOK BACK INTO THE ALTERATION RAYS... AND REVERSED THE PROCESS.
BUT... WHY? I CAN'T IMAGINE MODOK AS CAPABLE OF MERCY!
BUT MAYBE KATE--AS MS. MODOK--STRUCK A CHORD IN HIM HE NEVER KNEW WAS THERE.
MAYBE, HAVING LOVED HER, HE COULDN'T DESTROY HER... SO INSTEAD HE GAVE HER BACK.
AND NOW THAT I HAVE HER... I'LL NEVER LET HER GO!

NEXT ISSUE: Carl Potts has gone gallivanting off to the San Diego Convention and left Assistant Editor Ann Nocenti in charge. So who picks this very month to have an identity crisis? The Hulk! And he comes up to the Marvel offices demanding help! What problem could be so serious that the Hulk could not handle it? Was Ann able to help our Green Goliath out of his dilemma? Be here in 30 days to find out!

This must be the month for self-reflection because there's another character who must take a hard look at his life. THUNDERBOLT ROSS – *the* career military man – committed treason against his country. If a man betrays all that he stands for, what's left? Next issue we go back into Ross's past to explore the forces that shaped him, and re-live his raging conflict with his life-long nemesis – the Hulk.

MARVEL LIMITED SERIES

1 of 5

VAN LENTE
PORTELA
PALLOT
GURU eFX

SUPER-VILLAIN TEAM-UP™

"No man chooses evil because it is evil;
He only mistakes it for happiness, the good he seeks."
- Mary Wollstonecraft, A Vindication of the Rights of Men
MUST BALANCE THE EQUATION.
SUBTRACT THE VARIABLE.
BUT WHAT ABOUT OUR RELATIONSHIP?
ARRRRGH! ONLY YOU COULD THINK THAT A DRUNKEN HOOKUP DURING THE PROJECT: ADAPTOID COMPLETION CELEBRATION MEETS THE BASIC CRITERIA FOR A RELATIONSHIP, GEORGE...
LOOK, I THOUGHT I COULD LEARN SOMETHING FROM YOU, OKAY? I THOUGHT THAT YOUR SHY, STUTTERING DEMEANOR DISGUISED A BRILLIANT MATHEMATICIAN...
...BUT NO, YOU'RE JUST LIKE THIS DRIP I HAD A FLING WITH IN COLLEGE, BRUCE. I THOUGHT HE'D MAKE A GREAT PHYSICIST ONE DAY--
--BUT HE TURNED OUT TO BE A LITTLE MAN TRAPPED IN A LITTLER MAN'S BODY.
STOP PAGING ME! STOP LURKING AROUND MY QUARTERS! IT'S EMBARRASSING.
...NEED BRAVE VOLUNTEERS FOR THE LOTTERY TO BECOME THE SUBJECT PRIME IN A.I.M.'S GREATEST PROJECT TO DATE...
...A HYBRID OF MAN AND MACHINE, CAPABLE OF MILLIONS OF COMPLEX CALCULATIONS PER MILLISECOND...
OKAY, MONICA...
...WE'LL SEE WHO'S THE LITTLE MAN THEN...
A.I.M.
M.O.D.O.C.
MENTAL
ORGANISM
DESIGNED
ONLY FOR
COMPUTING

...DESIGNED ONLY FOR COMPUTING...
...ONLY FOR...
WAIT! I... Uh...
...I THINK I'VE CHANGED MY MIND...
CEASE YOUR PITIFUL MEWLING, TARLETON!
EVERYONE IN ADVANCED IDEA MECHANICS KNOWS YOU TO BE AN UNIMAGINATIVE DULLARD!
BUT YOUR BRAIN IS ABOUT TO UNDERGO A BILLION YEARS OF EVOLUTION IN A MATTER OF MOMENTS!
SOON, ONLY YOU WILL BE CAPABLE OF THE INFINITESIMALLY COMPLEX CALCULATIONS NECESSARY TO BRING PROJECT: COSMIC CUBE TO FRUITION!
THE SECRETS OF ALL CREATION ARE ABOUT TO BE LAID BARE BY YOUR GENIUS, GEORGE TARLETON!
FOR REASON'S SAKE, MAN, FACE THEM WITH SOME DIGNITY!
NOOO!

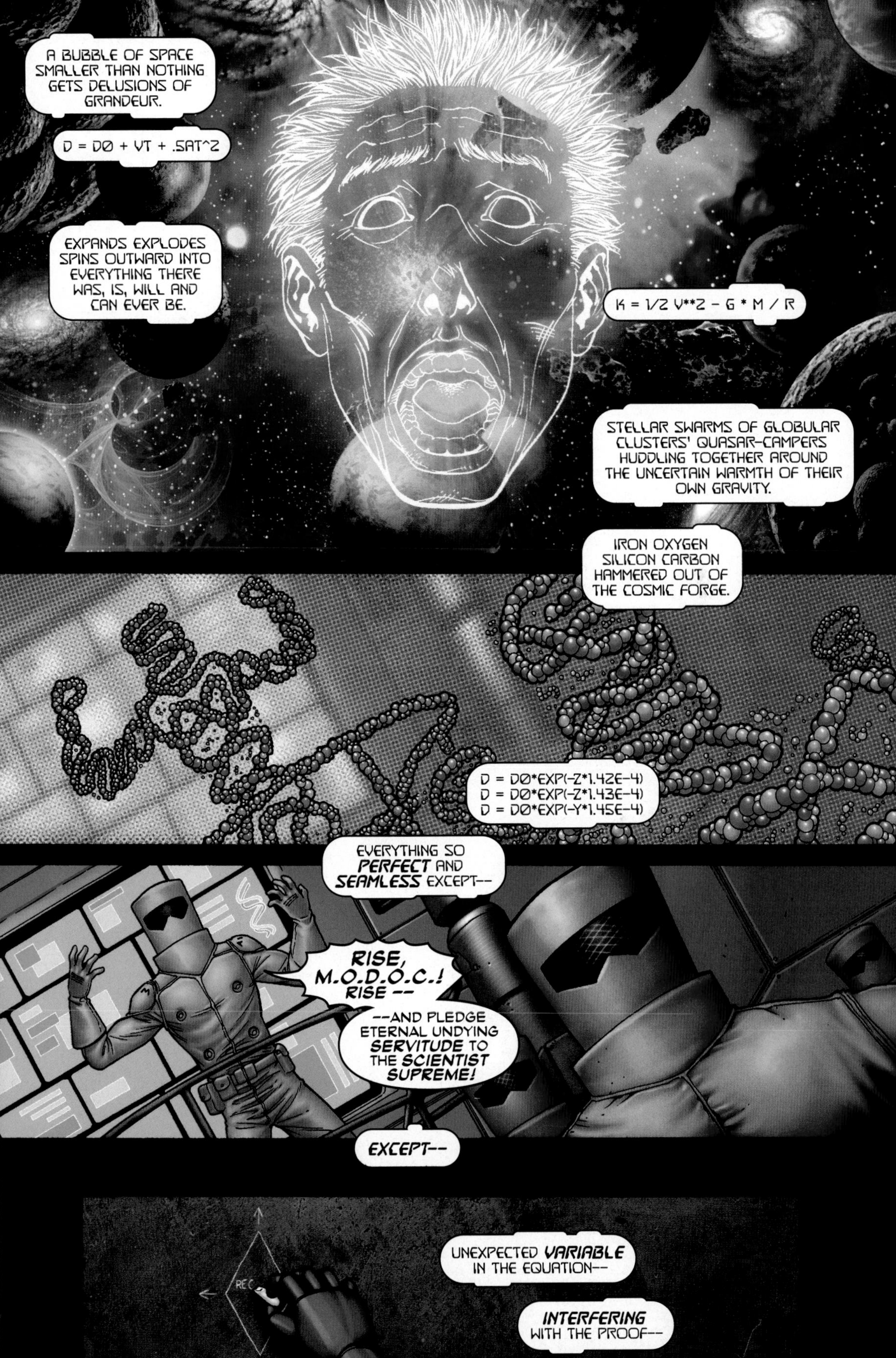
A BUBBLE OF SPACE SMALLER THAN NOTHING GETS DELUSIONS OF GRANDEUR.
D = DØ + VT + .5AT^2
EXPANDS EXPLODES SPINS OUTWARD INTO EVERYTHING THERE WAS, IS, WILL AND CAN EVER BE.
K = 1/2 V**2 - G * M / R
STELLAR SWARMS OF GLOBULAR CLUSTERS' QUASAR-CAMPERS HUDDLING TOGETHER AROUND THE UNCERTAIN WARMTH OF THEIR OWN GRAVITY.
IRON OXYGEN SILICON CARBON HAMMERED OUT OF THE COSMIC FORGE.
D = DØ*EXP(-Z*1.42E-4)
D = DØ*EXP(-Z*1.43E-4)
D = DØ*EXP(-Y*1.45E-4)
EVERYTHING SO PERFECT AND SEAMLESS EXCEPT--
RISE, M.O.D.O.C.! RISE --
--AND PLEDGE ETERNAL UNDYING SERVITUDE TO THE SCIENTIST SUPREME!
EXCEPT--
REC
UNEXPECTED VARIABLE IN THE EQUATION--
INTERFERING WITH THE PROOF--

LIFE.
WHY IS THERE LIFE?
YAAAAGHHH!
NO REASON, NO JUSTIFICATION FOR LIFE.
UNNECESSARY VARIABLE DOES NOT FIT.
SUBTRACT IT AND STATEMENT IS TRUE.
END ALL LIFE. BALANCE EQUATION. PERFECT, CLEAN, PURE.

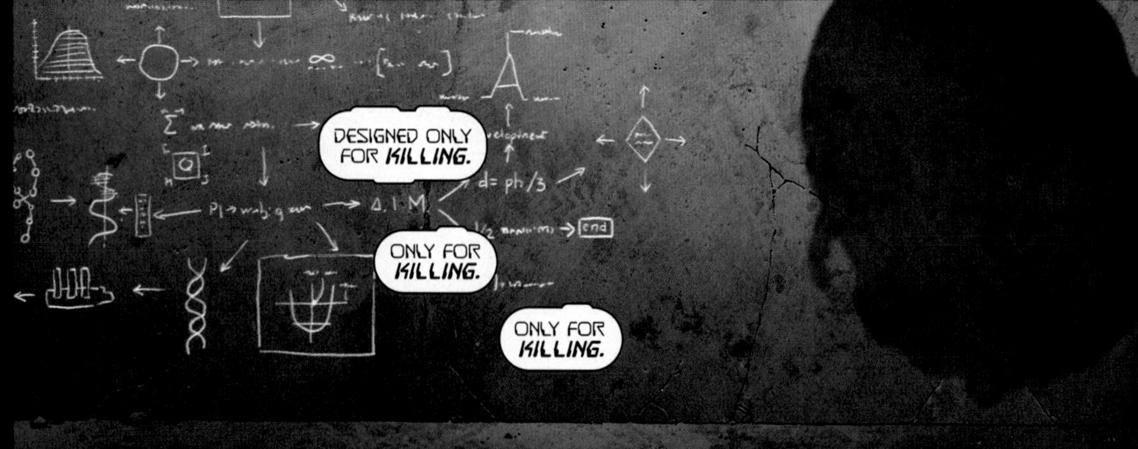
DESIGNED ONLY FOR KILLING.
ONLY FOR KILLING.
ONLY FOR KILLING.

RECRUIT MINIONS
ONLY FOR COMPUTING.
COMPUTING...
...REVENGE.

ACAPULCO...
ESTO PINTA MAL PARA EL ARMADILLO...
...¡EL CHUPACABRA LO TIENE DONDE QUIERE!
MISTAKEN FOR HAPPINESS
OR: "THE TEAM"

FSSSSSS!
CHUPACABRA ESTÁ SEDIENTO DE SANGRE DE SU CONTRARIO...
¡ESPEREN...! 'DILLO LANZA A 'CABRA POR ENCIMA DE SU HOMBRO--¡A UN BRAIN-BUSTER!
ROOOAARR
SLAMMM
AHORA CHUPACABRA ESTÁ JUSTO DONDE VA A LLEGAR EL FINISHER DE SU ANTAGONISTA...
...¡EL ROADKILL SLAMMER!
DIL-LO! DIL-LO!

SOLO UNA NOCHE
ARMADILLO
VS
<ANOTHER DAY, ANOTHER PURSE... YOU'RE ALMOST BORING ME HERE, NIÑO.>
<LET'S SEE... YOUR THIRTY-PERCENT SHARE MAKES IT A TEN-THOUSAND-PESO NIGHT FOR YOU, MY FRIEND!>
<OR $900 AMERICAN. BUT I GUESS YOU'RE THE BOSS...>
<...BIG PAPI.>
<YOU KNOW SOMETHING, NIÑO? YOU GOTTA WORK ON YOUR GRATEFUL FACE.>
<YOU AIN'T IN AMERICA NO MORE. NO MANAGER WILL TAKE YOU THERE-- NOT WITH YOUR SHEET.>
<AND YOU WERE A WASHOUT WITH THE RANGERS!>
<SO UNTIL THE FOOD PREPARATION INDUSTRY CREATES SOME EMPLOYMENT OPPORTUNITIES FOR GIANT ORANGE FREAKS...>
<...YOU BEST MAKE PEACE WITH THE FACT BIG PAPI IS THE BEST FRIEND YOU GOT.>
ANTONIO RODRIGUEZ...

AN INDIAN RESERVATION OUTSIDE HEARTSDALE, NEW MEXICO...
OUR PATIENCE IS OFFICIALLY AT ITS END, THOMAS.
WOULD YOU DENY ME THE RIGHT TO DEFEND MYS--
SILENCE, NEPHEW. FOR CENTURIES HE WHO WIELDS THE PUMA TOTEM HAS BEEN THE PROTECTOR OF OUR CLAN AND ALL ITS SECRETS...
...BUT NOW WE ELDERS MUST ASK:
WHO WILL PROTECT US FROM YOUR RECKLESSNESS?
PARTLY, WE KNOW, WE ARE TO BLAME...
FIREHEART C.E.O. INDICTED FOR OF BRIBERY, FRAUD;
Assets Froze
"...FOR, SO LONG AS YOU DID OUR BIDDING AS WELL, WE INDULGED YOU IN YOUR...THRILL-SEEKING. THIS CAREER YOU'VE BUILT FOR YOURSELF AS A CONTRACT KILLER.
"WE MAY BE OLD, BUT WE KNOW HOW TO READ A NEWSPAPER, THOMAS. WE KNOW YOUR HANDIWORK WHEN WE SEE IT.
"THE ASSASSINATION OF THAT VIETNAMESE GANG LEADER IN MADRIPOOR-- THAT WAS YOUR HANDIWORK. DO NOT TRY TO DENY IT."
DENY IT? I WANT TO CROW IT FROM THE ROOF-TOPS.
THE 4T'S CONTROLLED THE SEXUAL SLAVERY OF GIRLS FROM LAOS TO L.A. THE PLANET ALMOST SMELLS BETTER NOW THAT THEY'RE DEAD.
AND I NEED LAWYERS TO DEFEND MYSELF FROM THESE TRUMPED-UP CHARGES. LAWYERS REQUIRE MONEY. FOR MONEY I NEED JOBS--

LISTEN TO YOU COMPOUND YOUR ARROGANCE!
WHAT YOU NEED IS TO START THINKING OF YOUR TRIBE BEFORE YOURSELF FOR ONCE IN YOUR LIFE, THOMAS!
THOSE CHARGES ARE WHY THE COUNCIL ORDERED A HALT TO YOUR MERCENARY ACTIVITIES IN THE FIRST PLACE!
YOU MAY NOT LEAVE OUR SACRED LANDS UNTIL THE COUNCIL HAS DECIDED ON APPROPRIATE PUNISHMENT.
I WOULD STRONGLY SUGGEST YOU SPEND THIS TIME IN THE SWEAT LODGE, IN MEDITATION...
"...I'VE RARELY SEEN SOMEONE IN AS MUCH NEED OF GUIDANCE FROM HIS SPIRIT ADVISOR AS YOU."
THOMAS FIREHEART...
...HOW WOULD YOU LIKE TO MAKE FIVE MILLION DOLLARS?
YOU'RE JUST ABOUT THE WISEST SPIRIT ADVISOR I'VE EVER MET.

RENO, NEVADA...
...THE RIVER IS THE EIGHT OF DIAMONDS.
MR. KATZ'S NINE HIGH CARRIES THE POT...
NINE HIGH?!
HOW CAN YOU CALL ME ON A NINE HIGH?!?
HOW DID YOU KNOW I WAS BLUFFING?! SOME KINDA TELL...?!
TELL?
Heh
BUBELEH, YOU MIGHT AS WELL HAVE "I'D-GO ALL-IN PRE-FLOP-ON-A-THREE-DEUCE-UNSUITED" TATTOOED ON YOUR FOREHEAD...
SIR? CAN WE SEE YOU FOR A MOMENT, SIR?
THE VIEW DON'T GET ANY BETTER, BOYCHIK.
WE JUST DON'T THINK POKER'S YOUR GAME, SIR...
YOU EVER TRY RUSSIAN ROULETTE?
ENJOYING FLEECING MY CASINO, MR. FLUMM?

THIS IS DISCRIMINATION, THAT'S WHAT THIS IS! RACIAL PROFILING! PICK UP THE PHONE, IT'S THE A.C.L.U. CALLING!
I GOT YOU ON MISTAKEN IDENTITY, TOO! THE NAME IS KATZ!
AND I SAY IT'S FLUMM. MARVIN FLUMM...
...BETTER KNOWN IN LAW ENFORCEMENT CIRCLES AS THE TELEPATHIC NUISANCE, MENTALLO.
I CAN ONLY ASSUME YOU HAVEN'T STOPPED READING THE MINDS OF THE DEALERS AND PLAYERS SINCE YOU GOT HERE, SO THAT MAKES IT TWELVE-AND-A-HALF MILLION YOU OWE ME.
QUITE AN IMAGINATION YOU'VE GOT THERE.
ANY PROOF TO GO WITH IT?
ONLY THAT IT TAKES ONE TO KNOW ONE.
YOU SEE... I TOOK OVER THIS CASINO LAST WEEK.
PURPLE MAN! BUBELEH! PAL! HOW FORTUNATE! Heh, heh!
HERE I AM, SICK OF HAVING MY BRIDGEWORK REDONE EVERY THURSDAY BECAUSE OF THYROID CASES IN BODY STOCKINGS... THINKING I'D HAVE TO FLY SOLO IN MY NEW CAREER!
BUT LUCKY ME...FIRST JOB I DO, I RUN ACROSS AN ALLIED TRADESPERSON! WITH OUR COMBINED POWERS, WE COULD CASH IN THIS TOWN LIKE A WINNING LOTTO TICKET!
SORRY.
I SAW IT FIRST.
KLIK
KLIK
KLIK
KLIK
KLIK
KLIK
KLIK
KLI

BLAM
BLAM
BLAM
HE COULDN'T HAVE GOTTEN FAR!
FIND HIM, SLAVES!
JUST MY !@#$%! LUCK! FIRST JOB I PULL... FIRST FRICKIN' JOB!
GETTING SO A MUTANT CAN'T MAKE A DISHONEST BUCK ANYMORE!
MARVIN FLUMM...
FIXER! OL' BUDDY, OL' PAL... THOSE WERE THE DAYS! WE WERE AN UNBEATABLE TEAM, STICKING IT TO S.H.I.E.L.D. ...THE AVENGERS...THE MICRONAUTS!
GOD, HOW I HATED THE FRICKIN' MICRONAUTS...
...HOW WOULD YOU LIKE TO MAKE FIVE MILLION DOLLARS?

VE AL 1133 DE GOWANUS AVENUE EN BROOKLYN LA MEDIANOCHE DEL DIA CINCO...
...IN BROOKLYN AT MIDNIGHT ON THE FIFTH...
...ON THE FIFTH.
THIS SUMMONS WILL NOT BE REPEATED.
THAT IS ALL.
B-BUT...
...YOU MADE ME PROMISE I WOULDN'T DO BAD THINGS ANYMORE, MAMA.
YOU'RE SENDING ME KIND OF A M-M-MIXED MESSAGE, DON'T YOU THINK?
U-UNLESS... WHAT YOU'RE SAYING...
...IS THAT S-SOMETIMES YOU HAVE TO DO BAD THINGS IN ORDER TO DO GOOD...
REPO NOTIFICATION
FINAL NOT

BIG TROUBLE IN LITTLE CHINA 2
JACK BURTON STRIKES AGAIN

1133 GOWANUS

DAILY BUGLE
SPIDERMAN STILL MENACES NEW YORK

IF WE THREE AGREE TO WATCH EACH OTHER'S BACKS IT SHOULD MINIMIZE OUR RISK.
I'VE BEEN OUT HERE FOR FOUR HOURS AND SEEN NO SIGNS OF UNUSUAL ACTIVITY--OR ANY ACTIVITY AT ALL, FOR THAT MATTER.
A TITLE SEARCH SUGGESTS THAT THIS BUILDING IS EXACTLY WHAT IT LOOKS LIKE IT IS-- A GARAGE FOR ICE-CREAM TRUCKS-- ALBEIT A CONDEMNED ONE.
THE COMPANY THAT BUILT IT HAS BEEN IN CHAPTER ELEVEN SINCE THE EIGHTIES.
HEEEEY, ALL RIGHT, GET A LOAD OF THIS!
THE UNITED VILLAINS OF BENETTON! I LOVE IT!
EVENIN', GENTS. MENTALLO'S THE NAME, UNEXPLAINED PSYCHIC PHENOMENA IS THE GAME.
PAID YOUR RESPECTS TO OUR MYSTERIOUS HOST YET?
MERELY VERIFYING IT IS SAFE TO PROCEED--
SAFE, SCHMAFE! YOUR AMORAL LIFESTYLE HAS LEFT YOU A WEE BIT PARANOID, TOMMY-BOY!
WHAT? HOW DID YOU KNOW MY NA--
Oh. RIGHT. PSYCHIC.
THAT SUBLIMINAL TELE-SIGNAL? MANIFESTING AS A WISE MENTOR ARCHETYPE? KIDS' STUFF! PROFESSIONAL FELONS SUCH AS OURSELVES SHOULD HAVE NOTHING TO FEAR!
I'D PUT ON WHATEVER'S IN THAT BRIEFCASE IF I WERE YOU, FRIEND.
BUT Y-YOU'RE NOT ME, NOW A-ARE YOU?
I-I-I PROMISED SOMEONE I WOULDN'T--NOT UNLESS I A-A-ABSOLUTELY

MADRE DE DIOS...
...I GOT TO START HAVING VISIONS LIKE THIS MORE OFTEN.
IF YOU'RE FOND OF BREATHING, DON'T TAKE ANOTHER STEP.
WE RECEIVED A SUMMONS TO MEET AT THE CANAL SIDE OF THIS BUILDING.
THAT DOUGH WAS PROMISED TO US--!
POIT
HOLD ON. WE WERE TOLD TO REPORT TO THE STREET SIDE. MONEY WAS PROMISED US TOO, AND THERE SEEMS TO BE PLENTY TO GO AROUND.
NO NEED TO START THROWING PUNCHES AT THE FIRST SIGN OF ANOTHER COSTUME.
YEAH, WHAT YOU TAKE US FOR?
HEROES?

KRKK
POIT
NYAH, NYAH!
MADE YOU BLINK!
STOP HIM! HE'S TAKING OUR MONEY--
YOUR MONEY?!
SCHRAAAAAK
WITH THAT SCRATCH, I CAN FINANCE TURNING ME HUMAN AGAIN!

WOW! THE GORTON'S FISHERMAN! WHAT AN HONOR!
I LOVE YOUR FISH STICKS!
BOPP
UNHH
BUT YOU KNOW WHAT I LIKE EVEN MORE?
OTHER PEOPLE'S STUFF.
HEY.
NICE SKATE-BOARD.
YES. IT IS.
SO K-K-KEEP YOUR FILTHY HANDS OFF IT.
ZWOK
STRIKE QUICKLY-- BUT BE CAREFUL!
ONE OF US IS REALLY THE CHAMELEON!
NO, REALLY. YOU THINK?

I'M THINKING CHAMELEON'S THE ONE THAT JUST MORPHED INTO A GIANT PRAWN.
A GIANT--?
WHAT ARE YOU TALKING ABOUT?
SOMEBODY MIGHT BE PUTTING A MENTAL PROJECTION OVER YA, CHAM.
BE ME
I'M A STINKER.
THREE WORDS FOR YOU, SUGAR:
FLESH. EATING. ENZYME.
KLIK-KLAK
I GOT HER, I GOT HER!
Whoa, Whoa! PEOPLE, PEOPLE!
NOW DON'T GET ME WRONG, I LOVE GRATUITOUS FISTICUFFS AS MUCH AS THE NEXT RED-BLOODED AMERICAN.
BUT AM I TOTALLY MISSING SOMETHING HERE? WHAT ARE YOU ALL FIGHTING ABOU --
ENOUGH.

WHILE IT IS HEARTENING TO KNOW YOU CAN DEPLOY YOUR VARIOUS AND SUNDRY ABILITIES AS A GROUP AS WELL AS INDIVIDUALLY...
... NOW YOU MUST CONSERVE YOUR STRENGTH FOR THE NIGH-IMPOSSIBLE TASK AHEAD.
FOR I SHALL NOT GIVE YOU THE TREASURE OVER WHICH YOU BICKER AND BRAWL...
NOT, AT LEAST, UNTIL AFTER YOU EARN IT.
Heh
YOU'VE GOT A BIG HEAD.

DEFENSE RESPONSE TIME UNDER THREE SECONDS... JUST LIKE WE WERE LED TO EXPECT!
WHICH WAY TO THE HYPERNOVA CONTAINMENT CHAMBER, CHAMELEON?
RIGHT, THEN LEFT, THEN STRAIGHT, THEN RIGHT, THEN--

SHRAKK
AAAARGGH!
DAMN! CRAZY FLOATING MARBLES GOT AT OUR REAR A LOT QUICKER THAN WE PLANNED!
THEY'RE MADE OUT OF SOME KIND OF ORGANIC CERAMIC...MAY BE SUSCEPTIBLE TO ACIDIFIED DIMETHOXYPROPANE--
AAHHH!
SHRAKK
LASER! COME BACK HERE-- WE NEED SERIOUS REAR GUARD REINFORCEMENTS-- NOW!
ALRIGHT, PUMA, ALRIGHT! WHO DIED AND MADE YOU M.O.D.O.K.?
YOU KNOW HOW HARD IT IS TO DO A U-TURN AT THE SPEED OF LIGH--
--EEYYAAHHH!

!@#$! SUPER-VILLAINS! IT'S LIKE HERDING CATS!
PRETTY IRONIC, COMING FROM YOU, HOLMES.
I'M AN INDIAN, 'DILLO--
--WE LIVE ON IRONY!
HEH LEAST WE GOIN' OUT LAUGHIN'!
N-N-NUTS! THE CONTAINMENT CHAMBER'S J-J-JUST ON THE OTHER S-S-SIDE!
W-W-WE GOTTA FIGURE OUT A WAY TO GET TH-TH-THROUGH THERE!
NO PROBLEMO, MY STUTTERIN' PEEP!
UGH!
IF BY "WE" YOU MEAN "ME"--

AND BY "THROUGH", YOU MEAN "GO NOWHERE NEAR"!
HAH! IN YOUR FACE, SUCKERS! I--THE SPECTACULAR SPOT--HAVE PREVAILED...
...WHERE YOUR QUOTE-UNQUOTE "USEFUL" POWERS STUNK LIKE POOPY! TRIPLE-HAH!
AND TO THINK BEFORE THIS THE ONLY VILLAIN TEAM WHO WOULD HAVE ME WAS THE "LEGION OF LOSERS!"
BZZAAAAP

BUNGLERS.
INCOMPETENTS!
NOW DO YOU SEE?
YOU FACE NO BANK VAULT OR DIAMOND WHOLESALERS!
THIS IS NOT SOME INFANTILE REVENGE PLOT AGAINST THE SAME COSTUME WHO SENT YOU TO ATTICA THE LAST TIME YOU TRIED TO GET EVEN WITH HIM!
WE STEAL FROM THE INFINICIDE-- TEMPORAL CARTOGRAPHERS FROM THE END OF TIME!
THEIR TECHNOLOGY AND SUPER-POWERS ARE BEYOND YOUR IMAGINING!
foward
back
development
d=ph/3
end
WE CANNOT POSSIBLY HOPE TO PREVAIL BY FORCE!
IT IS ONLY THROUGH THE FRACTALLY BRILLIANT PLAN OF A MIND DESIGNED ONLY FOR KI-KI-KI-
--COMPUTING-- THAT WE CAN EVADE THEIR DEFENSES!

"THE INFINICIDE'S **BEACON** SHALL BE PHASED OUT OF THE TIMESTREAM AND INTO **THIS** ERA FOR ONLY A **BRIEF** PERIOD, WHILE THEY FINISH MAPPING THE CATACLYSMIC **WARS** RECENTLY WAGED BY OUR SO-CALLED **HEROES.**

"THEIR FORTRESS FLOATS **THIRTY STORIES** OVER THE TAKLAMAKAN **SALT WASTES** OF NORTHWESTERN **CHINA,** BROADCASTING A SUBLIMINAL **TELE-SIGNAL** TO PEOPLE AROUND THE GLOBE TOUCHED BY THE CONFLICT.

"THOUGH THESE NORMALS KNOW NOT WHY, THEY FIND THEMSELVES **INFECTED** WITH THE IRRESISTIBLE URGE TO **TRAVEL** TO THE BEACON WHERE THEIR MEMORIES MIGHT BE DOWNLOADED INTO THE INFINICIDE'S **CHRONO-MAP.**"

IN THE **CENTER** OF THE FLOATING FORTRESS LIES THE **OBJECT** OF OUR QUEST--ITS **POWER SOURCE--**

--A **HYPERNOVA** TRAPPED IN A **TEMPORAL BOTTLE**...AN **EXPLODING STAR** CONTINUOUSLY BURSTING AND RE-BURSTING IN AN **INFINITE LOOP**... PRODUCING MORE ENERGY THAN THE SUN COULD IN A **TRILLION YEARS.**

YES...THE **ULTIMATE** FUEL SOURCE.

OR THE ULTIMATE WEAPON.
WILL YOU POINT IT AT A.I.M.--OR THE AVENGERS?
THE INTRICACIES OF MY PLAN ARE SO COMPLEX I FEAR YOU WOULD GO MAD IF I SHARED THEM WITH YOU IN THEIR ENTIRETY.
FOR THE GOOD OF YOUR SANITY, I MUST INSIST THAT YOU FOCUS SOLELY ON THOSE INFINITESIMALLY MINISCULE STRANDS THAT PERSONALLY CONCERN YOU.
ONLY MY EVOLUTIONARILY-ACCELERATED BRAIN COULD HAVE DETECTED THE ARRIVAL OF THE BEACON IN THIS ERA--
ONLY I COULD HAVE THOROUGHLY SCANNED IT FROM AFAR TO CREATE THIS NIGH-PERFECT PSIONIC PSYMULATION WITH WHICH TO TRAIN YOU...
VATO LIKES TO HEAR HIMSELF TALK.
THEY'RE ALL LIKE THIS, SHUG'. JUST CLOSE YOUR EYES AND THINK ABOUT THE MONEY.

Oh, AND THANKS FOR ALL YOUR HELP DURING THE PSYMULATION, KRESKIN.
LOOKED LIKE YOU WERE MAKING FOOLS OF YOURSELVES JUST FINE WITHOUT ME.
YOU SIT ON YOUR HANDS DURING THE REAL JOB AND MY BOOT AND YOUR @$$ ARE GONNA GET REAL ACQUAINTED.
Ooooh. SCARY.
OY! I HAVEN'T SEEN SUCH A PITIFUL COLLECTION OF HAS-BEENS AND NEVER-WERES SINCE THE LAST TIME THE PARTRIDGE FAMILY HAD A REUNION SPECIAL.
BIG HEAD IS GOING TO REGRET LUMPING THE GREAT MENTALLO IN WITH THIS MESHUGGE LOT!
LAST TIME I CHECKED THE TERRORIST GRAPEVINE, ADVANCED IDEA MECHANICS HAD A HEFTY PRICE TAG ON M.O.D.O.K.'S ENCEPHALITIC CRANIUM.
IF I TIPPED OFF THEIR NEW SCIENTIST SUPREME TO HIS WHEREABOUTS, I'M SURE I COULD COLLECT A DANDY FINDER'S FEE...
...AND, IF I PLAYED MY CARDS RIGHT, COLLECT THE HYPERNOVA AFTER HUMPTY-DUMPTY GETS HIS YOLK SCRAMBLED!
A WISE BACKSTABBER ALWAYS HAS SOMEBODY WATCHING HIS BACK, THOUGH.
OUR EMPLOYER IS TOO MIRED IN RANTING MODE RIGHT NOW TO CATCH ME SCANNING THE SURFACE THOUGHTS OF MY TEAMMATES FOR POTENTIAL ALLIES.
LIVING LASER'S SHEER POWER HAS GOT TO COME IN HANDY...

GAAHHH! THIS IS A HUMAN MIND?!
LOOKS LIKE IT'S ALL LIGHT BOY CAN DO TO KEEP HIMSELF FROM DISSOLVING INTO QUANTUM STEW AT ANY MOMENT!
NO WAY I'M GONNA RISK HIM MERGING WITH THE UNIVERSE IN THE MIDDLE OF MY JOB!
SO WHAT'S YOUR STORY, TONTO?
DAMN! FIVE FEDERAL BRIBERY INDICTMENTS?
HE'S ACCUSED OF INFLUENCING SENATORS ON THE INDIAN AFFAIRS COMMITTEE TO SQUASH COMPETITORS OF FIREHEART ENTERPRISES' GAMING CONCERNS!
KITTY CAT'S OWN TRIBE HAS COMPLETELY DISTANCED THEMSELVES FROM HIM--THEY'RE GONNA LET HIM TAKE THE FALL ALONE!
HIS TRIAL STARTS NEXT MONTH, AND HE DOESN'T HAVE A DIME TO MOUNT A DEFENSE!
SCANNING THE REST OF HIS MIND... SEEMS LIKE IT'S A FRAME JOB... BUT IT FITS HIS NECK LIKE A NOOSE!
THEY FROZE HIS ASSETS--HE SPENT HIS LAST DROP O' CASH

JACKPOT! KITTY'S GONNA POUNCE AT EARNING SOME EXTRA SCRATCH BY TURNING MODDY OVER TO THE YELLOW LONGJOHNS!
HE'LL BE PUTTY IN MY HANDS...
SNIFF SNIFF
GRRRRR
OR NOT.
gulp
HOW DID HE DO THAT?!
HOW DID HE KNOW I WAS INSIDE HIS--
WHOA.
WHAT'S ALL THIS, MR. CHAMELEON?
WELL, I WILL SAY THIS ABOUT MY TEAMMATES...
...THEY CERTAINLY ARE FULL OF SURPRISES!

--I SAID, IS THAT CLEAR, MINION MENTALLO?
Wha--? Oh--Uh, CRYSTAL, FEARLESS LEADER!
EXCELLENT. THE INFINICIDE SHALL TELEPATHICALLY SCAN MINION CHAMELEON BEFORE THEY ALLOW HIM ONTO THEIR BEACON.
IT MATTERS NOT WHAT FORM HE TAKES--IF HIS THOUGHTS ARE NOT ALSO DISGUISED, HE WILL BE VAPORIZED WHERE HE STANDS!
GOTCHA! I'LL WRAP A PSYCHIC MASK AROUND THE OL' HIPPOCAMPUS! NO SWEAT!
BUT IT'S WALL-TO-WALL JIBBER-JABBER IN HERE--WHAT SAY WE FIND A QUIET PLACE TO DO SERIOUS BRAIN WORK, CHAMMY?
Er... ALRIGHT. YOU'RE THE EXPERT...
WE LEAVE FOR CHINA IN TWELVE HOURS! I EXPECT EACH ONE OF YOU TO DRILL IN YOUR PART OF THE PLAN UNTIL THEN, MY MINIONS!
WHY HE KEEP CALLIN' US MINIONS? THAT RACIAL?
NO, I DON'T THINK SO.
BETTER NOT BE.
BUST A CAP IN HIS @$$.
IF HE HAD ONE.

LOST MESA INDIAN RESERVATION...
MISTER FIREHEART! MISTER FIREHEART!
I LOOKED ALL OVER FOR TOMMY-- HIS TRAILER-- THE SWEAT LODGE--
BUT THEN I RAN INTO MR. MANY-ARROWS AT THE RESERVATION STORE--
"--HE SAYS HE SAW TOMMY HITCHHIKING OUT ON I-40 EARLY SUNDAY MORNING!
"TOMMY IS LONG GONE, MR. FIREHEART!"
BROOKLYN
DISOBEYING A DIRECT ORDER OF THE COUNCIL! NOW WE KNOW HE'S YOUR NEPHEW, JOE--
NO, I AGREE. THOUGH HE MAY BE MY OWN FLESH AND BLOOD, HIS DEFIANCE HAS PROVEN HIM UNWORTHY OF WIELDING THE PUMA TOTEM.
HE HAS LEFT US NO OTHER RECOURSE THAN TO STRIP HIM OF HIS POWER...
...FOREVER!

WHAT'S YOUR NAME?
RACHEL. RACHEL *KATZ*.
AND *WHERE* DO YOU LIVE?
FOURTH FLOOR WALK-UP ON AVENUE B.
DIDN'T YOU HEAR S.H.I.E.L.D.'S CALL TO EVACUATE THE *CITY*?
I DID, BUT I'M THE *STRINGER* FOR THE *FREE WEEKLY*.
I COULDN'T PASS UP THE CHANCE FOR A *STORY*...
...SO MY NEIGHBOR, *SCOTT BEGLEY*, AND I HID IN THE *ROOT CELLAR*...

...AND WE FOLLOWED THE SOUNDS OF FIGHTING...
...UNTIL WE FOUND...
GRAAAGH!

GOOD.
THESE *FALSE MEMORIES* OF THE OPENING SALVO OF HULK'S WAR AGAINST THE *HEROES* SHOULD ENTICE THE INFINICIDE TO WANT TO BEAM YOU *ABOARD*.
IS THIS GOING TO *STAND UP* UNDER THEIR PSYCHIC SCRUTINY?

TWO BLOCKS FROM THE HIDEOUT...
IMPLANTING PSIONIC DISGUISES WAS DAY ONE BASIC TRAINING IN S.H.I.E.L.D. PSYCH-OPS.
MUST BE WHY BIG HEAD RECRUITED ME FOR THIS TEAM, SINCE HE'S NO SLOUCH IN THE E.S.P. DEPARTMENT HIMSELF.
BETCHA DIDN'T KNOW I STARTED OUT AS ONE OF NICK FURY'S BOYS, DIDJA, CHAMMY?
OF COURSE I DID, FLUMM. I DO MY HOMEWORK.
I SHOULD'VE FIGURED. YOU'VE BEEN IN THE GAME LONGER THAN ANY OF US.
PROBABLY PICKED UP ON ALL KINDS OF SPECIALIZED TRADECRAFT.
LIKE, Gee, I DUNNO...
...EXPERTLY-IMPLANTED TELEPATHIC SHIELDS, FOR INSTANCE?
THERE A PROBLEM, MISS?
AAH! NO--I THOUGHT--
I THOUGHT I SAW--
I DON'T KNOW WHAT I SAW!
Heh WHAT DID YOU SAY? MENTAL ARMOR?
NO. THAT'S RATHER BEYOND MY EXPERTISE.
I DON'T KNOW WHY I WOULD NEED SUCH SHIELDING IN THE FIRST PLACE--

WHA--?
AHHHH!
WHOOOOM
THAT WAS CLOSE!
DIDN'T SEE THAT WAS A DEDICATED BUS LANE--
--WHAT? IT WASN'T THAT FUNNY.
WHY ARE YOU LOOKING AT ME LIKE THAT?
CHAMMY.
BUBELAH.
WE NEED TO TALK.

AND SO...
THE MINUTE I DETECTED THE MENTAL ARMOR I WAS ON TO YOU, BUT NOW THERE'S NO POINT IN EVEN DENYING IT.
AM I SUPPOSED TO HAVE THE SLIGHTEST CLUE WHAT YOU'RE YAMMERING ON ABOUT?
ENOUGH WITH THE ACT ALREADY, IT'S INSULTING. NEVER TRY TO B.S. A B.S.'ER.
THAT TELE-BLOCK IS PRETTY IMPRESSIVE--AND I DON'T KNOW HOW YOU'RE ABLE TO EMULATE CHAMMY'S POWERS--
BUT THE ONE THING YOU DIDN'T--YOU COULDN'T--DISGUISE--
--WAS THE RESIDUAL TRACE OF YOUR SPIDER-SENSE. I'D RECOGNIZE IT ANYWHERE...
...SPIDER-MAN.
THE AVENGERS HAVE YOU INFILTRATING M.O.D.O.K.'S GANG TO FIGURE OUT WHAT HE'S UP TO, Huh?
WELL, BETWEEN YOU, ME AND THE CANAL, HUMPTY-DUMPTY IS GONNA TAKE ME INTO HIS CONFIDENCE, LAY OUT HIS WHOLE SCHEME FOR ME, WHICH I THEN WOULD BE MORE THAN HAPPY TO SHARE WITH YOU AND YOUR TEAMMATES...
...FOR THE RIGHT PRICE, OF COU--
WHAT ARE YOU--
FLAME ON!

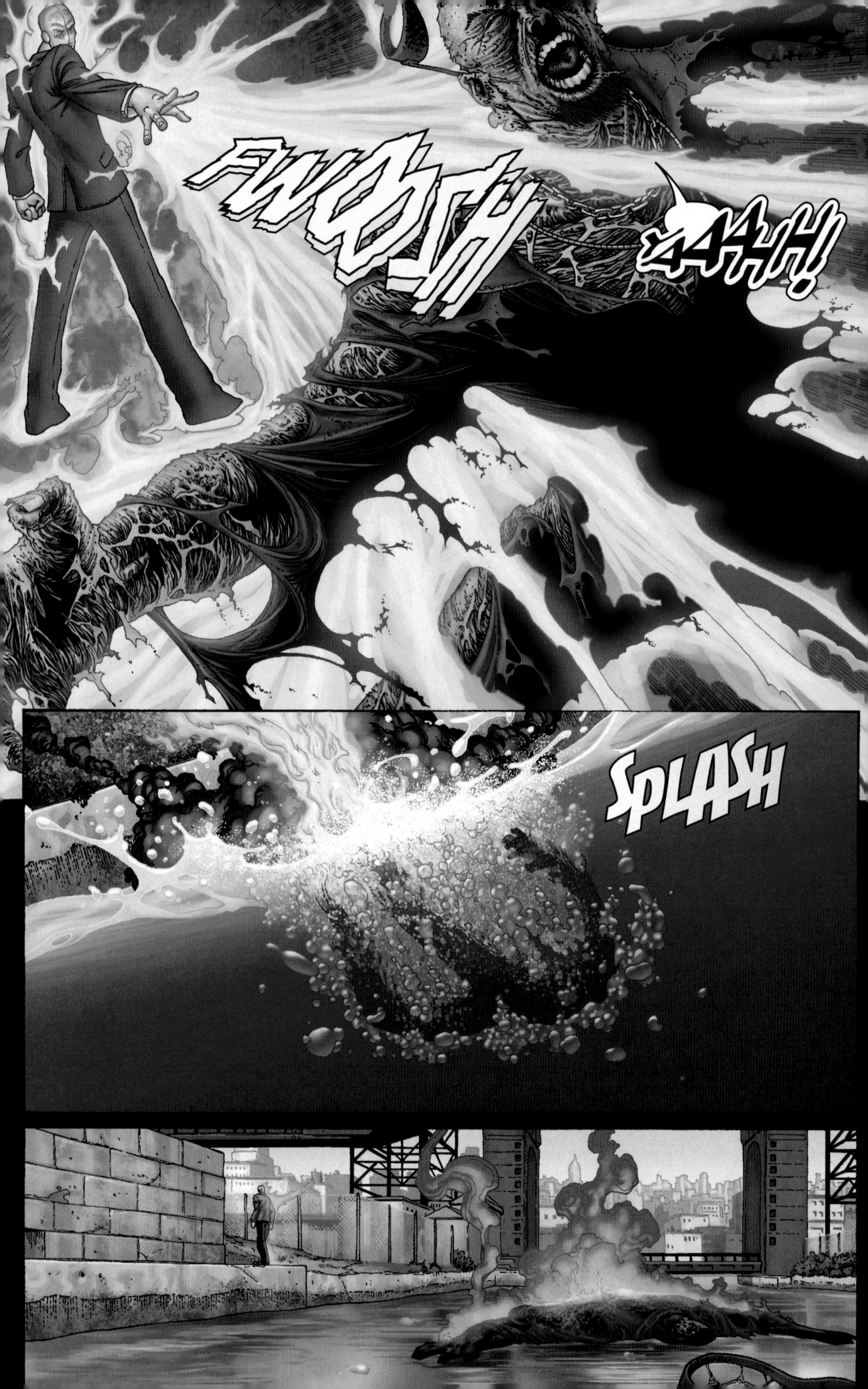
FWOOSH
AAAH!
SPLASH

BACK AT THE HIDEOUT...
HEY, NIGHTSHADE...
...AIN'T YOU THE CHICA WHO ONCE TURNED CAPTAIN AMERICA INTO A WEREWOLF?
THE FALCON, TOO--BACK WHEN THEY WERE PARTNERS.
SIGH THOSE WERE THE DAYS...SO MUCH SIMPLER, THEN. ALL A GIRL NEEDED WAS A SECRET HIDEOUT, A WEREWOLF SERUM AND A DREAM...
I HAD THEM BOTH ON THE ROPES, TOO--BUT THEN THE YELLOW CLAW HAD TO GO AND RUIN IT ALL.
YEAH, I HEARD THAT GUY'S A NIGHTMARE TO WORK WITH.
WHAT ABOUT YOU, TALL, FURRY AND MUTE? ANY "ALMOST GOT 'IM" STORIES?
NO. ONCE THE PUMA HAS ACCEPTED A CONTRACT, HE ALWAYS COMPLETES IT. THIS SHALL BE NO DIFFERENT.
WOW. THAT'S PRETTY IMPRESSIVE. SINCE I DON'T KNOW HOW YOU CAN MAINTAIN YOUR CAT-LIKE AGILITY...
...WITH THAT FLAGPOLE SO FAR UP YOUR BUTT.
I BEG YOUR--
I FOUGHT SPIDER-MAN ONCE!
HE WON!

SNEAKIN' UP ON US--
JUMPY FOR A GUY MADE ENTIRELY OUT OF ENERGY, LASER.
EVER TRY YOGA?
MINION CHAMELEON, YOU ARE FIFTEEN HUNDRED AND SEVENTEEN POINT FOUR TWO SECONDS LATE. MINION MENTALLO IS WITH YOU?
BAD NEWS, BOSS. MENTALLO PLANTED MY PHONY MEMORIES, THEN BAILED.
SAID HE DIDN'T FEEL SAFE BECAUSE NIGHTSHADE THREATENED HIM.
WHAT? I WAS JUST TALKIN' SMACK!
WHO'D HE PULL HIS LAST JOB WITH? MORMONS?
A-A-ALL ABOARD N-N-NAUTILUS JUNIOR.
SHE'S OUR F-F-FAST BOAT TO CHINA.
WAIT. MENTALLO FLED AFTER COMPLETING HIS TASK, BUT BEFORE COLLECTING HIS PAYMENT?
THERE IS A NINETY-NINE POINT FOUR NINE THREE PERCENT PROBABILITY AGAINST THAT OCCURRING.
I KNOW, IT'S WEIRD...
...BUT WHAT CAN I SAY?
IT'S WHAT HAPPENED.

TARGET IS SCANNING ADAPTOID'S SURFACE THOUGHTS...
WE'RE PLAYING BACK MEMORIES OF THE PARK...
A.I.M. CENTRAL COMMAND.
THERE. TARGET TOOK THE BAIT.
HE'S STILL SUSPICIOUS, BUT CAN'T PROVE THAT WASN'T WHAT HAPPENED.
THE PSYCHIC SHIELDING YOU PROVIDED THE ULTRA-ADAPTOID HAS NOT BEEN COMPROMISED, DR. RAPPACCINI.

SO, DEAREST MONICA, OUR ARRANGEMENT STANDS? FIVE MILLION NOW...
AND FIVE MILLION ONCE THE ULTRA-ADAPTOID CASHES IN THE OPEN CONTRACT ON YOUR WAYWARD CREATION?
INDEED. I APOLOGIZE FOR THE DELAY IN INITIAL PAYMENT, BUT WE FIRST HAD TO VERIFY YOUR IDENTITY.
A.I.M.'S INTEL HAD BEEN THAT THE CHAMELEON WAS DEAD--OR IN AN INSANE ASYLUM.
YES, WELL...
...THAT WOULD BE EXACTLY WHAT I WANTED YOU TO THINK.
FADED INTO THE BACKGROUND, IMPERCEPTIBLE...THAT'S WHERE A CHAMELEON IS MOST COMFORTABLE...
...AND WHERE I SHALL NOW RETURN.
TA.
A.I.M. IS QUITE FORTUNATE THAT CHAMELEON CONTACTED US THE SECOND HE RECEIVED M.O.D.O.K.'S TELEPATHIC SUMMONS.
AS IS THE WORLD.
THERE'S ONLY ONE USE THAT INSANE FREAK WOULD PUT THIS HYPERNOVA TO...

"...AS THE POWER SOURCE FOR A NEW COSMIC CUBE THAT HE WILL USE TO FULFILL HIS PERVERTED DESIGN.
"HIS 'MINIONS' DON'T EVEN REALIZE THAT THE REAL JOB THEY'RE BEING PAID TO PERFORM...
"...IS THE UNMAKING OF ALL LIFE ON EARTH!"
PREVENGE
OR: "THE PLAN"

MARVEL LIMITED SERIES
3 of 5

VAN LENTE
PORTELA
PALLOT
GURU eFX

SUPER-VILLAIN TEAM-UP™

XINJIANG UYGUR AUTONOMOUS REGION, CHINA:
MINION CHAMELEON NOW TREADS ONE OF THE MOST INHOSPITABLE PLACES ON EARTH...THE TAKLAMAKAN SALT WASTES.
THE LOCAL TRIBESMEN CALL IT "THE LAND OF DEATH."
NO RAIN. NO ANIMAL LIFE.
ALMOST NO PLANT LIFE.
APPROACHING: POTENTIAL ABDUCTEE_
INITIATING: PSYCHIC SCAN_
EXTRACTING: RELEVANT MEMORIES_

IT IS ONE OF THE FEW PLACES ON EARTH ONE COULD LEAVE A PSYCHICALLY CLOAKED FORTRESS FROM THE END OF TIME INDEFINITELY.
CONCLUSION: SUBJECT CONTAINS MEMORIES USEFUL FOR CONSTRUCTION OF CHRONO-MAP_
RECOMMENDATION: TELEPORT SUBJECT ABOARD BEACON_
FLOATING FIFTY STORIES ABOVE THE SALT PLAINS, THE BEACON COMMANDS PERFECT SIGHT LINES IN EVERY DIRECTION FOR ONE HUNDRED KILOMETERS.
IMPOSSIBLE TO SNEAK UP ON FROM THE AIR.
OR FROM THE GROUND.
ON TOP OF THE GROUND, THAT IS...
KRONCH KRONCH KRONCH

HE'S IN.
THANK GOD.
ptui
MY MOUTH IS FULL OF SALT.
KRONCH
KRONCH
KRONCH
WHERE THE MONEY IS
OR: "THE JOB"

HE'S IN, DR. RAPPACCINI.
A.I.M. CENTRAL COMMAND.
IT'S IN, FERGUSON.
THOUGH OUR ULTRA-ADAPTOID HAS DUPLICATED THE CHAMELEON'S APPEARANCE, PERSONALITY AND POWERS, DO NOT FORGET THAT OTHERWISE IT IS A MINDLESS MACHINE.
WHEN I BECAME SCIENTIST SUPREME I SWORE TO REVERSE MY THANKFULLY DECEASED PREDECESSOR'S PITIFUL TRACK RECORD OF A.I.M. INVENTIONS THAT TURN AROUND AND TRY TO DESTROY US.
THUS OUR ULTRA-ADAPTOID HAS NO INDEPENDENT WILL OF ITS OWN.
AND, LEST IT GET TOO POWERFUL TO EVER THREATEN US...
"...OUR ANDROID IS BEAMED ONLY A FEW POWERS AT A TIME, FROM A VAST DATABASE COLLECTED OFF EVERY HERO THE SUPER-ADAPTOID EVER FOUGHT--VIA SATELLITE!
"I WILL ASSUME DIRECT CONTROL OF EVEN ITS SPEECH AND MOTOR FUNCTIONS NOW THAT WE HAVE REACHED THIS CRITICAL JUNCTURE."
I TRUST THE DELICIOUS IRONY OF USING A LOYAL A.I.M. CREATION TO DESTROY A RENEGADE ONE IS NOT LOST ON YOU MEN.
AND ONCE M.O.D.O.K. IS DEAD--AND THE TARGET OF HIS HEIST IS IN OUR POSSESSION--THAT STAIN ON OUR HISTORY SHALL AT LAST BE ERASED.
HERS TOO, RIGHT, SINCE SHE AND THAT FREAK ACTUALLY KNOCKED BOOTS? >SNICKER<

WHO SAID THAT?!?
HENDRICKS. I MIGHT HAVE KNOWN.
ONE: I WILL NOT TOLERATE ANY DOUBLE STANDARD, HENDRICKS!
IF I WAS A MAN, YOU WOULD NOT BE SNICKERING!
TWO:
HE DIDN'T LOOK LIKE THAT WHEN WE DID IT!
AND THREE:
AAAAAAAA
KRUNCH
HENDRICKS' DUTY STATION IS VACANT. MATTHEWS, REPLACE HIM.
YES, MA'AM.

THE INFINICIDE'S BEACON...
klak
klak
klak
MINION CHAMELEON, THE GUARDS APPROACH. SHAPESHIFT INTO ONE OF THEM, NOW!
DISCREPANCY: NEW ABDUCTEE NOT / REPEAT NOT / AT TARGET LOCATION_
RUN: SEARCH PROGRAM / TARGET: NEW ABDUCTEE_
"GOTTA SAY I'M EARNING MY PAY HERE.
"NEVER TRIED TO PICK A GENETIC KEYPAD LOCK BEFORE."
NEVER TRIED TO SYNTHESIZE THE GENES OF A CREATURE FIVE BILLION YEARS AHEAD OF MY TIME WITHOUT A TISSUE SAMPLE BEFORE, EITHER.
BUT A MUTAGEN MIST OF UNSTABLE MOLECULES AND X-FACTOR SKIN CELLS...
"...SHOULD DO THE TRICK."
SSSSS

BLOOP
SSSHHHHHH
THE INFINICIDE HAS RELEASED CLOUDS OF SENSOR DUST AROUND THE PERIMETER OF THE CONTAINMENT PLATFORM.
WHRRRRR
WAIT FOR THE BLIND SPOTS IN THE CAMERA VIEW, MINION CHAMELEON.
YOU SHALL HAVE SIX SECONDS, MINION PUMA.
I ONLY NEED FOUR.

WHRRRR
NOW.

FWAP
GOOD. YOU SUCCESSFULLY EVADED THE DUST.
NOW WAIT FOR THE CAMERA TO SWIVEL AWAY AGAIN...
WAIT FOR IT...
NOW, MINION LASER! PROCEED BEYOND THE RANGE OF THE VISIBLE SPECTRUM!
ONCE MINION PUMA REMOVES THE BEACON'S POWER SOUCE, YOU NEED TO THROW OFF SUFFICIENT ALPHA PARTICLES TO FOOL THE INFINICIDE'S ENERGY LEVEL MONITORS...
...LONG ENOUGH FOR HIM TO RETURN TO MINION SPOT'S WARP HOLE AND SECURE OUR PRIZE.
SSSSSH! YOUR INCESSANT MONOLOGUING ISN'T HELPING MY EQUILIBRIUM ANY, M.O.D.O.K.

COUPLE MINUTES GONE BY...GUESS EVERYTHING'S GOING OKAY IN THERE, Huh?
MAYBE.
MAYBE IT STOPPED BEING OKAY LONG BEFORE WE GOT HERE.
WHOLE MENTALLO THING DON'T SIT RIGHT, Huh?
HELL NO. BUCKETHEAD WAS NO FOOL. HE SKIPPED FOR A REASON.
IF HE SMELLED SOMETHING ROTTEN WITH THIS SETUP, I DON'T BLAME HIM.
HOW COME BIG HEAD KNOWS SO MUCH ABOUT THIS INFINICIDE CREW AND THEIR CRIB?
WHY IS HE COOLIN' HIS HEELS BACK IN BROOKLYN WHILE WE GOT OUR @$$ES HANGING OUT IN THE BREEZE HERE?
YOU SO SUSPICIOUS, WHY DON'T YOU SPLIT TOO, CHICA?
"'CAUSE AFTER MY LAST RUN-IN WITH THE BLACK PANTHER, I MADE ONE LAST GO AT CIVILIAN.
"I'M ALL SELF-TAUGHT--I GOT NO FANCY DEGREES--SO THE BEST MED JOB I COULD GET WAS ANSWERING PHONES AT ST. VINCENT'S, IN THE VILLAGE.
"UNTIL I POINTED OUT A BAD DIAGNOSIS BY ONE OF THEIR HOTSHOT DOCTORS, THAT IS.
"HE DID SOME GOOGLING--FIGURED OUT WHO I WAS--AND THAT I LIED ABOUT MY RECORD ON MY JOB APPLICATION.
"I GOT M.O.D.O.K.'S TELE-OFFER JUST AS UNEMPLOYMENT RAN OUT."
I DIDN'T SKIP FOR THE SAME REASON YOU DIDN'T, 'DILLO. SAME REASON NONE OF US DID.
I USED UP ALL MY SECOND CHANCES. THIS JOB IS ALL THAT STANDS BETWEEN ME AND THE BOTTOM OF A REAL LONG FALL.
AND WHAT REALLY BOTHERS ME...
...IS THAT M.O.D.O.K. KNOWS IT TOO...
...AND THAT'S WHY HE HIRED US IN THE FIRST PLACE.

HERE, SPOT, TAKE IT.
LASER, IT'S TIME.
WHRRRR
C'MON, WE HAVE TO GO!
LASER...?
LASER!
CONFIRM: AUDIBLE ANOMALY_
...
NO ANOMALY... DETECTED.

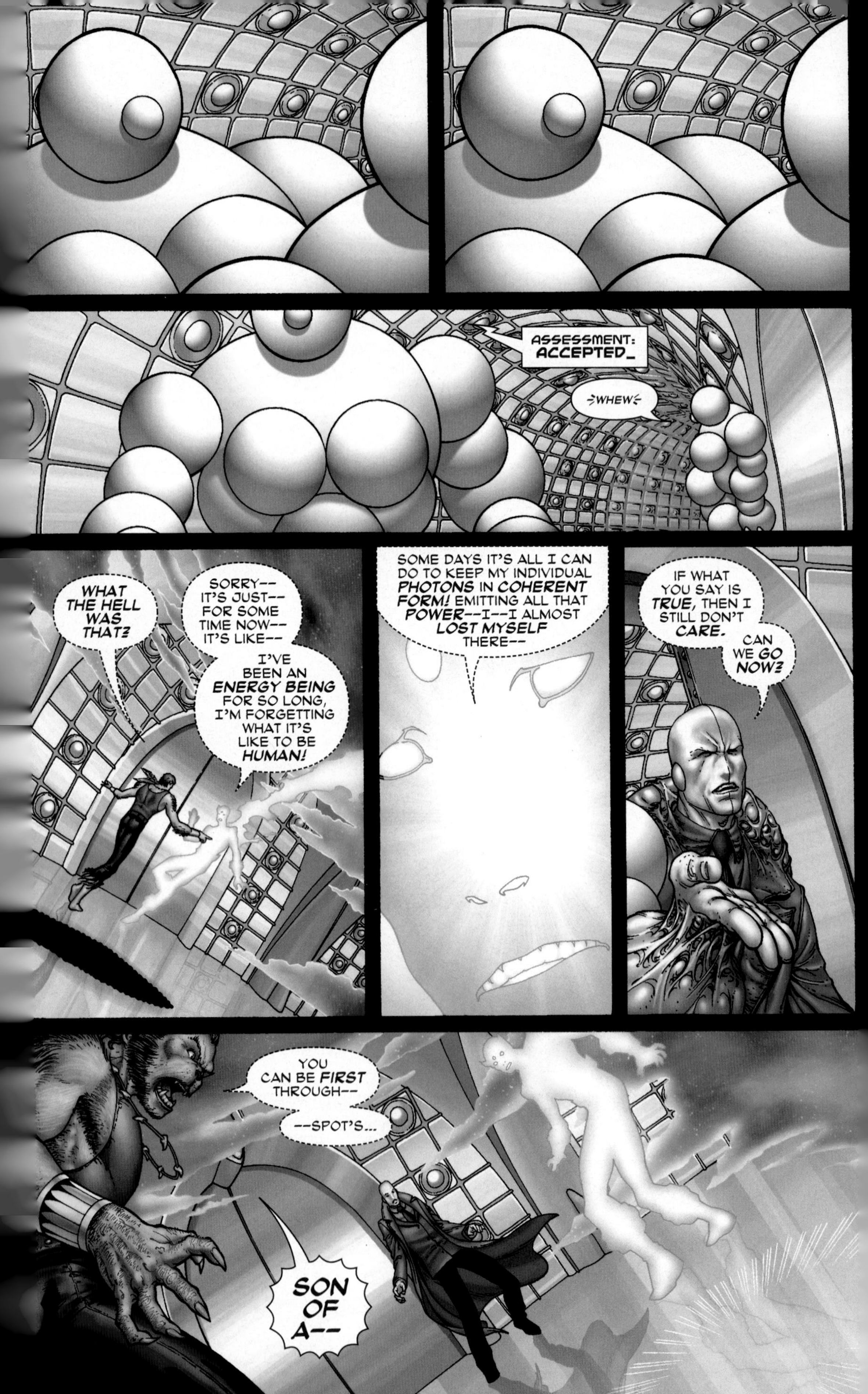
ASSESSMENT: ACCEPTED_
WHEW
WHAT THE HELL WAS THAT?
SORRY-- IT'S JUST-- FOR SOME TIME NOW-- IT'S LIKE--
I'VE BEEN AN ENERGY BEING FOR SO LONG, I'M FORGETTING WHAT IT'S LIKE TO BE HUMAN!
SOME DAYS IT'S ALL I CAN DO TO KEEP MY INDIVIDUAL PHOTONS IN COHERENT FORM! EMITTING ALL THAT POWER--I--I ALMOST LOST MYSELF THERE--
IF WHAT YOU SAY IS TRUE, THEN I STILL DON'T CARE.
CAN WE GO NOW?
YOU CAN BE FIRST THROUGH--
--SPOT'S...
SON OF A--

WHAT ABOUT YOU, SPOT? THE WHOLE REASON WE HAD TO DIG THIS TUNNEL SO CLOSE WAS FOR YOU TO BE IN RANGE FOR YOUR HOP-SPOTS TO GET INSIDE.
WHAT DO YOU THINK ABOUT--
SPOT?
AAAH...
>SLURP!<
POLYSACCHARIDES... CARBOXYMETHYL-CELLULOSE... SUCROSE!
>SLURP!<
REVENGE FUEL...
>SLURP!<
BROOKLYN, WE HAVE A PROBLEM.
WHA--? MINION NIGHTSHADE! WHY ARE YOU BREAKING THE TELEPATHIC SILENCE PUMA REQUESTED? HAS THE AWAY TEAM RETURNED?
YEEEEEEEAH... ABOUT THEM...
WHRRRR KLIK
BWOOP
BWOOP
BWOOP
RUN?
RUN.

BWOOP BWOOP BWOOP
IS IT JUST ME, OR WHEN WE FOUGHT THOSE THINGS DURING M.O.D.O.K.'S PSYMULATION, DIDN'T WE, UH... ...DIE?
IT ISN'T YOU! C'MON! THIS WAY!
IS THERE A WAY OUT OF HERE? THERE AREN'T EVEN ANY WINDOWS FOR ME TO PASS OUT OF!
"M.O.D.O.K. HAS BETRAYED HIS MINIONS--"
--AS WE PREDICTED, DOCTOR!
DROP THE PRETENSE--UNLEASH THE FULL POWER OF THE ADAPTOID!
NO. IT'S TOO SOON. I HAVE PLANS OF MY OWN FOR THAT HYPERNOVA, AND THE TRUST OF THESE "VILLAINS" MAY YET ALLOW ME TO GET IT.
AIM
DO YOU HAVE EVEN THE SLIGHTEST CLUE WHERE YOU'RE GOING?
I SMELL A FAMILIAR ODOR THIS WAY...

Ah.
WELL.
THIS EXPLAINS A LOT...
...SUCH AS WHY MODOK HAS SUCH AN AFFINITY FOR THE INFINICIDE.
DIDN'T HE MENTION A.I.M. RAN HIM THROUGH AN EVOLUTIONARY ACCELERATOR?
WHAT?
WHY ARE YOU LOOKING AT ME LIKE THAT?

LOST MESA INDIAN RESERVATION...
AND SO IT IS DONE.
FOR DISOBEYING THE COUNCIL'S ORDER NOT TO LEAVE OUR TRIBAL LANDS, THOMAS FIREHEART HAS BEEN STRIPPED OF THE PUMA TOTEM.
NOW ANOTHER MUST BE FOUND TO TAKE HIS PLACE.
AND QUICKLY, JOSEPH. THE ATTACKS ON HIM WERE CLEARLY BUT A PRELUDE TO AN ASSAULT ON LOST MESA ITSELF.
I KNOW, BROTHERS. WOULD THAT WE COULD HAVE PROTECTED MY NEPHEW, BUT UNTIL HE LEARNS SELFLESSNESS...
"...I FEAR HE IS BEYOND ANYONE'S HELP."
POIT
THE TAKLAMAKAN SALT WASTES...
Heh, Heh. SAYONARA, SUCKERS!
ONE WHO VALUES HIS LIFE AS PRECIOUS DOES NOT USE THE LANGUAGE OF THE IMPERIALISTS OF NIPPON WITHIN MY HEARING, SPOT.

WHOA, Hey, NO NEED TO GET CRANKY THERE, MANDARIN. IT'S YOUR MONEY.
I'D TELL YOU DIRTY LIMERICKS IN ESPERANTO IF YOU WANTED ME TO!
THAT WON'T BE NECESSARY.
YOU HAVE THE ITEM YOU DESCRIBED IN YOUR E-MAIL?
IF YOU'VE GOT MY FIFTEEN MILLION BUCKS, I DO!
INCREDIBLE... IT IS AS YOU SAID. THE PERPETUAL ANNIHILATION OF A POCKET UNIVERSE...
...A SELF-SUSTAINING FUEL SOURCE OF NIGH-INFINITE POWER.
I KNEW YOU'D LOVE IT, MANDY! LUCKY FOR ME I KNEW HOW TO GET IN TOUCH WITH YOU.
'COURSE, IT HELPS THAT I SWIPED THE KINGPIN'S ROLODEX AFTER HE FIRED ME AS HIS HEAD RESEARCHER!
YES...MY LATE FATHER KEPT A FILE ON YOU.
YOUR BIZARRE CONDITION IS A RESULT OF YOUR FAILED ATTEMPT TO REPLICATE THE DARKFORCE POWERS OF THE TEENAGE HERO, CLOAK.
THE SAME POWER HARNESSED BY FATHER'S BLACK LIGHT RING!
WHAT ARE YOU DOIN'? WE HAD A DEAL!

SO WE DID.
AND I PAID YOU FOR THE HYPERNOVA, AS I PROMISED.
BUT YOU HAVE ALREADY BETRAYED YOUR ORIGINAL EMPLOYER-- AND CONDEMNED YOUR TEAMMATES TO CERTAIN DEATH.
ONE SUCH AS YOU IS WITHOUT HONOR. WHAT IS TO STOP YOU FROM BETRAYING ME TO M.O.D.O.K., SO LONG AS THE PRICE IS RIGHT?
I W-WOULDN'T DO THAT--YOU GOTTA BELIEVE ME--
I AM AFRAID TRUSTING YOU IS A CHANCE I CANNOT AFFORD TO TAKE.
Uhhh...
NO... NO...
NOOOO!

NO!
F-FOR THE FIRST TIME...IN MY LIFE...I...CANNOT FEEL MY SPIRIT HELPER GUIDING ME...
...WHY... WHY HAS THE PUMA TOTEM ABANDONED ME...?
TAKE PUMA THAT WAY! I'LL SLOW THEM DOWN!
ARE YOU HIGH?
JUST GO!
NOW THEY'RE OUT OF VIEW! I CAN SEE WHAT THIS ANDROID CAN DO!
TRANSMIT TO ME THE POWERS OF SPIDER-MAN!
RUN: ANNIHILATION PROGRAM_
THE POWERS OF INVISIBLE WOMAN!
TARGET: LOST_
RUN/SWITCH: OPTICS: INFRARED--

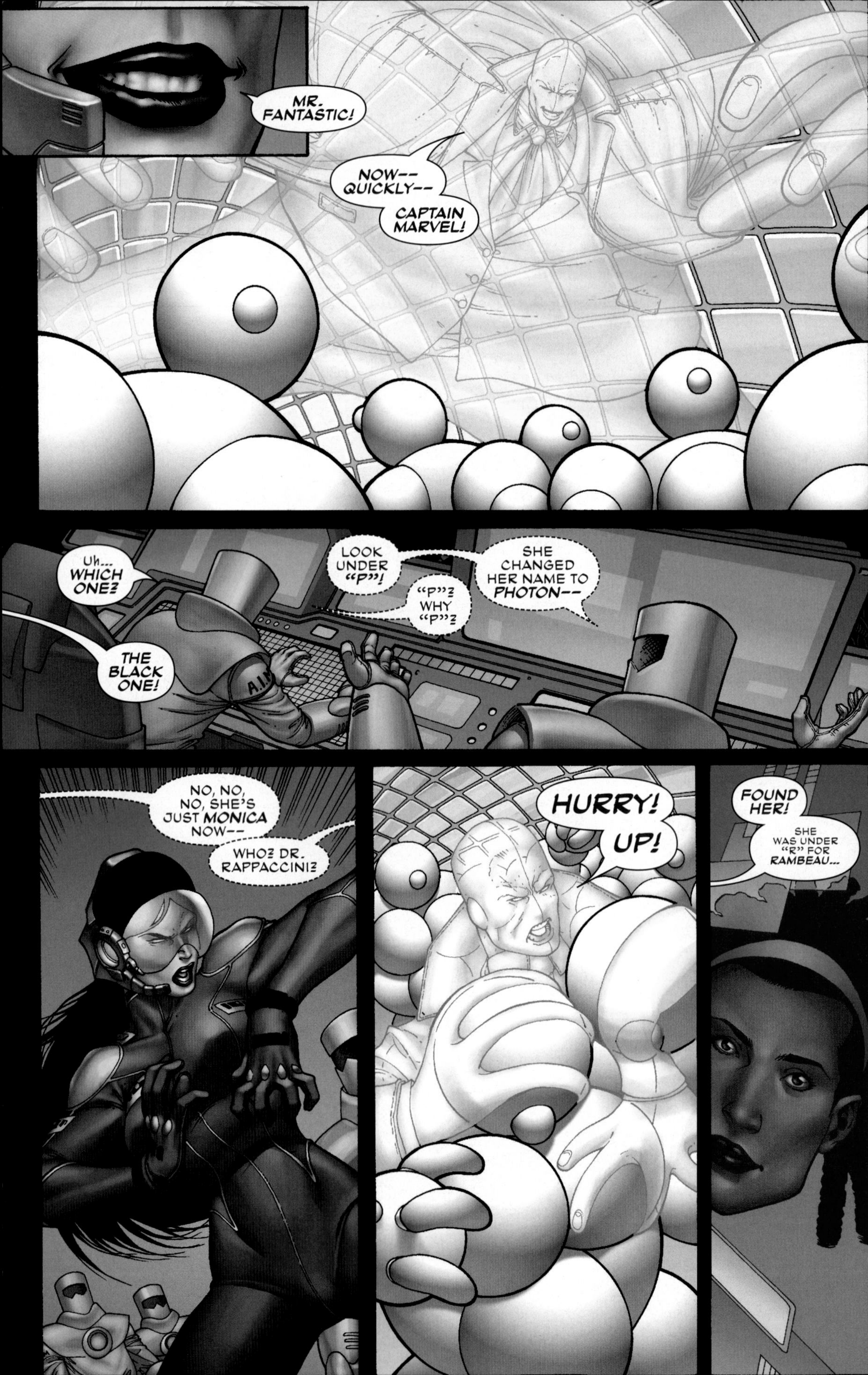
MR. FANTASTIC!
NOW-- QUICKLY--
CAPTAIN MARVEL!
Uh... WHICH ONE?
THE BLACK ONE!
LOOK UNDER "P"!
"P"? WHY "P"?
SHE CHANGED HER NAME TO PHOTON--
NO, NO, NO, SHE'S JUST MONICA NOW--
WHO? DR. RAPPACCINI?
HURRY!
UP!
FOUND HER!
SHE WAS UNDER "R" FOR RAMBEAU...

ZZZROOOW
HA HA HA!
I COULD GET USED TO THIS!
THESE SO-CALLED HEROES AREN'T USING THEIR POWERS TO THEIR FULLEST POTENTIAL!
LOOK OUT, FIREHEART! SLOW MEANS DEAD!
WHO CARES...NO LIFE WORTH LIVING WITHOUT TOTEM...
YOU KNOW WHAT I WOULD GIVE TO BE IN YOUR SHOES, KITTY? A NORMAL HUMAN AGAIN?
I'M GONNA KEEP YOU ALIVE LONG ENOUGH TO KNOCK SOME SENSE INTO YOU!
HOW IS HE?
HEY, IT'S NOT LIKE THINGS COULD GET ANY WORSE!

DON'T SAY THAT.
"DON'T EVER SAY THAT."
IS THIS REALLY A GOOD IDEA?
YOU GOT A BETTER ONE, I'M TAKIN' REQUESTS!
TOPSIDE WE MIGHT GET SOME SENSE OF WHAT'S--
Uh-oh.
THE BEACON'S GOT NO POWER! IT'S FALLING RIGHT ON--

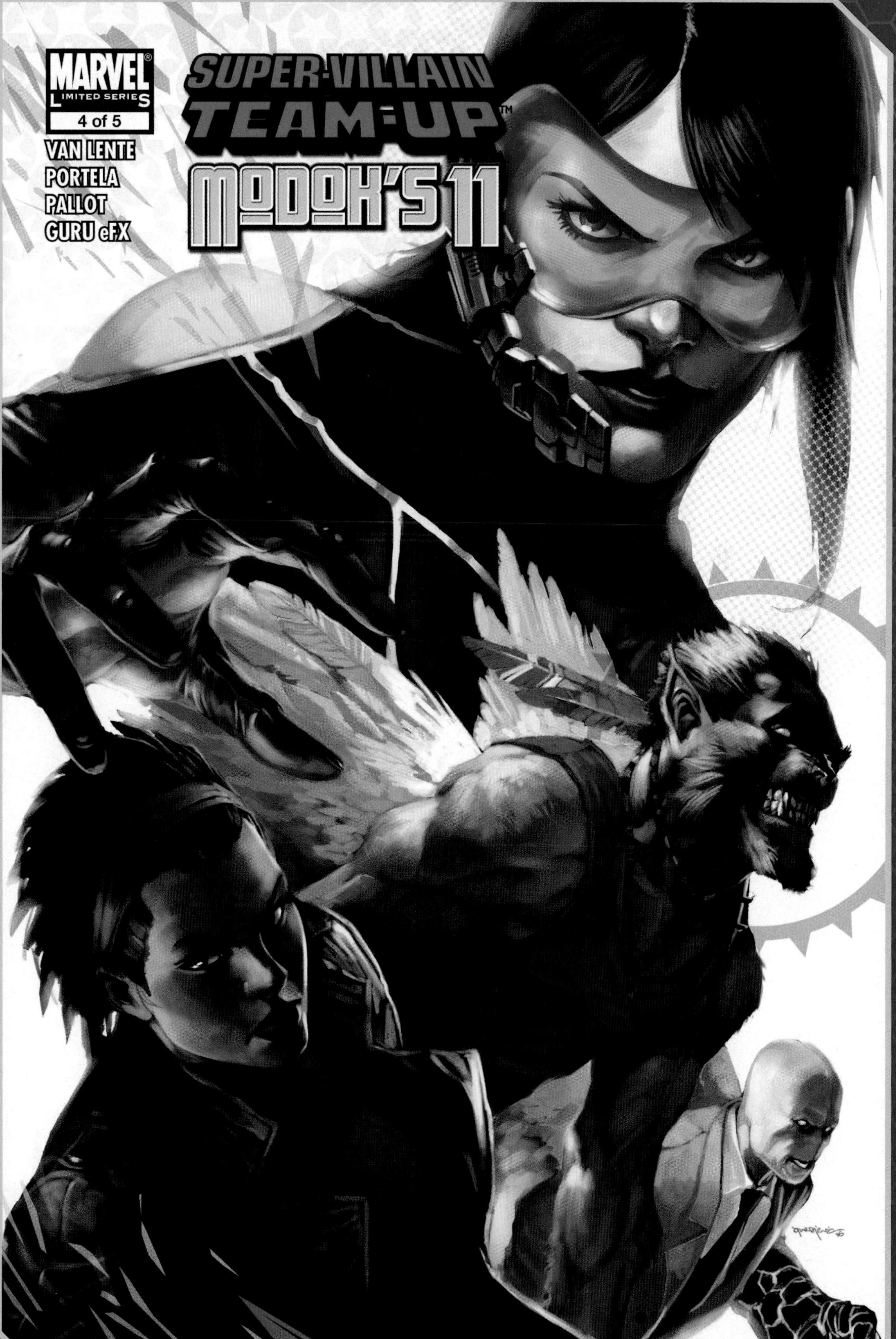

SUPER-VILLAIN TEAM-UP™

MODOK'S 11

VAN LENTE
PORTELA
PALLOT
GURU eFX

I have seen men die from treading on water and fire, but I have never seen a man die from treading the course of virtue.

--Confucius

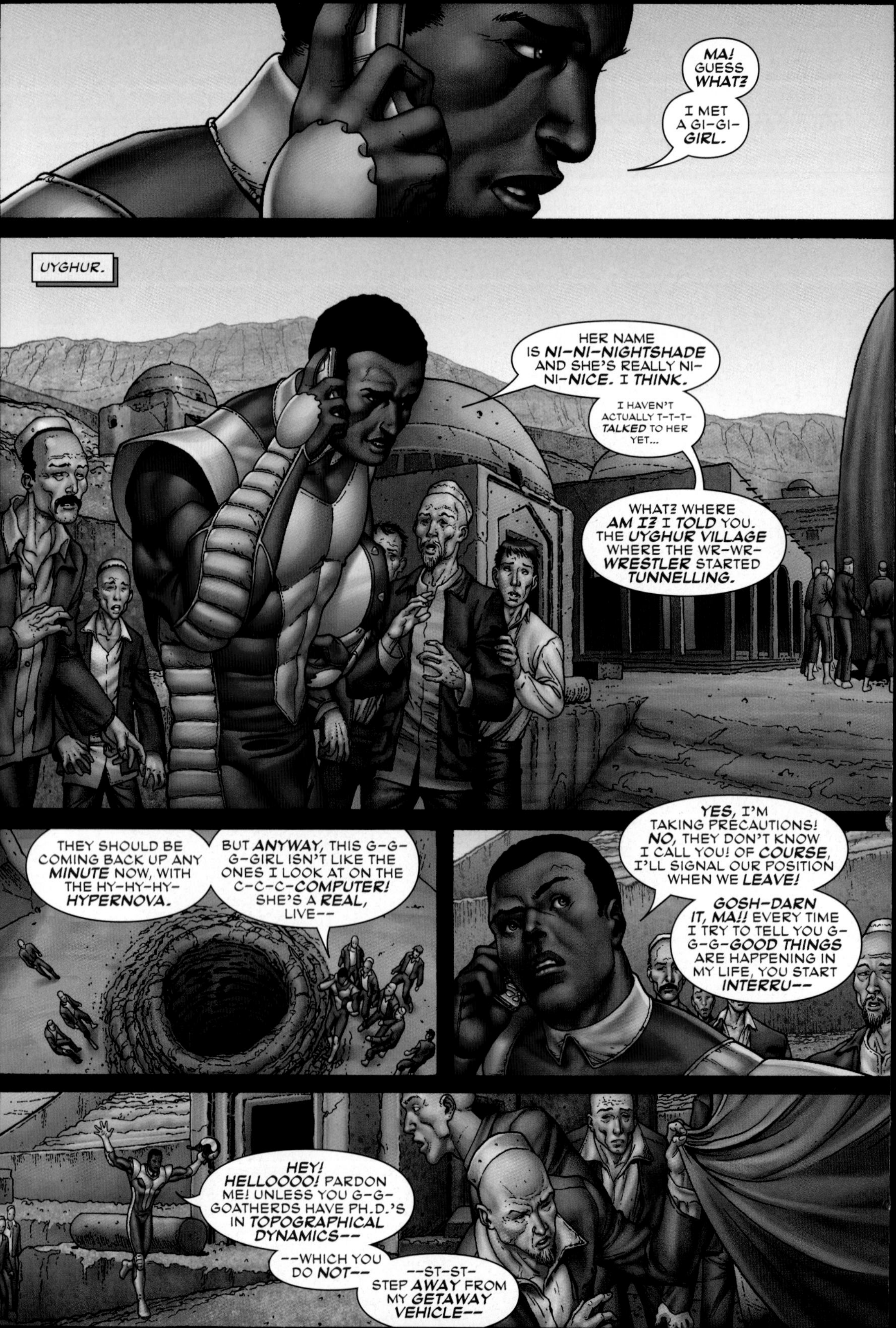

MA! GUESS WHAT?

I MET A GI-GI-GIRL.

UYGHUR.

HER NAME IS NI-NI-NIGHTSHADE AND SHE'S REALLY NI-NI-NICE. I THINK.

I HAVEN'T ACTUALLY T-T-T-TALKED TO HER YET...

WHAT? WHERE AM I? I TOLD YOU. THE UYGHUR VILLAGE WHERE THE WR-WR-WRESTLER STARTED TUNNELLING.

THEY SHOULD BE COMING BACK UP ANY MINUTE NOW, WITH THE HY-HY-HY-HYPERNOVA.

BUT ANYWAY, THIS G-G-G-GIRL ISN'T LIKE THE ONES I LOOK AT ON THE C-C-C-COMPUTER! SHE'S A REAL, LIVE--

YES, I'M TAKING PRECAUTIONS! NO, THEY DON'T KNOW I CALL YOU! OF COURSE, I'LL SIGNAL OUR POSITION WHEN WE LEAVE!

GOSH-DARN IT, MA!! EVERY TIME I TRY TO TELL YOU G-G-G-GOOD THINGS ARE HAPPENING IN MY LIFE, YOU START INTERRU--

HEY! HELLOOOO! PARDON ME! UNLESS YOU G-G-GOATHERDS HAVE PH.D.'S IN TOPOGRAPHICAL DYNAMICS--
--WHICH YOU DO NOT--
--ST-ST-STEP AWAY FROM MY GETAWAY VEHICLE--

MA?
“GOTTA GO.”

Whoa.
WHY AREN'T WE DEAD?
A.I.M. CENTRAL COMMAND:
IT'S CALLED AN INVISIBLE FORCE FIELD, MORON.
SUE RICHARDS INVISIBLE WOMAN
HEH GOOD ONE, LARRY.
CAN WE PLEASE JUST KILL THESE LOSERS NOW, DR. RAPPA--
SSSSH!! INCREASE PARABOLIC HEARING BY 75%!
SOME KIND OF RUMBLING OR GRINDING GETTING CLOSER--
"YO! ESES!"
LITTLE HELP?
RRRMMMMMMM

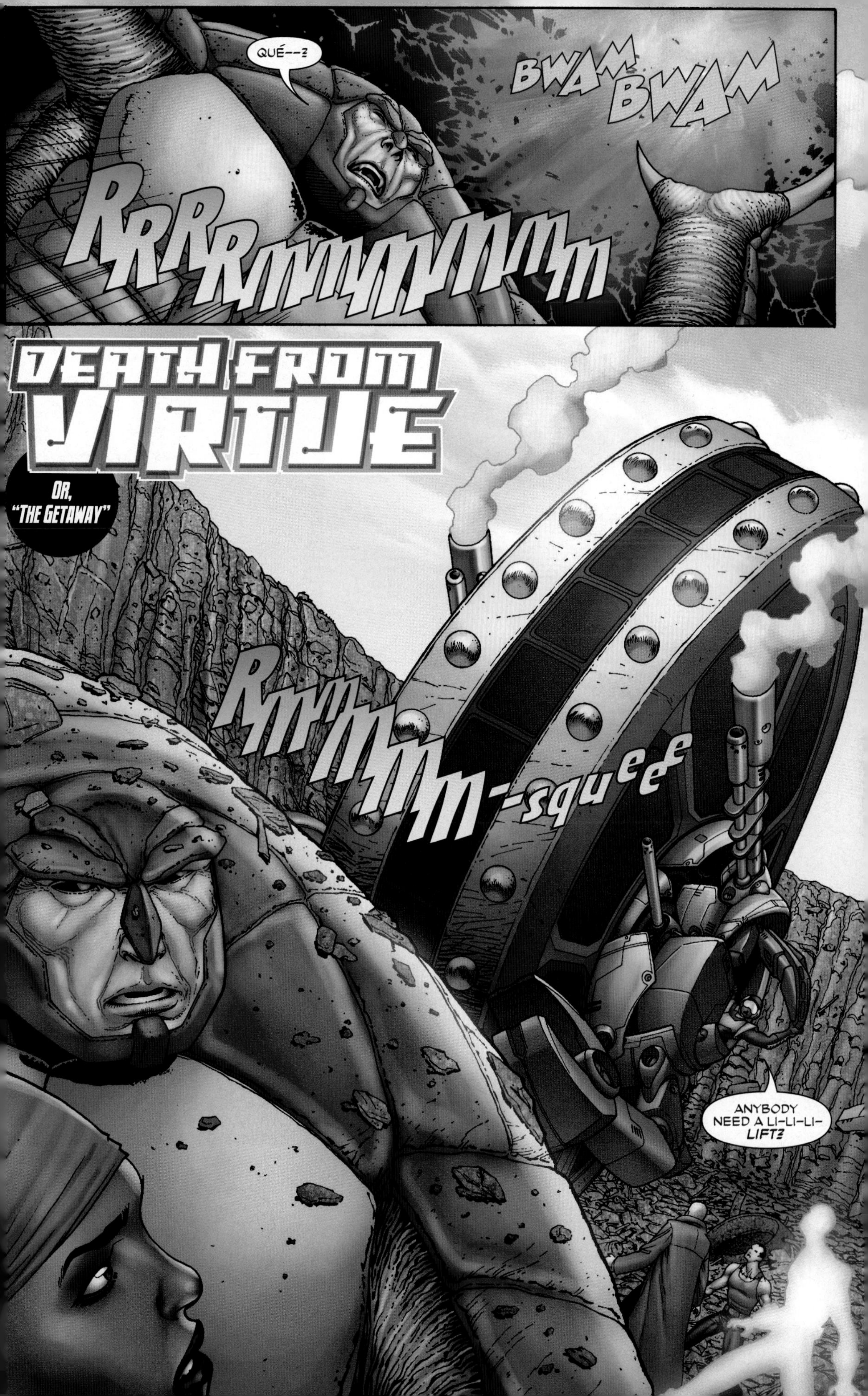
QUÉ--?
BWAM BWAM
RRRRMMMMMMMM
DEATH FROM VIRTUE
OR, "THE GETAWAY"
RMMMMMM-squeee
ANYBODY NEED A LI-LI-LI-LIFT?

WHAT THE HELL IS THIS THING?
B-B-BIG WHEEL!
A DISGRUNTLED CLIENT TRIED TO M-M-M-MURDER ME WITH IT ONCE!
BUT IT'S A CLASSIC T-T-T-TINKERER DESIGN! I COULDN'T JUST WASTE IT!
MY TOTEM... GONE...LIKE HALF MY SOUL... RIPPED OUT OF ME...
HEY, PUMA, YOU LOOK DIFFERENT, SOMEHOW...
...YOU SWITCH COSTUMES?
COZY ENOUGH FOR YOU?
G-G-G--
TALK AT ME, M.O.D.O.K.!
I HAVE COMPLETED MY PSIONIC SCAN OF THE AREA! THE MANDARIN IS PROCEEDING NORTH BY NORTHWEST AT APPROXIMATELY 420 MPH!
AVAILABLE DATA SUGGESTS AN 87.39% PROBABILITY THAT THE SPOT BETRAYED US AND SURRENDERED THE HYPERNOVA TO HIM!
PURSUE HIM, MY MINIONS, OR OUR CONTRACT IS FORFEIT!!!
AGAIN WITH THE "MINIONS"...
SHOULD WE WORRY ABOUT THE INFINICIDE?
Nah...
...I THINK THEY'VE HAD ALL OF THE TWENTY-FIRST CENTURY THAT THEY CAN TAKE.

HOW WILL WE KNOW THIS MANDARIN WHEN WE SEE HIM?
WELL, I'M GONNA GO OUT ON A LIMB, HERE...
...AND GUESS THAT'S PROBABLY HIM.
GOOD.
I FEEL CRAMPED IN HERE, AND I HAVE NO CORPOREAL BODY.
I'LL TELL YOU WHEN I'VE FOUND THE HYPERNOVA BY BEAMING MY VOICE BACK TO YOU IN THE FORM OF RADIO WAVES.

<LOOK WHAT I HAVE BROUGHT YOU, FATHER.>
<A PERPETUAL MOTION MACHINE FROM THE END OF TIME.>*
<ONCE WE REACH THE VALLEY OF SPIRITS, I SHALL AT LAST ACHIEVE ONE OF YOUR FONDEST DREAMS...>
<...AND USE THIS ETERNALLY EXPLODING STAR TO IGNITE THE HEART OF AXONN-KARR'S FALLEN SPACE-SHIP.>
<WITH THE FULL POWER OF A MAKLUAN BATTLE CRUISER AT OUR FINGER-TIPS...>
*TRANSLATED FROM--WHAT ELSE?--MANDARIN. -MULTILINGUAL MARK

<...I SHALL BE SCATTERING YOUR ASHES ACROSS THE RUINS OF BEIJING WITHIN THE WEEK.>
KKIIII-YIIII--
YOU BRAIN-DEAD, JUNIOR?
YOU CAN'T HONG-KONG-PHOOEY A GUY MADE OUT OF ENERG--
ZWOW
AAAHH!

KRAK
ARTHUR PARKS.
THE LIVING LASER.
MY FATHER EMPLOYED YOU SEVERAL TIMES IN HIS WAR AGAINST THE IMPERIALIST, TONY STARK.
I AM NOT MY FATHER.
HE SENT ME TO A MONASTERY WHEN I WAS VERY YOUNG, SO I MIGHT GAIN COMPLETE MASTERY OVER MY LIFE-ENERGY...
...MY CHI.
I...I FELT THAT. FOR THE FIRST TIME IN YEARS...
...A HUMAN TOUCH.
DO IT. PLEASE DO IT AGAIN...
MASTERY OVER CHI-FLOW ALLOWS ME TO DETECT ENERGY DISRUPTIONS ON MY SHIP EVEN BY INTRUDERS OUTSIDE THE VISIBLE SPECTRUM--
WOK
YES... MORE...
SMACK
THUD

--AND ALLOWS ME TO METE OUT PUNISHMENT TO THE SAME!
SMAK
THUD
SOUNDS LIKE LIGHT BOY'S TAKING A WORSE BEATING THAN I DID LAST TIME I CAGE-MATCHED LOS HERMANOS VAMPIROS!
THIS IS OUR CHANCE TO NAB BACK OUR SCORE!
KEEP THIS CARNIVAL RIDE STEADY, RACER!
O-OKAY, NIGHTSHADE...
BU-BU-BUT YOU CAN CALL ME B-B-B-B--
SPWOOSH
A COUPLE CHROMO-TWEAKS OF THE SILKWORM, AND YOU GOT YOURSELF AN ORGANIC ROPE BRIDGE AS STRONG AS CABLE!
EXCEPT I THINK YOU'RE TOO HEAVY, EVEN FOR IT, 'DILLO. SORRY.
TAKE THE WHEEL--WE'LL BE RIGHT BACK!
YEAH, YEAH.
IT'S GLANDULAR.

WHAP
AND TO THINK THE WEST AND THE MAOISTS LUMPED MY FATHER IN WITH YOU SO-CALLED "VILLAINS!"
WHAT AN INSULT! HE WAS NOTHING LIKE YOUR KIND.
HELLO, YOU BIG, BEAUTIFUL HYPERNOVA, YOU. MISS US?
WHAT ABOUT LIVING LASER?
WHAT ABOUT HIM?
THE SPOT TOLD ME ABOUT ALL OF YOU.
SHRAKK
COWARDS AND PARASITES--ALL WITHOUT HONOR--WILLING TO SELL EACH OTHER OUT FOR A FEW EXTRA DOLLARS.
LIAR! LASER SAVED MY LIFE IN THE BEACON--HE'S NO COWARD!
AND I HAVE HONOR! I AM DUTY-BOUND TO SAVE HIM!
FITTING, THEN, TO CRUSH YOU--AS ONE WOULD ANY OTHER VERMIN.
N-NO--W-WAIT--GAK!
YOU COULD'VE CHOSEN A MORE CONVENIENT TIME TO SUDDENLY GET MORALS, PUMA.
WITHOUT POWERS, YOU'RE TALKING SUICIDE--
BETTER TO DIE IN DEFENSE OF ONE'S PEOPLE THAN LIVE AS A PAWN--
--DISCARDED, FORGOTTEN, ONCE YOUR USEFULNESS HAS EXPIRED!

THIS MUST BE WHAT THE PUMA SPIRIT--MY UNCLE--WAS TRYING TO TEACH ME--
--TO PUT MY TRIBE BEFORE MY-SELF--
--IN A NOBLE CAUSE, EMPOWERED BY VIRTUE--
--THIS IS WHAT IT MEANS TO WIELD THE PUMA TOTEM!
AND I WILL NEVER FAIL IT AGAIN!
RROOOAARR
WEREWOLF SERUM?
I CALL IT A LYCANTHRO-CATALYST--IT CHEMICALLY SWAPS OUT ANOTHER FORM A MUTANT OR OTHER SUPERHUMAN MIGHT HAVE IMPRINTED ON HIS DNA...
...BUT, BASICALLY, YEAH, WEREWOLF SERUM.

EVEN THOUGH HE'S ALL FURRY AGAIN, PUMA'S GONNA NEED PLENTY OF BACKUP! C'MON!

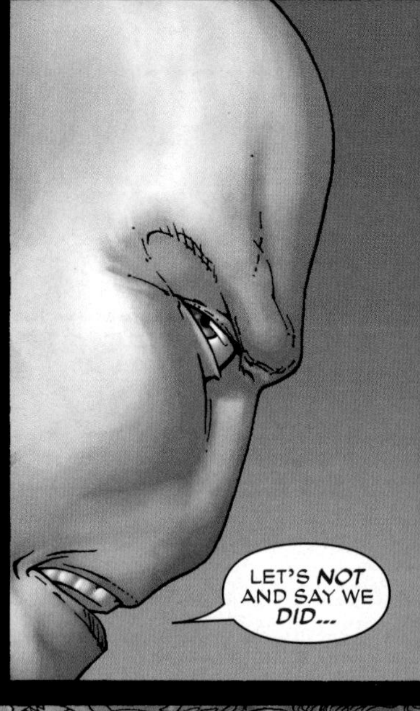
LET'S NOT AND SAY WE DID...

WHA...?

Oh, NO...

NO!!!

DOES ANYONE ON THIS TEAM ACTUALLY WORK FOR WHO THEY SAY THEY WORK FOR?!?

MANDARIN!

"PUMA," I PRESUME?
SLASH

YOU APPEAR TO BE MORE *SKILLED* THAN YOUR *TEAM-MATE.*

I AM THE CULMINATION OF *TEN GENERATIONS* OF BREEDING AND *MEDICINE* TO CREATE THE *PERFECT WARRIOR* OF THE *LOST MESA KISÂNI!*
FWOOOSH

AND I WILL *NOT* ALLOW MY FRIENDS TO BE *THREATENED!*
ZWOK

THE PRIDE OF AN ENTIRE *PEOPLE*, EH?

WHAT A HORRENDOUS BURDEN.

IF I WERE IN YOUR POSITION, I WOULD BE CONCERNED...

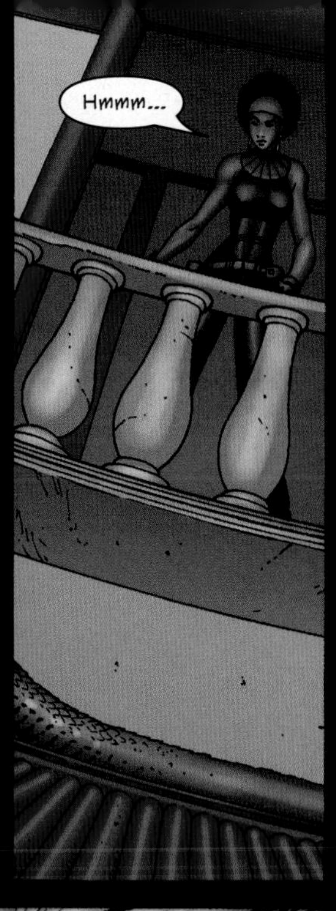
Hmmm...

...ABOUT HOW MY SUDDEN DISINTEGRATION WILL REFLECT ON THEM!

RACER!

KRASH

YO.
MANDY.
GUESS WHAT?
I GOT YOUR DAD.
YOU DON'T LET ME, KITTY, AND LIGHT BOY WALK OUTTA HERE, WITH THE HYPERNOVA...
...ONE SQUIRT OF INDUSTRIAL SOLVENT WILL TURN POPS INTO PREBIOTIC TOE JAM.
YOU DIG?
WITCH! HOW DARE YOU DISHONOR MY FAMILY?!?
I WILL BURN YOU AND FREEZE YOU AT THE SAME TIME!
I WILL BLAST YOUR CORPSE INTO ATOMS BEFORE IT HITS THE GROUND--
WAVING THOSE RINGS AROUND IS GIVIN' ME A REAL BAD CASE OF THE ITCHY TRIGGER FINGERS...
YOU SHOOT HIM, YOU DIE NEXT!!

HEEEEY! ALL RIGHT! YOU GOT IT, RACER!
BUT--
--I'M DOWN HERE, YO! BRING IT HERE--
¿QUÉ COÑO ES ESO...?
TOLD YOU WE SHOULD'VE KILLED THEM WHEN WE HAD THE CHANCE.
LARRY, YOU SO DO NOT WANT HER TO HEAR YOU SAY THAT...
A.I.
THAT TOUGH TALK AIN'T HELPIN' YOUR POPS NONE, MANDARIN!
LET MY GUYS GO FIRST!
DROP HIM OR DIE! NOW!
POINT THAT GUN AWAY FROM MY FATHER!!

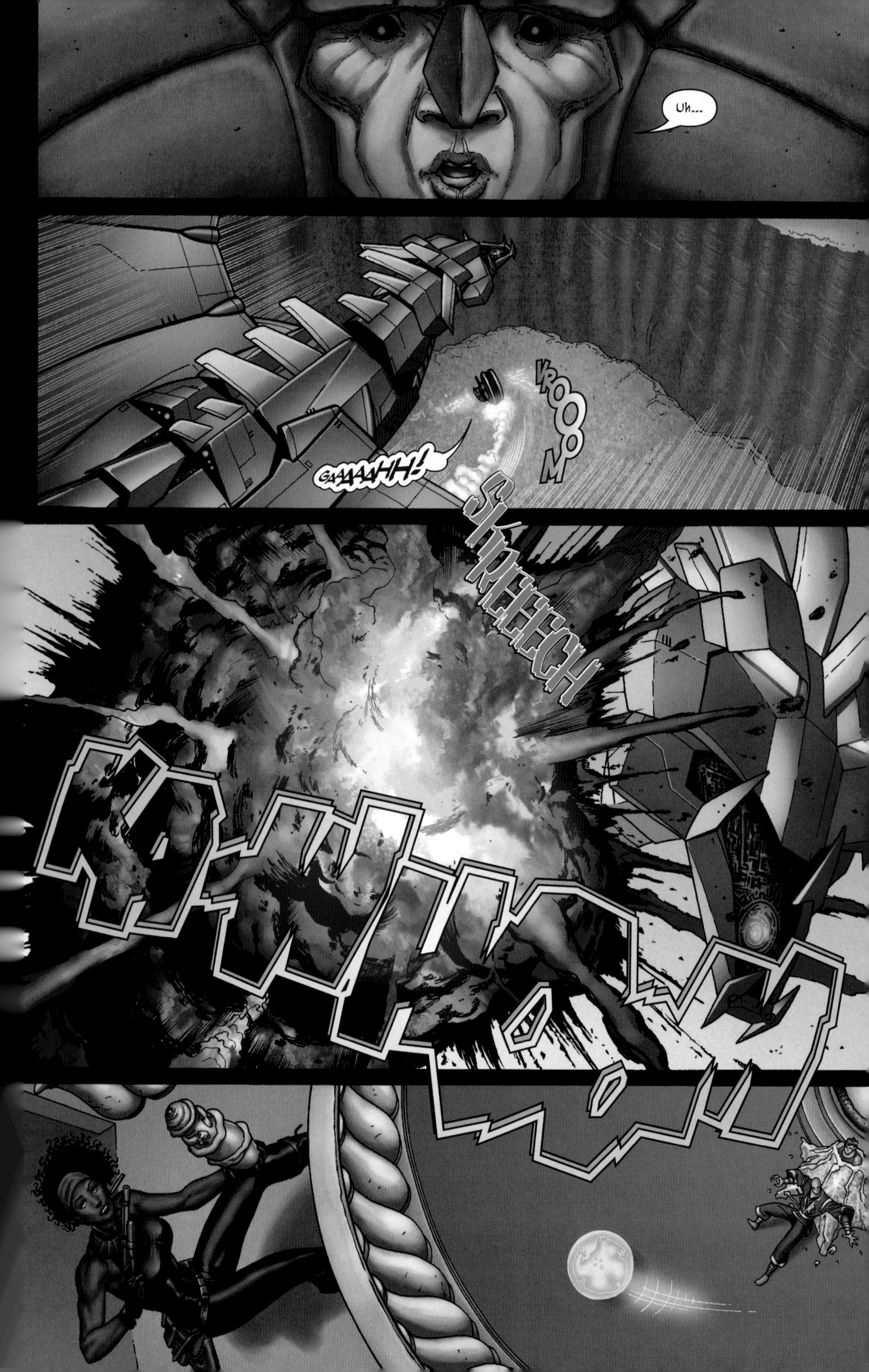
Uh...
VROOOOM
GAAAAAHH!
SKREEECH

RRRGH!
AAAHH!
SLASH
FWAP
THWOOOM!

MAMA! MAMA! THE PLAN HAS CHANGED! YOU DON'T NEED TO AMBUSH US--I'VE GOT THE HY-HY-HYPERNOVA!
I'M BRINGING IT TO YOU AT THE R-R-R-RENDEZVOUS POINT!
YOU GOT MY M-M-MONEY?!
THE DEAL IS YOU DON'T GET DIME ONE UNTIL THE HYPERNOVA IS SAFE AND SOUND IN OUR HANDS.
AND...MR. FARRELL...FOR GOD'S SAKE... FOR THE LAST TIME...
...STOP CALLING ME MOTHER.

MARVEL®
LIMITED SERIES
5 of 5

VAN LENTE
PORTELA
PALLOT
GURU eFX

SUPER-VILLAIN TEAM-UP™

MODOK'S 11

A man who wishes to make a profession of goodness in everything must necessarily come to grief among so many who are not good. Therefore, it is necessary for a prince, who wishes to maintain himself, to learn how not to be good.

--Niccolò Machiavelli, "The Prince"

UYGHUR.

"DR. RAPPACCINI!"

A.I.M. CENTRAL COMMAND.

AS YOU SUSPECTED...

...THERE IS AN EXHAUST VENT ANTERIOR TO THE REAR WHEELS OF RACER'S SKATE-BOARD!

MARK IV SKATEBOARD

DOWNLOAD THE TARGETING COORDINATES INTO THE ADAPTOID IMMEDIATELY--

"--ALONG WITH MAXIMOFF'S POWERS."

GET IN THE GUNNER'S CHAIR, NORIKO.

WHATEVER THAT...WINGED THING IS, IT'LL BE HERE FIVE SECONDS AFTER RACER IS.

YOU GOT IT, BOSS.

JUDGING BY THEIR VELOCITY, THEY SHOULD BE IN OUR LAPS IN TWENTY, MAYBE THIRTY--

Uh-oh. THAT CAN'T BE GOOD.
sput sput sput
NO!!!
WHAT ARE THE ODDS OF THAT?
SCARLET WITCH'S HEX BOLTS HAVE WORKED THEIR DESIRED EFFECT, DR. RAPPACCINI.
SPIDER-MAN
Ohhhhhh...

AT LAST!
I HOLD IN MY HANDS THE GREATEST POWER SOURCE IN THE HISTORY OF THE MULTIVERSE!
THE FINAL KEY TO THE ULTIMATE VICTORY OF ADVANCED IDEA MECHANI--
WHAT?
WHAT NOW?!
ZEWWW
PRELIMINARY SCANNING INDICATES THAT WE'VE SECURED A, UH--
--SOLID LIGHT HOLOGRAM.
I'VE... HAD...
A.I.M.
ENOUGH!

NEARBY.
FFFF... GGGKKK... Eerrrr...
NNNGGG... NO PAIN.
PAIN IS A FUNCTION OF THE MIND.
AND WHERE THERE IS NO MIND, THERE CAN BE NO--
BZZZZT
YAAAHH!
NNRRR!!!
NOW.
WHERE WERE WE?

SHRAKKK
AAAAA!
NEVER HAD MUCH USE FOR BLING, MYSELF.
BUT THESE ARE DECORATIVE AND FUNCTIONAL. CAN'T KNOCK THAT.
WITCH! YOU ARE NOT WORTHY OF WEARING FATHER'S SANDALS, MUCH LESS HIS RINGS!
YEESH! YOU RANT WORSE THAN OUR BOSS, MANDARIN.
GIVE IT A REST, WILL YA? YOU'RE GIVIN' VILLAINY A BAD NAME!
SEE HOW A COMMON FOE CAN UNITE US "DISHONORABLE" TYPES?

NO MATTER.
YOU SHALL ALL DIE SCREAMING.
I'VE HAD IT UP TO HERE WITH THE DOUBLE-CROSSES AND TRIPLE-CROSSES AND QUADRUPLE-CROSSES!
NO MORE STEALTH, NO MORE SUBTERFUGE!
I'M JUST GOING TO RIP YOUR LIMBS OFF UNTIL ONE OF YOU TELLS ME WHERE THE HYPERNOVA IS!
YES! BRILLIANT!
ATTACK SOMEONE THAT CAN ABSORB POWERS!

NO WONDER M.O.D.O.K. CHOSE YOU LOT AS HIS MINDLESS MINIONS!
CAN'T YOU TELL WHEN YOU'VE BEEN HAD?
FOR ONCE, THE CHAMELEON ISN'T SOMEBODY ELSE...
...SOMEBODY ELSE IS THE CHAMELEON.
AND IS THAT A WOMAN'S VOICE COMING OUT OF HIM ALL OF A SUDDEN? WHAT THE HELL?
PUMA. I SHIFTED MY VISION TO LOOK AT CHAMEL--
...Uh, WHOEVER... IN THE FULL ELECTROMAGNETIC SPECTRUM.
A) THIS IS CLEARLY AN ARTIFICIAL LIFE-FORM WE'RE DEALING WITH.
AND B) IT'S RECEIVING SOME KIND OF A SIGNAL FROM GEOSYNCHRONOUS ORBIT.
COULD BE THAT THAT'S HOW WHOEVER OWNS IT, CONTROLS IT.
THE INNER CORE OF MY SHIP... ≥KOF≤ IS MADE OUT OF MAKLUAN... EXTRATERRESTRIAL MATERIALS.
DESIGNED TO BLOCK RADATION--UP TO AND INCLUDING COSMIC RAYS--FOR INTERSTELLAR TRAVEL--≥KOF≤
LOOK-- LOOK FOR MARKINGS--
I UNDERSTAND.
HOLD IT OFF AS LONG AS YOU CAN.

FOOLS! WHY ARE YOU FIGHTING?
THE M.O.D.O.K. CREATURE DOESN'T DESERVE YOUR LOYALTY! HE HAS LIED TO YOU FROM THE VERY START!
I'M NOT SURE WHAT YOU THINK THE EMPLOYMENT OPPORTUNITIES ARE FOR GIANT FLOATING HEADS, BUT I CAN TELL YOU, THEY'RE FAIRLY POOR!
M.O.D.O.K. DOESN'T HAVE TWO DIMES TO SCRAPE TOGETHER!
THE MILLIONS HE SHOWED YOU--HIS FANCY HEADQUARTERS--ALL PSIONIC ILLUSIONS!
MENTALLO FIGURED THIS ALL OUT--BEFORE I KILLED HIM!
I HAVE NO DOUBT M.O.D.O.K. WOULD HAVE SIMPLY SLAIN YOU, HAD YOU SUCCEEDED IN BRINGING THE HYPERNOVA TO HIM.
IN THAT SENSE, I OFFER YOU MORE THAN HE HAS--
YOUR LIVES!
BUT I WILL JUST KILL YOU OUT OF SHEER FRUSTRATION IF, IN THE NEXT FIVE SECONDS, YOU DO NOT TELL ME--
WHERE?
IS?
THE HYPERNOV--

SQUEEEE
AAGHH!
WHAT HAPPENED? WHAT HAPPENED? WE LOST CONTACT?
OUR SIGNAL TO THE ADAPTOID HAS BEEN BLOCKED!
SORRY, LADY. WHAT YOU SAY MIGHT BE TRUE...
...BUT WE'RE PROFESSIONALS. IF M.O.D.O.K. WANTS TO BREAK HIS WORD, THAT'S HIS BUSINESS. BUT FOR US...
...A CONTRACT IS A CONTRACT.
AND WE'RE GOING TO FULFILL IT.

¡LO SIENTO, VATOS! THE CRASH DUMPED ME HALFWAY UP THE MOUNTAIN AND THE ROADKILL SLAMMER SEEMED LIKE THE FASTEST WAY TO GET DOWN HERE.
WHAT'D I MISS?
Eh...
...NOTHING MUCH.
BUT STILL, THIS BEGS THE QUESTION...
...WHERE IS THE HYPERNOVA?
IT NEVER LEFT THE MANDARIN'S SHIP.
I PLACED A SOLID HOLOGRAM NEXT TO IT...
...AND WARPED LIGHT AROUND THE REAL ONE, RENDERING IT INVISIBLE--
--UNTIL I HAD THE OPPORTUNITY TO OPEN IT.

WHAT YOU SMOKING, LIGHTBOY? YOU CRACK THAT THING OPEN JUST A HAIR AND YOU'RE GONNA UNLEASH THE END OF THE UNIVERSE!
WITHOUT THE PROPER CONTAINMENT FIELD, WE'LL ALL BE KILLED--
C'MON, AIN'T YOU CROOKS EVER HEARD OF EINSTEIN? E=MC²?
I'LL USE UP ALL THAT POWER CONVERTING MYSELF FROM ENERGY BACK INTO MATTER!
THIS IS MY ONLY CHANCE TO BECOME NORMAL AGAIN!
THAT'S OUR SCORE YOU'RE MESSIN' WITH! WE DON'T BRING IT IN, WE DON'T GET PAID!
I SWEAR ON MY FATHER, IF YOU EXPEND THE HYPERNOVA I WILL SIMPLY KILL YOU THE MINUTE YOU TURN HUMAN.
BUT BEFORE THEN--FOR JUST A SECOND, MAYBE TWO--I'LL FEEL THE MOUNTAIN AIR ON MY FACE--THE SMOKE IN MY NOSTRILS--
--I'LL SQUINT IN THE GLARE OF THE DESERT SUN.
WHEN THE MANDARIN HIT ME--I WAS ABLE TO REMEMBER WHAT IT WAS LIKE TO FEEL THINGS, LIKE A REAL PERSON--
I KNOW IT'S A PRETTY CRAPPY THING TO DO, AFTER YOU GUYS RISKED EVERYTHING TO SAVE ME.
BUT IF I DON'T DO THIS, I STILL WON'T REALLY HAVE A LIFE.
...I'M SORRY.
LASER, NO--

"AND THEN, JUST LIKE THAT...
"...HE WAS GONE."

BROOKLYN.
FOUR DAYS LATER.
SO. WHAT YOU'RE SAYING IS...
...YOU DON'T HAVE THE HYPERNOVA?
NO, OF COURSE WE DON'T HAVE THE !@#%! HYPERNOVA!
YO, WE'RE JUST LUCKY THE FLASH DISTRACTED MANDARIN LONG ENOUGH FOR US TO ESCAPE!
YOU HAVE A LOT TO ANSWER FOR, M.O.D.O.K.!
OH DO I, NOW?
HELL, YEAH! FOR ONE THING, LOOKS LIKE THAT "ADAPTOID" WAS RIGHT--YOUR H.Q. AND THE DOUGH WERE FAKE!
AND HALF YOUR "MINIONS" TURNED OUT TO BE TURNCOATS!
CHAMELEON WORKED FOR A.I.M.--RACER FOR S.H.I.E.L.D.--SPOT FOR MANDARIN--
WE THREE ARE THE ONLY ONES WHO DIDN'T TRY TO SHANK YOU!
THAT'S GOTTA BE WORTH SOMETHIN', EVEN IF WE DIDN'T BRING BACK THE--

HOW...?
THERE WAS A 64.25% CHANCE THAT ONE OF YOU WOULD BETRAY ME.
WITH SPOT, AN UNSTABLE PERSONALITY AT BEST, THAT PROBABILITY LEAPT TO 78% EVEN.
SO I TOOK THE PRECAUTION, ONCE YOU LEFT OUR HIDEOUT...
...OF PRESERVING ONE OF HIS WARPHOLES FOR MY OWN USE.

DO NOT FORGET THAT IN ORDER FOR OBJECTS TO PASS INTO ONE OF SPOT'S SPOTS AND OUT THE OTHER...
...THEY FIRST HAVE TO PASS THROUGH THE INTERMEDIARY REALM OF THE DARK DIMENSION...
...WHERE I WAS ABLE TO INTERCEDE...
...AND PASS A REPLICA OFF TO SPOT.
WHAT? YOU MEAN YOU LET US RISK OUR COLLECTIVE BACON HAULING AFTER MANDARIN WHEN YOU KNEW ALL HE HAD WAS A FAKE?
MENTALLO'S DISAPPEARANCE INDICATED A 98.7% CHANCE THAT CHAMELEON WAS A TRAITOR.
I COULD NOT WARN YOU WITHOUT WARNING HIM.
THEN MAYBE WE SHOULD CLEAR OUT OF HERE. HAVE YOU CALCULATED THE PROBABILITY THAT A.I.M. KNOWS EXACTLY WHERE THIS PLACE IS?
INDEED.

BOOM
I WOULD PLACE IT AT APPROXIMATELY 100.00%...
...SINCE I E-MAILED THEM DIRECTIONS.
TSK-TSK. MONICA.
ALWAYS WITH THE ROBOTS.
THIS OBSESSION WITH CONTROL BETRAYS A DEEP-ROOTED INSECURITY--
SHUT UP, FREAK!!
I'M TRYING TO TELL YOU YOU'VE WON. I'M NOT GOING TO WASTE ANY MORE A.I.M. RESOURCES TRYING TO STEAL THE HYPERNOVA FROM YOU.
BUT I HAVE BROUGHT ONE BILLION DOLLARS IN UNTRACEABLE BILLS. THAT OUGHT TO KEEP YOU IN GLUCOSE PACKS FOR THE FORESEEABLE FUTURE.
AND THE PROMISE OF A TRUCE BETWEEN YOU AND ME.

THERE WAS A TIME WHEN I WOULD HAVE GIVEN YOU THE HYPERNOVA--OR ANYTHING YOU DESIRED--FOR FREE, DEAREST MONICA.
AREN'T YOU SORRY YOU BROKE UP WITH ME?
DON'T YOU UNDERSTAND, GEORGE?
I NEVER BROKE UP WITH YOU.
BECAUSE WE WERE NEVER DATING!!
WE SPENT ONE NIGHT TOGETHER!! ONE!! HOW PATHETIC DO YOU HAVE TO BE--
SHUT UP! SHUT UP BACK THERE!!
STOP SNICKERING!
MY REDUCED CIRCUMSTANCES ARE DUE ALMOST ENTIRELY TO A.I.M.'S INCESSANT HOUNDING.
I HOPE THIS MARKS A NEW ERA OF COOPERATION BETWEEN US, MONICA.
DON'T PUSH IT.
NOW, MY MINIONS, AS PROMISED--FIVE MILLION DOLLARS EACH...
WITH A BONUS OF THE REDIVIDED SHARES OF THE FIVE WHO BETRAYED ME...
...FOR A TOTAL OF $10,250,000!
ALL RIGHT! ADIOS, CRUDDY TIJUANA AMPHITHEATERS!
HELLO, A HALFWAY DECENT DEFENSE...
NEED ANY HELP PROVING YOUR INNOCENCE, KITTY?
AS MUCH AS I CAN GET...
...AND I CAN PAY HANDSOMELY FOR IT, TOO.
NOW YOU'RE TALKIN', ESE!
WHY BREAK UP SUCH A PROFITABLE TEAM?

THAT NIGHT.
THE CONTAINMENT FIELD SHALL BE FULLY POWERED IN T-MINUS FOURTEEN HOURS, DR. RAPPACCINI.
THEN A.I.M. SHALL HAVE A BRAND-NEW COSMIC CUBE BEFORE THE DAY IS OUT...
...AND WE'LL AT LAST BE ABLE TO HUNT DOWN THAT ENCEPHALITIC MANIAC--
--AND DESTROY HIM ONCE AND FOR ALL!
WHOA-- WAIT A MINUTE--
ENERGY LEVELS SPIKING--
AROOGA AROOGA
RECRUIT MINIONS
TEMPORAL BOTTLE'S BREAKING DOWN--
--BUT THE CONTAINMENT FIELD ISN'T FULLY POWERED--
RECRUIT MINIONS
SECURE HYPERNOVA

THERE'S ONLY ONE EXPLANATION--
THE TEMPORAL BOTTLE STARTS TO DECAY ONCE TAKEN OUT OF THE INFINICIDE'S BEACON AND PLACED INTO THE REGULAR TIMESTREAM!
SECURE HYPERNOVA
SELL HYPERNOVA
M.O.D.O.K. MUST HAVE CALCULATED PRECISELY HOW LONG IT'D TAKE THE BOTTLE TO DISINTEGRATE!
A.I.M.
EVACUATE. POWER SURGE UNCONTAINABLE. EVACUATE.
I HAVE BECOME ONE WITH THE ALL.
LASER--?
NOW I JUST LIKE TO WATCH.
GO BOOM.
PRETTY.

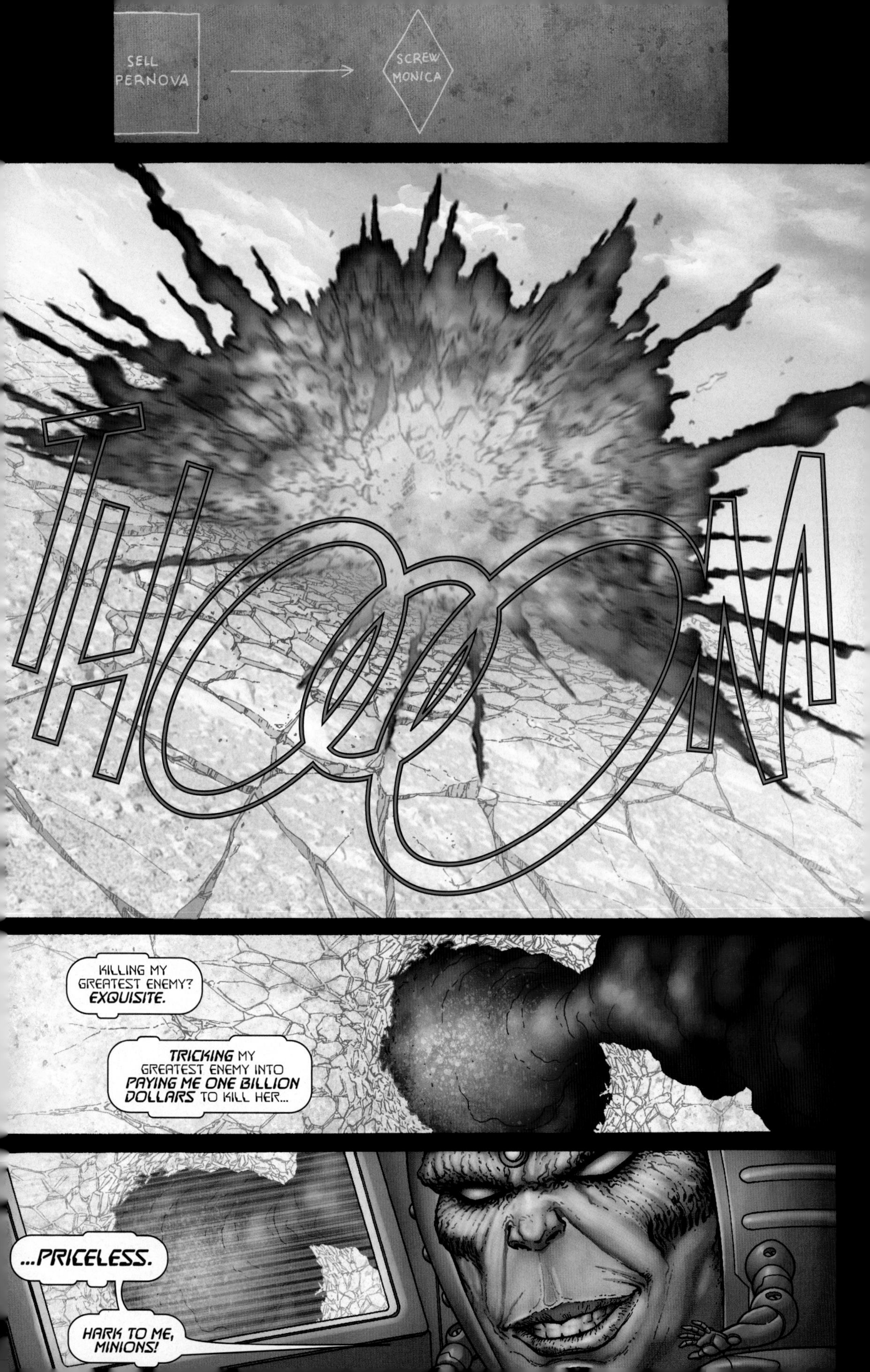

SELL PERNOVA

SCREW MONICA

THOOM

KILLING MY GREATEST ENEMY? ***EXQUISITE.***

TRICKING MY GREATEST ENEMY INTO ***PAYING ME ONE BILLION DOLLARS*** TO KILL HER...

...PRICELESS.
HARK TO ME, MINIONS!

TODAY I DESTROYED MY EX-GIRLFRIEND!
TOMORROW... THE WORLD!
ALL HAIL M.O.D.O.K.!
YES! ALL HAIL ME!
HOW NOT TO BE GOOD
OR, "THE PAYOFF"
FFTG

MARVEL
ONE-SHOT
1
BELAND
DOE
Fantastic Four
IN... ¡ATAQUE DEL M.O.D.O.K.!

WE HAVE AN EXPRESSION IN PUERTO RICO... "WHEN IT RAINS IN PONCE, PEOPLE DON'T GO OUT."

SO ON A NIGHT LIKE THIS, WHEN IT'S REALLY COMING DOWN, YOU CAN FEEL SOMETHING'S GOING TO HAPPEN.

SOMETHING BAD.

I COULD HEAR THE EXPLOSION FROM HERE ON VIGÍA HILL. THIS IS THE THIRD TIME IT'S HAPPENED IN A WEEK.

NO TIME FOR THE STAIRS.
UGH...THIS ALWAYS KILLS MY ANKLES.

BY NOW I AM SURE THE *POLICÍA* HAVE ARRIVED.
FARMACON
I HOPE TO GOD THEY'RE SMART ENOUGH TO STAY OUTSIDE.
POLICIA

WILO... I DON'T LIKE THE LOOKS OF THIS...
ANOTHER PHARMACEUTICAL BREAK-IN, JUAN CARLOS. THIS TIME, HOWEVER, WE'LL CATCH THEM. THIS ENDS NOW.

THE POLICE HAVE BEEN MADE A LAUGHING-STOCK BY THESE CRIMINALS ALL WEEK. NOW WE SHALL HAVE THE LAST LAUGH, MY FRIEND.
AY, WILO... I'M NOT SURE I WANT TO FACE WHATEVER COULD MAKE A HOLE IN A WALL THIS SIZE.

FREEZE!! DO NOT... EH...?
¿QUÉ ES ESO...?

SQUEE??!

HEH HEH... *THERE* ARE YOUR LITTLE CRIMINALS, WILO.
DIOS... DAMNED MONKEYS. THEY'RE A *CURSE.* THEY MUST HAVE FOLLOWED THE CROOKS IN AFTER THEY LEFT.
CALL ANIMAL CONTROL AND TELL THEM TO...

WILO...?
DIOS... JUAN CARLOS...

CHHCK CHHCK CHHCK CHHCK

RUN!!!
BRATATATATATATATATATAT

FARMACON
FIND COVER!!! I'LL CALL FOR BACKUP!!!

WILO... LOOK...!!
¿QUÉ...?

GET OUT OF HERE, BOTH OF YOU!! IT'S NOT SAFE!!

CRNCHHH

¡EL VEJIGANTE!

THE DEMON EXISTS!

I'M NOT A DE... AY, FORGET IT. MIRA, ¡VÁMONOS!!

FOOMP

FOOMP

FOOMP

WILO!! LISTEN TO THE MAN!! RUN!!

WHEN I SAY VÁMONOS, SEÑOR... I MEAN...

UNNNH... THAT... HURT ...MANAGED TO GET THIS POLICEMAN TO SAFETY... HIS PARTNER... LOOKS OKAY TOO... WHOA...
EVERYTHING GETTING DARK... HANG IN THERE, HERO...
CAN'T... LOSE CONSCIOUSNESS... NOW...
STUPID STUPID LEADER...!!!
MASTER SAY WE NOT TO BE SEEN!
THEN MAYBE MASTER SHOULD BE HERE TO MAKE SURE WE NOT SEEN. YOU NOT CALL ME STUPID AGAIN OR...
SQUEE!! THIS FUN!! WE BLOW UP MORE THINGS NOW!!
NO. WE GO NOW.
UGH. WHO DIE AND MAKE YOU BOSS?!!
MASTER MAKE ME BOSS!! HE SAY IT LOTS OF TIMES BUT YOU NOT EVER LISTEN!!
IT TRUE. HE NOT LISTEN EVER.
UNNNNHHHHH...
GET UP...!! BEFORE THEY... GET...
...AWAY...

ANYTHING ON LAST NIGHT'S REFINERY EXPLOSION IN CATAÑO...?
ONLY THE EXPLOSION ITSELF. NOT THE ACTUAL CAUSE.

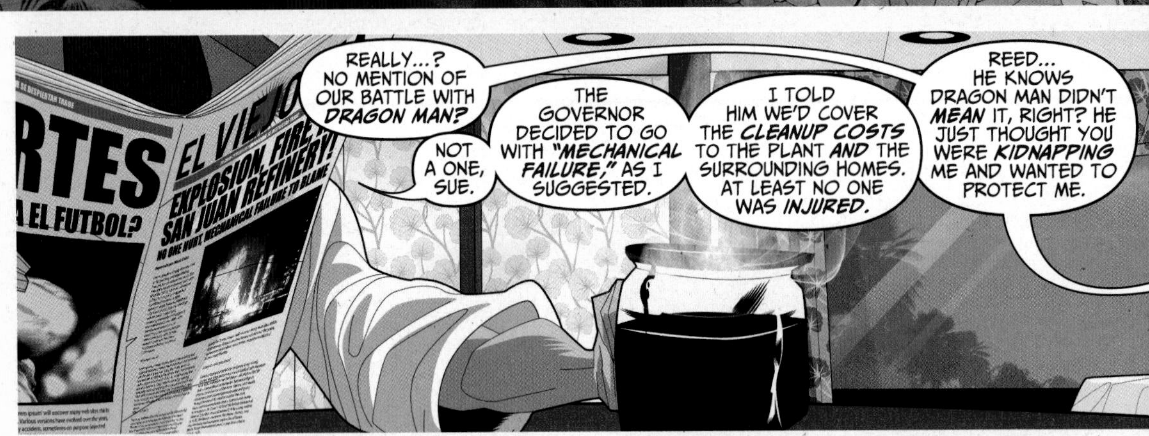
REALLY...? NO MENTION OF OUR BATTLE WITH DRAGON MAN?
NOT A ONE, SUE.
THE GOVERNOR DECIDED TO GO WITH "MECHANICAL FAILURE," AS I SUGGESTED.
I TOLD HIM WE'D COVER THE CLEANUP COSTS TO THE PLANT AND THE SURROUNDING HOMES. AT LEAST NO ONE WAS INJURED.
REED... HE KNOWS DRAGON MAN DIDN'T MEAN IT, RIGHT? HE JUST THOUGHT YOU WERE KIDNAPPING ME AND WANTED TO PROTECT ME.
EL VIEJO
EXPLOSION, FIRE SAN JUAN REFINERY!
NO ONE HURT, MECHANICAL FAILURE TO BLAME
RTES
A EL FUTBOL?

I FULLY EXPLAINED DRAGON MAN'S CONNECTION TO YOU, DARLING. I JUST WISH HE'D LET US ENJOY A VACATION NOW AND THEN.
REFILL..?
I FIND IT CUTE. AND ¡SÍ, GRACIAS!
...
SO...
IT'S YOUR TURN TO ASK.
EL VIEJO DIA
RTES
A EL FUTBOL?

I THOUGHT IT WAS YOUR TURN.
NNNNOPE. I ASKED MY QUESTION BACK IN THE FANTASTICAR. REMEMBER..?
"WHO'S YOUR FAVORITE MATHEMATICIAN?"
AH, YES. JOHANN CARL FRIEDRICH GAUSS.

SO... MY TURN...
MAKE IT A GOOD ONE, DEAR. THIS WILL BE NUMBER TWENTY.
YOUR FINAL QUESTION.
HMMMM... LET ME THINK THEN...

TOO MANY CHOICES...?
OH, I ALREADY HAVE IT. IF YOU'RE WILLING TO ANSWER, THAT IS.
OH, YOU SOOOO DON'T KNOW ME, DARLING. I'LL ANSWER ANYTHING YOU ASK.
OKAY.
HERE IT IS. IT'S SIMPLE.
DO YOU RECALL THE MOMENT YOU REALIZED I WAS THE ONE FOR YOU?

THE EXACT MOMENT...?
MM-HMMM.
WOW. A ROMANTIC ONE. THAT CAME OUT OF NOWHERE. I THOUGHT YOU'D ASK ME ABOUT THEORETICAL COSMOLOGY.
I'M READY, MY DEAR.
UMMM... OKAY. YOU REALLY WANT TO KNOW?

"THE MONTH WAS APRIL... ON A THURSDAY. 9:30 A.M.
"I JUST MOVED INTO MY FIRST APARTMENT. AND, OF COURSE, JOHNNY BAILED ON ME FOR SOME REDHEAD HE MET.
"AND HE DIDN'T SET UP MY STEREO LIKE HE PROMISED.
"UGH...I WAS SO MAD AT HIM THAT DAY.

"YOU OFFERED TO HOOK IT UP FOR ME, SO I'D AT LEAST HAVE MY MUSIC TO LISTEN TO WHILE I UNPACKED.
"AFTER A COUPLE OF HOURS, YOU WERE READY TO UNVEIL YOUR WORK."
OKAY... ARE YOU READY...?
READY FOR WHAT? AND...WHERE'S MY TURNTABLE AND ALBUM COLLECTION?

HERE. READ THIS.
OKAY... UMMM... "SYSTEM..."
A LITTLE LOUDER.
AHEM "SYSTEM... PLAY ROLLING STONES... SYMPATHY FOR THE DEVIL."

IT'S CALLED A "VOICE-TO-COMMAND ANALYZER."
IT USES THE AUDIO OF YOUR OWN VOICE TO TRIGGER AN ACTION REQUEST IN THE SYSTEM.
BUT... WHERE ARE MY ALBUMS..?
DIGITIZED. ALL OF THEM.
IT'S SOMETHING I'M HELPING SOME FRIENDS WITH OUT IN PALO ALTO. THE MUSIC IS STORED AS AN AUDIO FILE FORMAT, THEN...
REED...THIS IS... INCREDIBLE...

"AT THAT MOMENT, I THOUGHT ABOUT WHAT LIFE MIGHT *BE* LIKE WITH SOMEONE LIKE *REED RICHARDS.*
"THAT IT WOULD *NEVER* BE BORING.
"NOT WITH SOMEONE WHO HAD A MIND LIKE *THAT.*
"*EVERY* DAY WOULD BE INTERESTING."

AND YOU KNOW *WHAT?* I WAS RIGHT. ALL MY DAYS WITH YOU *HAVE* BEEN INTERESTING.
THANK YOU, MY DEAR.

SO...NOW IT'S *YOUR* TURN. WHAT'S *YOUR* FINAL QUESTION FOR *ME?*
NOOOOO... I NEED *TIME* TO THINK ABOUT THIS ONE. I WANT TO MAKE SURE IT'S *GOOD.*
THIS GAME HAS BEEN *FAR* TOO FUN TO END ON SOMETHING FRIVOLOUS, OR UNORIGINAL.
I HAVE TO MAKE YOU GIVE UP SOMETHING *GOOD.*
VERY WELL, THEN. NO PRESSURE.

BBRRINNGGGG
?
IF THAT'S *BEN,* ASK HIM WHERE WE CAN GET THAT *"MOFONGO"* DISH HE WAS TELLING US ABOUT.

HELLO?
YES, THIS IS HE. HOW MAY I HELP YOU?
OH. *HELLO,* OFFICER ARROYO.
...
I *SEE...*
INTERESTING...
OH NO.
I *NEVER* LIKE IT WHEN YOUR CALLS INVOLVE WORDS LIKE *"OFFICER"* AND *"INTERESTING."*

YOU DON'T SAY...
WELL, IT SOUNDS LIKE THE SPECIES KNOWN AS MACACA MULATTA... MORE COMMONLY KNOWN AS RHESUS MACAQUE. YES...
THEY'RE TYPICALLY BETWEEN 20.7 AND 22.9 CENTIMETERS IN HEIGHT...
REED... IT'S MOFONGO DAY... DON'T...

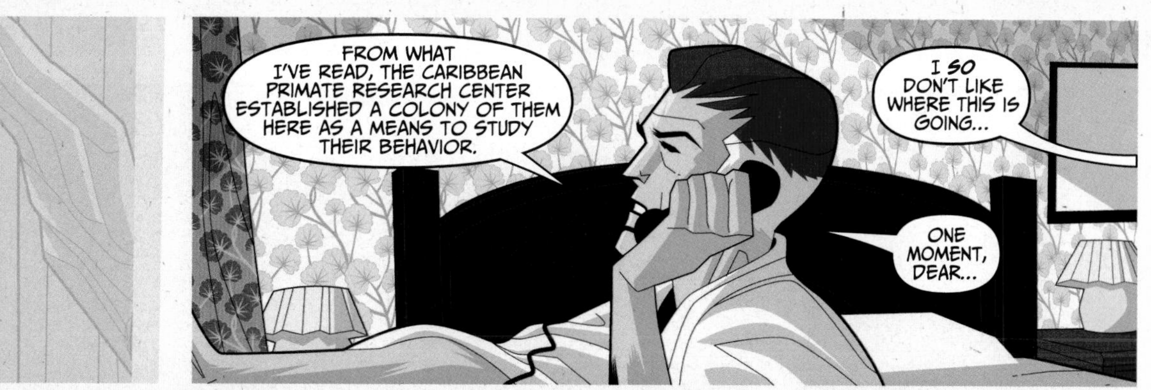
FROM WHAT I'VE READ, THE CARIBBEAN PRIMATE RESEARCH CENTER ESTABLISHED A COLONY OF THEM HERE AS A MEANS TO STUDY THEIR BEHAVIOR.
I SO DON'T LIKE WHERE THIS IS GOING...
ONE MOMENT, DEAR...

I'D HAVE TO EXAMINE THE CRIME SCENE, FIRST. THERE MAY BE SOME MICRO-EVIDENCE THAT CAN TELL US MORE ABOUT...
REED RICHARDS... DO NOT STRETCH OUT THE WINDOW WHEN I'M...
...EVEN GIVEN THE INTELLIGENCE OF THAT SPECIES, THERE'S LITTLE CHANCE THAT THEY WOULD EVEN REMOTELY BE ABLE TO HANDLE THE TYPE OF SOPHISTICATED WEAPONRY YOUR MEN ENCOUNTERED.

I'M SORRY, MY DEAR. THERE'S A SITUATION INVOLVING PRIMATES AND STATE-OF-THE-ART WEAPONRY.
SIGHHHH... I KNOW HOW YOU ARE ABOUT MYSTERIES. MEET ME FOR LUNCH.
COUNT ON IT. LOVE YOU.
MM-HMMM.

OFFICER ARROYO, I CAN BE THERE IN FIVE MINUTES.
NO NEED TO PICK ME UP. IT'LL BE NICE TO STRETCH MY LEGS A BIT.

UNHHH... MUST'VE CAUGHT SOME SHRAPNEL FROM THE EXPLOSION...

THIS IS THE *THIRD* TIME I'VE CROSSED PATHS WITH THOSE LITTLE GREMLINS.

AND IT'S THE *THIRD* TIME I'VE HAD MY *HEAD* HANDED TO ME.

I MAY BE *SEMI-IMMORTAL*... BUT IT DOESN'T MEAN THESE WOUNDS DON'T... *HURT.*
I NEED TO TAKE SOME TIME AND LET MY BODY... *NNH*... *HEAL* ITSELF.

STILL GETTING *USED* TO ALL THIS. THIS NEW BODY. THE NEW POWERS. MY NEW LIFE.
I MIGHT HAVE... *PUSHED* MYSELF TOO HARD BACK THERE... TAKING ON THOSE MISSILES... AND THE EXPLOSION...
WHEW... FEELS GOOD TO *RELAX.*

MUÑOZ LABS WOULD BE... THE NEXT... LOGICAL TARGET.
I'LL REST... FOR NOW... THEN HEAD OVER THERE AND...
...SEE... WHAT I... CAN... DO...

AND HOW WAS EVERYTHING, MRS. STORM?
OH. MY. *GOD.*
THIS WAS THE GREATEST MEAL *EVAHHH.*
I TAKE IT YOU ENJOYED YOUR FIRST *MOFONGO?*
HA HA HA... I'M *GLAD* YOU LIKED IT.
MOFONG

NGO

IT'D *BETTER* BE. YOU MISSED A *FABULOUS* LUNCH.

I HAVE *NO* DOUBT, DARLING. AND I *APOLOGIZE,* BUT UNFORTUNATELY...

I NEED YOU TO BE ON THE *LOOKOUT* FOR A CREATURE THE POLICE CALL *"EL VEJIGANTE."*

LIKE THE *COSTUMES* THEY WEAR HERE DURING CARNIVALS.

OFFICIALS ARE TELLING ME HE'S APPEARED AT ALL THREE BREAK-INS, *INCLUDING* LAST NIGHT.

FROM WHAT THEY SAY, THIS CREATURE IS EXTREMELY *AGILE* AS WELL AS *POWERFUL.* SO... PLEASE *DO* BE CAREFUL.

SIGH...YOU OWE ME SOME QUALITY BEACH TIME WHEN THIS IS OVER, MR. RICHARDS. DO YOU NEED ME TO JOIN YOU?
NOT AT THE MOMENT, DARLING. WE'RE STILL COLLECTING INTEL. I'D RATHER YOU JUST RELAX FOR NOW.
THAT I CAN DO. LOVE YOU.

I'LL MEET UP WITH YOU SHORTLY. THANK YOU FOR BEING PATIENT, DARLING.
HOW DEEP IS THE WATER YOU'RE IN?
ABOUT JULES VERNE LEVEL.
ANY IDEAS ON HOW WE CAN ELIMINATE THESE VERMIN, DR. RICHARDS?

WE OWE MOST OF OUR MEDICAL BREAK-THROUGHS TO THIS "VERMIN," OFFICER. AS WELL AS OUR ACHIEVEMENTS IN SPACE EXPLORATION.
SO I WOULD SUGGEST YOU CURB YOUR HATRED TOWARD SUCH AN IMPORTANT CREATURE.
I'M SURE THEY'RE ALSO VICTIMS HERE.

SEÑOR RICHARDS... I HAVE JUST ABOUT HAD IT WITH GUN-TOTING MONKEYS IN YELLOW JUMP-SUITS...NO MATTER HOW ADORABLE PEOPLE FIND THEM.
I'M SORRY...

DID YOU SAY YELLOW JUMPSUITS?

WOW, THAT WAS QUICK! SHOULD I GET MY SWIMSUIT AND...
IT'S A.I.M.!
ADVANCED IDEA MECHANICS? THOSE IDIOTS IN THE BEEKEEPER OUTFITS?
I UNDERSTAND YOUR FRUSTRATION... BUT THEIR ORGANIZATION DOES CONSIST OF SCIENTIFIC GENIUSES OBSESSED WITH DESTROYING THE WORLD AS WE KNOW IT.

BUT WHY WOULD THEY...
...?!

REED, DEAR... DO ME A FAVOR. TRACK MY LOCATION ON THE G.P.S. AND GET HERE AS SOON AS YOU CAN.
IS EVERYTHING ALL RIGHT?
JUST DO IT. GOTTA RUN!

GOTCHA.

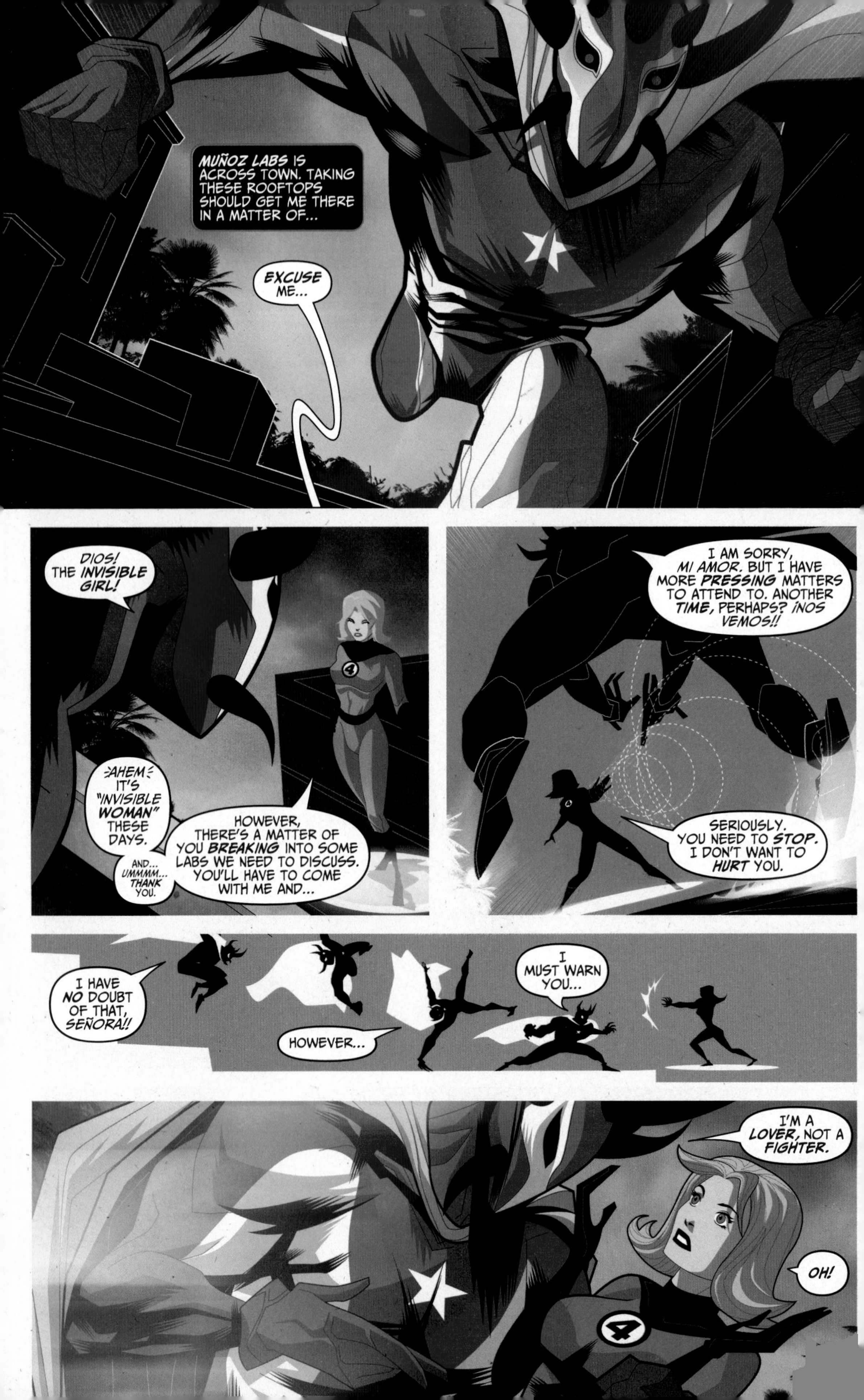

MUÑOZ LABS IS ACROSS TOWN. TAKING THESE ROOFTOPS SHOULD GET ME THERE IN A MATTER OF...
EXCUSE ME...

DIOS! THE INVISIBLE GIRL!
AHEM IT'S "INVISIBLE WOMAN" THESE DAYS.
AND... UMMMM... THANK YOU.
HOWEVER, THERE'S A MATTER OF YOU BREAKING INTO SOME LABS WE NEED TO DISCUSS. YOU'LL HAVE TO COME WITH ME AND...

I AM SORRY, MI AMOR. BUT I HAVE MORE PRESSING MATTERS TO ATTEND TO. ANOTHER TIME, PERHAPS? ¡NOS VEMOS!!
SERIOUSLY. YOU NEED TO STOP. I DON'T WANT TO HURT YOU.

I HAVE NO DOUBT OF THAT, SEÑORA!!
HOWEVER...
I MUST WARN YOU...

I'M A LOVER, NOT A FIGHTER.
OH!

I ENJOYED THIS DANCE, ¡MI AMIGA! WE MUST DO IT AGA--

SLAM!
OOOF!!!

AH... I DO SO HATE IT WHEN VILLAINS CAN BECOME INTANGIBLE.
VILLAIN?! ARE YOU CRAZY?!

I THINK WE COULD ALL DO WITH A TIME-OUT. LET'S ALL TAKE A MOMENT AND BREATHE.
CAREFUL, DEAR.
NO NEED TO BE, DARLING...

I HAVE A FEELING HE MEANS US NO HARM.
WE'RE LISTENING, VEJIGANTE. WHAT'S YOUR STORY?
YOUR WIFE IS AS INSIGHTFUL AS SHE IS BEAUTIFUL.

I DO HAVE A STORY, SEÑOR FANTÁSTICO... BUT IT IS NOT ONE I AM PROUD OF.

"I WAS A SOLDIER IN IRAQ.
"I ENLISTED AFTER THE EVENTS OF 9/11, AND WAS PROUD TO JOIN THE CAUSE...DESPITE HOW MY PARENTS, WHO ARE INDEPENDISTAS, DISAPPROVED OF MY DECISION.
"WE WERE SENT TO FIGHT AN ENEMY UNLIKE ANY OTHER. AND WE HAD NO CAPTAIN AMERICA TO LEAD US TO VICTORY.
"YOU WANT TO KNOW WHAT FEAR IS? FEAR IS DRIVING A HUMVEE ON THE STREETS OF IRAQ.
"YOU DREAD EVERY INCH OF THAT ROAD...AND FOR GOOD REASON.
"I.E.D.
"IMPROVISED EXPLOSIVE DEVICE. IT WENT OFF BEFORE ANYONE COULD REACT.
BOOM!
"THE WORLD SUDDENLY TURNED RED AS BODY PARTS FLEW PAST ME.
"IT WAS MY FIRST TASTE OF COMBAT. COMPLETE CHAOS ERUPTED AS BULLETS AND EXPLOSIONS FILLED THE AIR.
"THERE WERE SCREAMS OF THE WOUNDED MIXED IN WITH SOLDIERS SHOUTING COMMANDS TO EACH OTHER.
"AND I FROZE.
"FOR A WHILE, I COULDN'T HEAR A THING. NOT THE GUNFIRE OR THE BOMBS EXPLODING...OR MY SERGEANT SCREAMING HIS ORDERS AT ME.
"IT WAS LIKE TRYING TO HEAR UNDERWATER. I COULDN'T MAKE ANYTHING OUT EXCEPT THE SOUND OF MY HEART POUNDING. NO MATTER HOW I TRIED...I COULDN'T GET MYSELF TO DO ANYTHING.
"I WAS ABSOLUTELY TERRIFIED.

"THEN... SUDDENLY... MY HEARING CAME BACK TO ME...

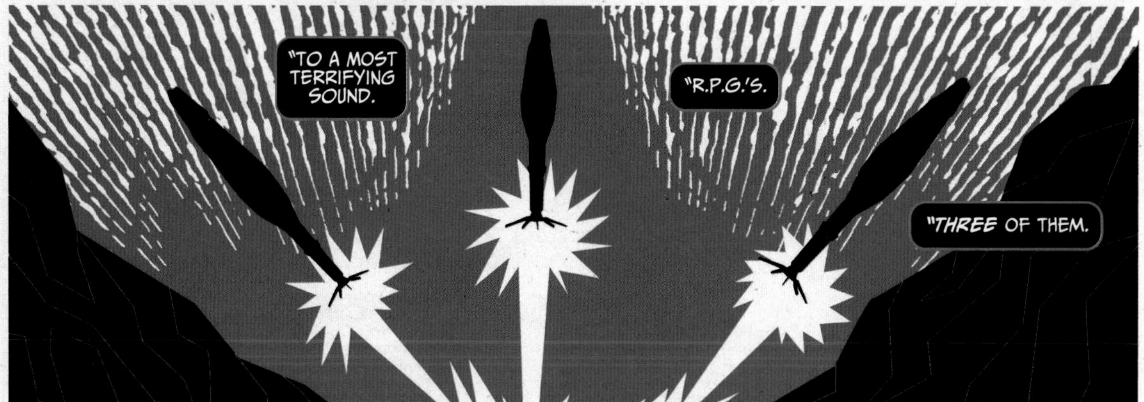

"TO A MOST TERRIFYING SOUND.
"R.P.G.'S.
"THREE OF THEM.

"I SHOULD HAVE HELPED MY SERGEANT WITH THE WOUNDED. SHOULD HAVE HELPED THEM GET TO SAFETY.

"BUT MY SURVIVAL INSTINCTS TOOK OVER. AND I FLED. AS FAST AS MY LEGS COULD CARRY ME.

"I MADE IT TO SAFETY.
"MY TEAM, HOWEVER...
"GONE.
"NONE SURVIVED.

"I SPENT TIME IN A V.A. HOSPITAL. NOT SO MUCH FOR THE PHYSICAL WOUNDS... BUT THE MENTAL.
"THERE WAS NO CURE FOR THE GUILT I CARRIED FROM THAT DAY ON. THEY TRIED ALL TYPES OF THERAPY... ALL KINDS OF DRUGS. NONE OF IT HELPED.
"I WAS DISCHARGED AND SENT BACK TO THE ISLAND. A SHELL OF A PERSON WHO MIGHT AS WELL HAVE DIED ON THAT FIELD.
MOTEL
"I DUMPED MYSELF IN A LOCAL FLOPHOUSE AND LIVED IN A BOTTLE FOR A NUMBER OF YEARS.
"COULDN'T PUSH THE ALCOHOL DOWN FAST ENOUGH... AND IT STILL DID NO GOOD.
"I WAS TOO WEAK TO LIVE... BUT DIDN'T HAVE THE WILL TO END MY LIFE.
"I HAD BECOME A NOWHERE MAN."
MIGUEL RODRIGUEZ...
¿QUÉ...?
I HAVE COME TO OFFER YOU...

...REDEMPTION.

"I COULDN'T UNDERSTAND WHAT WAS HAPPENING. WAS THIS A DREAM?
WAS I STILL IN A STUPOR?"
LEAVE MY HEAD... DEMON... BEFORE I...
SILENCE!

MY TIME HERE IS BRIEF, MORTAL... SO ALLOW ME TO SPEAK.
THIS GUILT AND SHAME YOU CARRY-- I, TOO, HAVE SHARED THAT WEIGHT.
IT NEARLY DESTROYED ME. BUT I WAS GIVEN A CHANCE TO MAKE THINGS RIGHT AGAIN.
TO BALANCE THE SCALES.

I AM A VEJIGANTE. THIS LINEAGE DATES BACK AS FAR AS TIME ITSELF.
AS THOSE BEFORE ME, I CHOSE TO ASSUME THIS FORM AND DEFEND PUERTO RICO AGAINST ALL EVIL.
UNTIL I HAVE PROVEN MYSELF WORTHY ENOUGH TO MOVE ON.
AND NOW, AFTER A HUNDRED YEARS AT MY POST, THAT TIME HAS COME FOR ME.

AND THUS IT IS UP TO ME TO SELECT MY SUCCESSOR. ONE WHO IS IN NEED OF REDEMPTION.
YOU ARE MY CHOICE, MIGUEL. REST NOW... AND DECIDE WITH A CLEAR MIND.
BUT I... OHHHH...

"I AWOKE THE NEXT MORNING, CLEAR-HEADED FOR THE FIRST TIME IN NEARLY FIVE YEARS.
"I ALMOST DIDN'T BELIEVE IT ALL HAPPENED...

"...UNTIL I SAW THE MASK ON THE FLOOR.
"A CHANCE FOR REDEMPTION. A CHANCE TO LIVE AGAIN.

"THERE WAS ONLY ONE ANSWER.
"I CHOSE 'YES.'"

THE ISLAND HAS SINCE BEEN UNDER MY PROTECTION. IT HAS NOT BEEN EASY...
AND, TO BE HONEST, I AM STILL TRYING TO UNDERSTAND WHAT POWERS I HAVE AND HOW THEY WORK...
BUT I VOWED TO BE A BETTER HERO THAN I WAS A SOLDIER.
SO THEN WHY FLEE THE SCENE YESTERDAY AFTER SAVING THE POLICE?
CERTAINLY YOU COULD HAVE PROVIDED VALUABLE INFORMATION TO THE AUTHORITIES.
NO OFFENSE, AMIGO... BUT IT WAS NOT LONG AGO WHEN BEING ASSOCIATED WITH YOUR KIND... MEANT BEING HUNTED AS AN ENEMY OF THE STATE.

I WANTED TO DO GOOD, BUT ON MY OWN TERMS.
THAT'S STILL NO REASON TO...

REED... SPIDER-MAN HAS ALWAYS BEEN A VALUABLE ALLY TO US.
AND HE'S ALSO HAD HIS ISSUES WITH PUBLIC OPINION. WE'VE ALWAYS PAID ATTENTION TO HIS ACTIONS, RATHER THAN HEARSAY.
I HAVE THE SAME GUT FEELING ABOUT THIS PERSON. I FEEL HE'S TELLING THE TRUTH.

VERY WELL, THEN, I'LL TRUST YOUR JUDGMENT, DEAR.
IF MY WIFE SAYS YOU CAN BE TRUSTED, THAT'S ALL I NEED TO KNOW.
REALLY? THAT QUICK?

FIND ANYTHING, REED?
THIS.
BIOTECH COMPOUNDS USED TO CREATE A CHIMERA EFFECT.
IN THEORY, CHIMERA EFFECTS FUSE GENETIC CODES OF DIFFERENT SPECIES. ONLY THE HIGH EVOLUTIONARY HAS BEEN SUCCESSFUL AT IT.
IN THIS CASE, I'D SURMISE A.I.M. IS ENHANCING THE INTELLIGENCE OF THE LOCAL PRIMATES. BUT WHY?

A.I.MONKEYS. NOW I'VE SEEN IT ALL.
BUT THE MECHANICS NEEDED WOULD REQUIRE MORE POWER THAN THE LOCAL GRID COULD SUPPLY.
OYE... IF IT'S POWER YOU NEED, I KNOW THE PERFECT SOURCE.
WE NEED TO GET TO RINCÓN.

WOOOO-HOOOO!!!
I LOVE IT WHEN I GET TO DRIVE!!
VERDAD... YOU DRIVE LIKE A TRUE PUERTO RICAN, SUSANA! PEDAL TO THE METAL!
SUE SHARES JOHNNY'S LOVE OF VELOCITY.
MY HUSBAND, ON THE OTHER HAND, DRIVES LIKE AGATHA HARKNESS.

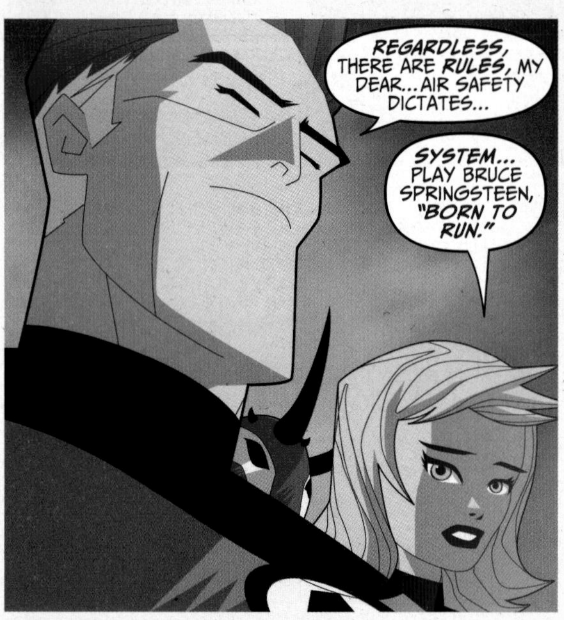
REGARDLESS, THERE ARE RULES, MY DEAR...AIR SAFETY DICTATES...
SYSTEM... PLAY BRUCE SPRINGSTEEN, "BORN TO RUN."

SIGH... THAT'S NOT WHY I DESIGNED THIS SOUND SYSTEM, DARLING.
I'M SORRY... WHAT?!
YOU NEVER GET TIRED OF DOING THAT, DO YOU...?

IT'S MORE EFFECTIVE THAN JOHNNY'S METHOD OF COVERING HIS EARS AND GOING "NAH-NAH-NAH-NAH."
WE ARE NEARING THE NUCLEAR PLANT, SEÑORA STORM. IT'S JUST UP AHEAD.

A WORD OF CAUTION, MY FRIENDS. THAT FACILITY HAS BEEN DORMANT FOR DECADES...
BUT I FEAR THIS IS NO LONGER THE CASE. I AM SENSING ENERGY PATTERNS FROM WITHIN.
YOU CAN SENSE...
AND ONE INDIVIDUAL WITH BIOELECTRONIC ENHANCEMENTS.
M.O.D.O.K.

¿QUIÉN ES EL M.O.D.O.K....?
MENTAL ORGANISM DESIGNED ONLY FOR KILLING. HIS BUSINESS IS DEATH. ON A GRAND SCALE.
THREE MILLION PEOPLE ON THIS ISLAND WOULD MAKE A VERY TEMPTING TARGET, ¿VERDAD?
INDEED. AND THE NUCLEAR PLANT WOULD ALLOW THEM TO DESIGN NEW WEAPONS OF MASS DESTRUCTION.
UGH. I HATE THAT PHRASE.

HMMM. A BOILING NUCLEAR SUPERHEATER REACTOR FACILITY.
IT HAS BEEN DECOMMISSIONED SINCE THE LATE '60S. HOW COULD THEY POSSIBLY GET IT UP AND RUNNING SO QUICKLY?
WHEN YOU'RE AVOIDING DETECTION, SPEED IS OF THE ESSENCE. THEY EXCEL AT IT.

ANYONE ELSE FEEL LIKE CHARLTON HESTON?
I'M GUESSING THEY'VE BEEN GENETICALLY EVOLVED TO BECOME PART OF THEIR WORK FORCE.
BUT WHY GO THROUGH ALL THAT WHEN YOU CAN JUST HIRE HUMANS?
THEY LOOK ADORABLE IN THOSE TINY SUITS.
I KNEW YOU WOULD SAY THAT.
SHUSH, DEAR.

I CAN SNEAK DOWN THERE AND...
NOT TO WORRY, FRIEND. ALLOW ME...

...SO ME TELL HIM, "THAT NOT BANANA."
THAT SOOO NOT TRUE.

SSHPUNKT

I HAVE TO ADMIT, THAT IS VERY FUN TO WATCH.
I'VE BEEN WITH HIM FOREVER AND I STILL FIND IT AWESOME.
THANK YOU, DARLING.
NOW IF YOU WOULDN'T MIND...?

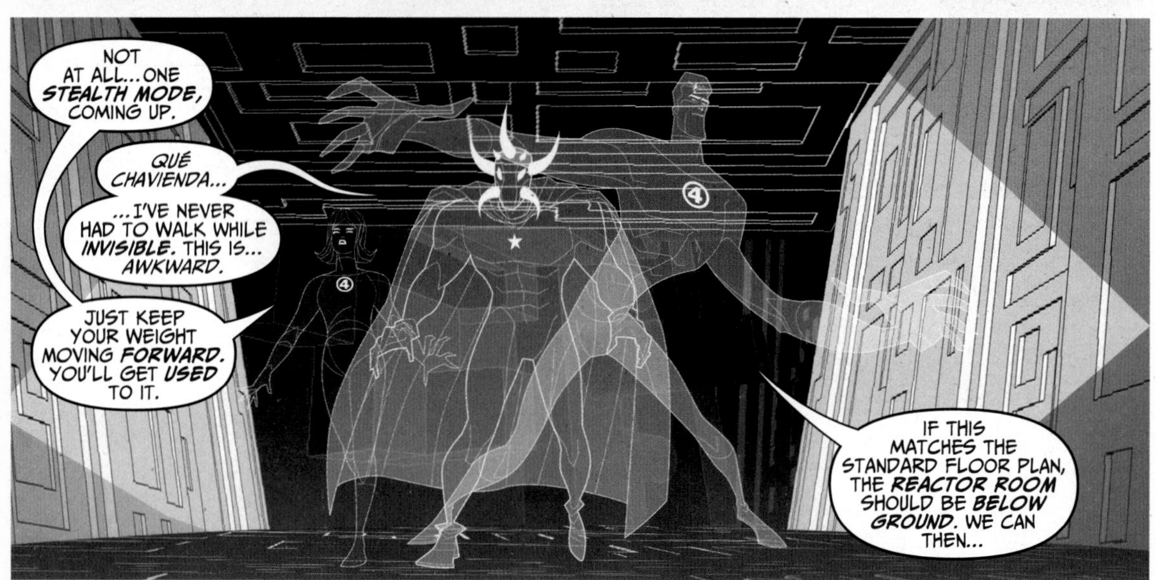
NOT AT ALL...ONE STEALTH MODE, COMING UP.
QUÉ CHAVIENDA...
...I'VE NEVER HAD TO WALK WHILE INVISIBLE. THIS IS... AWKWARD.
JUST KEEP YOUR WEIGHT MOVING FORWARD. YOU'LL GET USED TO IT.
IF THIS MATCHES THE STANDARD FLOOR PLAN, THE REACTOR ROOM SHOULD BE BELOW GROUND. WE CAN THEN...

BRRZZZZKKKTTT

TELL MASTER M.O.D.O.K. WE CATCH SOMETHING.
SOMETHING BIG.

EVERY TIME I FIND A NEW PLACE TO SET UP SHOP, THE VERMIN EVENTUALLY TRY TO SNEAK IN.
IT'S WHY I INSTALLED THOSE NEURO-SHOCK FLOORS. ANY LIVING CREATURE OVER TWENTY POUNDS SETS THEM OFF.
AGENT 9558...INFORM GENETICS TO INCREASE OUR UNIT OUTPUT BY 88.9382%. IT APPEARS WE HAVE BEEN COMPROMISED.
YEP.
THAT FIELD SHOULD HOLD OUR PRISONERS UNTIL WE'VE REACHED OUR QUOTA. THEN WE'LL BE RID OF THEM WHEN WE FLUSH THE FACILITY.
YEP.

YOU THREE MAY WATCH AND MARVEL AT HOW EFFICIENTLY AN ORGANIZATION SUCH AS A.I.M. CAN OPERATE.

GUESS AGAIN, CABEZUDO. IF YOU HAVE PLANS FOR WORLD DOMINATION, YOU WILL HAVE TO DO IT ELSEWHERE!

THE WORLD...? NO.
WE'RE LOOKING TO CONQUER A MORE DAUNTING ENEMY.
THE RECESSION.

IT TAKES A.I.M. UP TO FOUR YEARS AT A COST OF FOUR MILLION DOLLARS TO TRAIN AN AGENT.
THESE PRIMATE MINIONS, ON THE OTHER HAND, CAN BE CREATED INSTANTLY FOR NEARLY A THIRD THE COST.
THEY ALLOW A.I.M. TO ELIMINATE SALARIES AS WELL AS INSURANCE, OVERTIME, HOLIDAY PAY AND RETIREMENT PACKAGES.
IT IS COST-EFFECTIVE--
--PROVIDING A.I.M. WITH AN INCREASED BUDGET TO CREATE DEADLIER WEAPONRY ON A MORE PRODUCTIVE TIMETABLE.

I'LL SAY THIS--THEY MAY BE NUTS, BUT A.I.M. MAKES A QUALITY FORCE FIELD.
ANY IDEAS, REED?
PERHAPS. THE FLUCTUATING ENERGIES IN THIS FIELD MAY HOLD US IN...

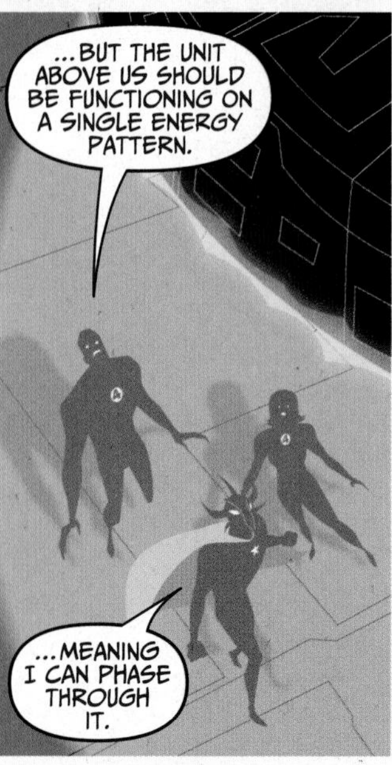
...BUT THE UNIT ABOVE US SHOULD BE FUNCTIONING ON A SINGLE ENERGY PATTERN.
...MEANING I CAN PHASE THROUGH IT.

MY THOUGHT EXACTLY.
SEE IF YOU CAN REACH THE CIRCUIT BREAK-ERS.

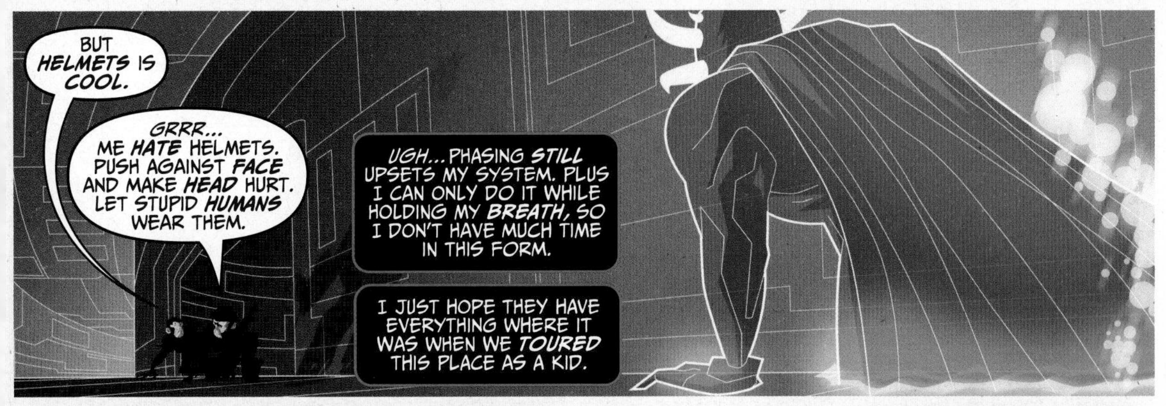
BUT HELMETS IS COOL.
GRRR... ME HATE HELMETS. PUSH AGAINST FACE AND MAKE HEAD HURT. LET STUPID HUMANS WEAR THEM.
UGH...PHASING STILL UPSETS MY SYSTEM. PLUS I CAN ONLY DO IT WHILE HOLDING MY BREATH, SO I DON'T HAVE MUCH TIME IN THIS FORM.
I JUST HOPE THEY HAVE EVERYTHING WHERE IT WAS WHEN WE TOURED THIS PLACE AS A KID.

CONTRA... MORE OF THOSE MONKEY AGENTS.
I NEED TO TAKE THEM OUT QUICK AND QUIET-LIKE.

BUT HELMET MAKE FEEL LIKE PART OF TEAM! YOU NOT FEEL SOMETHING MISSING?
ME? NOPE. DEALING WITH STUPID COLLAR RUBBING NECK WRONG WAY.
ALSO THINK YELLOW MAKE ME LOOK FAT.

SQUEEEE...!!
FFZZAMMMMM

GREAT. HE GOT A SHOT OFF. LOOKS LIKE THE SOUND HAS ALERTED MORE AGENTS...
AND I'M LOSING MY INTANGIBLE FORM!
THIS JUST GETS BETTER AND BETTER! C'MON, MIGUEL...GET IT TOGETHER!!

HE'S BEEN UP THERE FOR A WHILE NOW...AND THIS FIELD IS STILL UP AND RUNNING.
HOW DO YOU THINK HE'S DOING?
GIVEN HE'S NEW AT THIS...? LET'S JUST SAY IF HIS LUCK IS ANYTHING LIKE SPIDER-MAN HAS TOLD US OF HIS FIRST YEAR AS A HERO...

"...NOT VERY WELL."
DIOS! EVERYONE OFF!! DON'T MAKE ME GET ALL TITO TRINIDAD ON YOU!
SOUND ALARM!! HORNY MAN TRY TO ESCAPE!!
"HORNY MAN"? REALLY?! THAT'S WHAT YOU DECIDE TO CALL ME? THANKS.
AS IF MY SELF-ESTEEM WASN'T LOW ENOUGH...
ME HIT ALARM!! SQUEEE!!!

NO...
NO...
NOOOO...
HANDS OFF THE PRETTY BUTTON!!
YOU NOT STOP ME! AM BEST BUTTON-PUSHER IN ORGANIZATION!! ME...

OH, PLEASE SHUT UP.
YEESH. EVEN MY ENGLISH IS BETTER THAN YOURS, AND I GOT A C+...!
THANK YOU, PONCE HIGH SCHOOL, CLASS OF '99!!
OOFS!!!

HOW ABOUT THAT? I FINALLY SCORED A VICTORY! COUNT ONE FOR THE GOOD GUYS! WHEW!
BE CAREFUL, MIGUEL, YOU MAY ACTUALLY GET THE HANG OF THIS.
tik

CHUNNGGG
OH-OHS....
POWER HAS BEEN SEVERED!! BUT HOW DID THEY...
THE BORICUA!
QUICKLY!! RE-ROUTE ALL RESERVE POWER TO THE HOLDING CHAMBERS BEFORE...

MASTER!! HEROES GO BYE-BYE!! HEROES GO BYE-BYE!!
GRRR...WE HAVE TO UPGRADE VOCABULARY ON THE NEXT ROUND OF MINIONS...

THEY'VE FREED THEMSELVES!! INITIATE IMMEDIATE REACTOR SHUTDOWN! BLOW THE REACTOR!!
PSST...!

BOO.

THIS IS FUN! I COULD DO THIS ALL DAY!!
THAT SHOT WAS ME ANNOYED, M.O.D.O.K.... YOU DON'T WANT ME ANGRY.
STAND DOWN. NOW.

NONE MAY DEFEAT M.O.D.O.K.! YOU WILL ALL BE ELIMINATED AT THE HAND OF A.I.M.!! THE CORE IS OVERHEATING AS WE SPEAK!!
YOUR MISERABLE EXISTENCE ON THIS PLANET IS AT AN END!!

WE DON'T HAVE MUCH *TIME!* WE NEED TO TAKE THEM OUT AND STOP THAT CORE FROM *OVERHEATING!*

BWWARMFF
I THINK *NOT*, WOMAN.
UNNFF!!

MONSTER!! IF YOU'VE *HURT* HER...

I DO NOT *HURT* PEOPLE. I AM M.O.D.O.K.-- I *KILL!*
BETTER MEN THAN *YOU* HAVE TRIED TO KILL US. THEY'VE ALWAYS *FAILED!*

GET TO THE CONTROLS, REED! I'LL TAKE ON M.O.D.O.K!
I CALL DIBS ON THE MONKEYS!

FOOM

STRETCHY MAN GO BOOM.
WELL DONE, 94558.

STILL ALIVE. IMPRESSIVE.
VEJIGANTES CANNOT BE KILLED, ABUSADOR. IT'S PART OF THE JOB.
KEEP HITTING ME...AND I JUST...UNHH...GET BACK UP...
NO. YOU WILL NOT.
EVENTUALLY, YOU WILL BE DESTR--
NNNH!
WHAT IS--?

QUIET, CREATURE!
THERE IS... NNGH!
ATTACKING ME... UNHHHH!!! BUT I AM M.O.D.O.K.!!! WHO IS...

THAT IS A TWENTY-POUND FORCE FIELD BALL COMPRESSING YOUR BRAIN STEM, YOU BOBBLE-HEADED FREAK...
NNGGGHH...I...AM... UNNNH...M.O.D.O.K....

AND I AM SUSAN STORM. I AM A WIFE... A MOTHER OF TWO...

BUT MOST OF ALL...
I...AM...ON... VACATION!!!

NOW HERE'S WHAT'S GOING TO HAPPEN.
YOU'RE GOING TO SURRENDER AND FIX ALL THIS GARBAGE YOU CREATED...
OR I'M GOING TO CONDENSE THAT FORCE FIELD RIGHT HERE AND NOW...AND WATCH YOU STROKE OUT. ¿ME ENTIENDES?
FEMALE...!! M.O.D.O.K.... WILL...
ARRRGGGHHHH!!!!

I SAID...¿ME ENTIENDES?!
UUNHH!! M.O.D.O.K. ...WILL...
...STAND... DOWN...
NOW TURN THE CONTROLS OVER TO MY HUSBAND, THEN SIT THERE AND SHUT UP UNTIL THE AUTHORITIES ARRIVE.

THEN I'LL REMOVE THE FIELD.
AS SHE COMMANDS, MY MINIONS.
SQUEE... SEE-THROUGH LADY SCARY. ME GIVE UP.
ME TOO!

WOW. YOU BROUGHT OUT THE BIG GUNS AND USED YOUR ANGRY MOMMA VOICE.
I TOTALLY DID.
MIRA... I NEARLY WENT HOME TO CLEAN MY ROOM.
HA HA!

I STILL SAY THEY LOOK ADORABLE.
AY... VERDAD.
FOR SOMEONE WHO'S NEW AT THIS, YOU DID A GREAT JOB.
YOU SHOULD BE PROUD OF YOURSELF.
SERIOUSLY. MONKEYS?
YEP.
PRETTY RIDICULOUS. BUT THEY'RE CUTE AS A BUTTON.
...

I HOPE YOU'RE ABLE TO FIND PEACE, MIGUEL.
REDEMPTION WILL TAKE SOME TIME TO ACHIEVE, SEÑORA STORM. BUT I'M READY TO TAKE THAT JOURNEY.

WELL...IT'S NICE TO KNOW PUERTO RICO HAS SOMEONE LIKE YOU TO LOOK OUT FOR IT. WE'VE BECOME VERY ATTACHED TO THIS PLACE.
IF YOU'RE EVER IN NEW YORK, YOU HAVE AN INVITATION TO STAY WITH US!
A FLATTERING OFFER, SUSANA...BUT I CANNOT TAKE YOU UP ON IT.

AS A VEJIGANTE...I AM BONDED TO THE ISLAND. SHOULD I EVER LEAVE IT, THIS FORM WILL DISAPPEAR.
SO YOU'RE TRAPPED HERE...?
TRAPPED? HOW CAN I FEEL TRAPPED IN THE PLACE MY HEART BELONGS?
I LOVE WHAT I AM DOING.

THEN WE'LL DO DINNER WHEN WE VISIT! PROMISE ME THAT.
VEJIGANTES DON'T EAT, MI AMOR...
...BUT I WILL BE HAPPY TO WATCH YOU ENJOY SOME CHILLO FRITO... WITH A SIDE OF ARAÑITAS, OF COURSE.
IT... GLADDENS ME THAT WE HAVE MET.
EVERYTHING'S TAKEN CARE OF, DARLING. WE'RE FREE TO RESUME OUR VACATION GETAWAY.

¡NOS VEMOS, AMIGOS! I LOOK FORWARD TO SEEING YOU BOTH AGAIN!
ENJOY YOUR TIME ON MY ISLAND AND MAY YOU ENJOY THE LOVE IT INSPIRES IN US ALL! ¡SALUD!!
NOW, MY DEAR...AS I RECALL, I OWE YOU A SUNSET ON THE BEACH. SHALL WE..?
YOU HAVE TO ASK?
LEAD ON, SEÑOR FANTÁSTICO!

SOOOO... I HAVE MY *FINAL QUESTION* FOR YOU. BUT I *KNOW* YOU WON'T *ANSWER* IT.
OH, *REALLY?* BECAUSE...?
BECAUSE IT'S YOUR *DEEPEST* SECRET.
ONE THAT ME, BEN AND JOHNNY HAVE BEEN CURIOUS ABOUT FOR *YEARS.*
AND THAT IS...?
YOU HAVE TO *SWEAR* TO ME YOU'LL *ANSWER* IT.
FINE. I *SWEAR* I WILL ANSWER IT.
OKAY, THEN... MY TWENTIETH QUESTION FOR YOU IS...
...WHY *"MISTER FANTASTIC"?*

"YOU SPOKE EARLIER OF THAT DAY I CREATED YOUR SOUND SYSTEM. REMEMBER?"
BEATLES... ABBEY ROAD... "HERE COMES THE SUN."
OH MY GOD, REED... I COULD DO THIS FOREVER!!!
THIS IS BEYOND INCREDIBLE!!!!
WELL, IT'S NOTHING ANY M.I.T. NERD COULDN'T FIGURE OUT.
NERD?
REED, MY DEAR...
ANYONE WHO CAN DO WHAT YOU JUST DID IN TWO HOURS...

...IS MR. FANTASTIC IN MY BOOK!
LET ME TRY SOME ELVIS... "VIVA LAS VEGAS"!
"YOU SAID IT SO MATTER-OF-FACTLY, IT'S NO WONDER YOU DON'T RECALL SAYING IT.
"BUT IT HAD SUCH A PROFOUND IMPACT ON ME AS A PERSON.
"BECAUSE, UP TO THAT MOMENT, WHEN SOMEONE SPOKE OF MY INTELLIGENCE...IT WAS IN A DEPRECATING FASHION.
"BEN WOULD JOKINGLY CALL ME 'EGGHEAD' OR 'BIG BRAIN.' WHILE OTHERS LABELED ME A 'NERD' OR 'BOOKWORM.'

"BUT SUDDENLY, THERE YOU WERE... A WOMAN WHO WAS SO COMPLETELY OUT OF MY LEAGUE...
"LABELING MY INTELLIGENCE AS SOMETHING TO BE CELEBRATED...NOT SIMPLY JOKED ABOUT.
"SOMEONE LIKE YOU THOUGHT I WAS MR. FANTASTIC.

"WHICH IS WHY, THAT NIGHT WE OBTAINED OUR POWERS...AND IT WAS TIME FOR US TO COME UP WITH OUR NAMES...
"I ALSO MADE THE MOST OBVIOUS CHOICE."
AND I'LL CALL MYSELF...MISTER FANTASTIC!

THAT'S A TRUE STORY?
TRUE STORY.
SWEAR TO GOD?
SWEAR TO GOD.

THAT'S QUITE POSSIBLY THE MOST INCREDIBLY ROMANTIC THING ANYONE HAS EVER TOLD ME... IN MY LIFE.
REMEMBER, MY LOVE--THIS STAYS BETWEEN US. NO ONE FINDS OUT.
ESPECIALLY YOUR BROTHER.
OH, JOHNNY WOULD DESTROY YOU.
I'D RATHER HAVE DR. DOOM KNOW THAN JOHNNY.

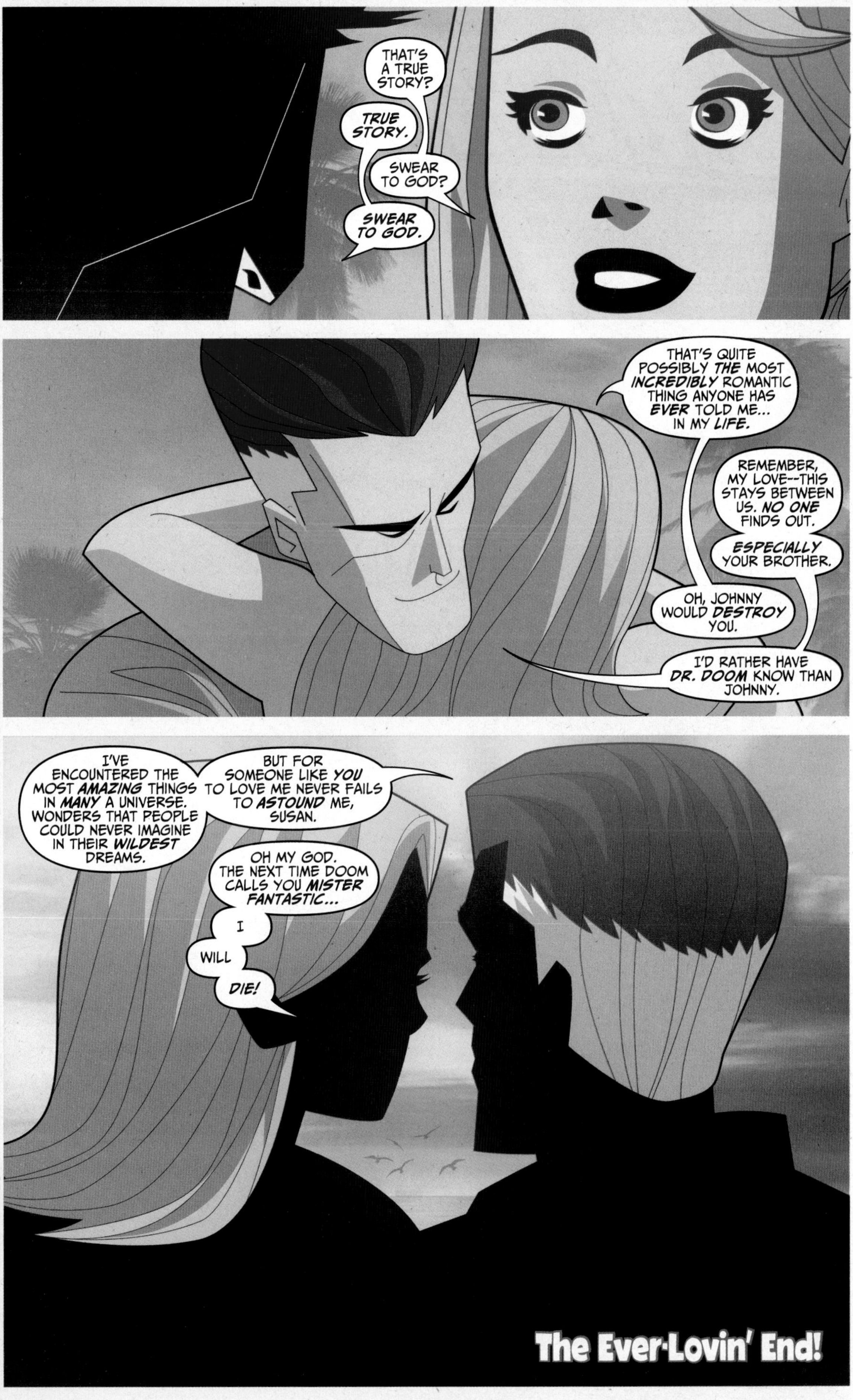

I'VE ENCOUNTERED THE MOST AMAZING THINGS IN MANY A UNIVERSE. WONDERS THAT PEOPLE COULD NEVER IMAGINE IN THEIR WILDEST DREAMS.
BUT FOR SOMEONE LIKE YOU TO LOVE ME NEVER FAILS TO ASTOUND ME, SUSAN.
OH MY GOD. THE NEXT TIME DOOM CALLS YOU MISTER FANTASTIC...
I
WILL
DIE!
The Ever-Lovin' End!

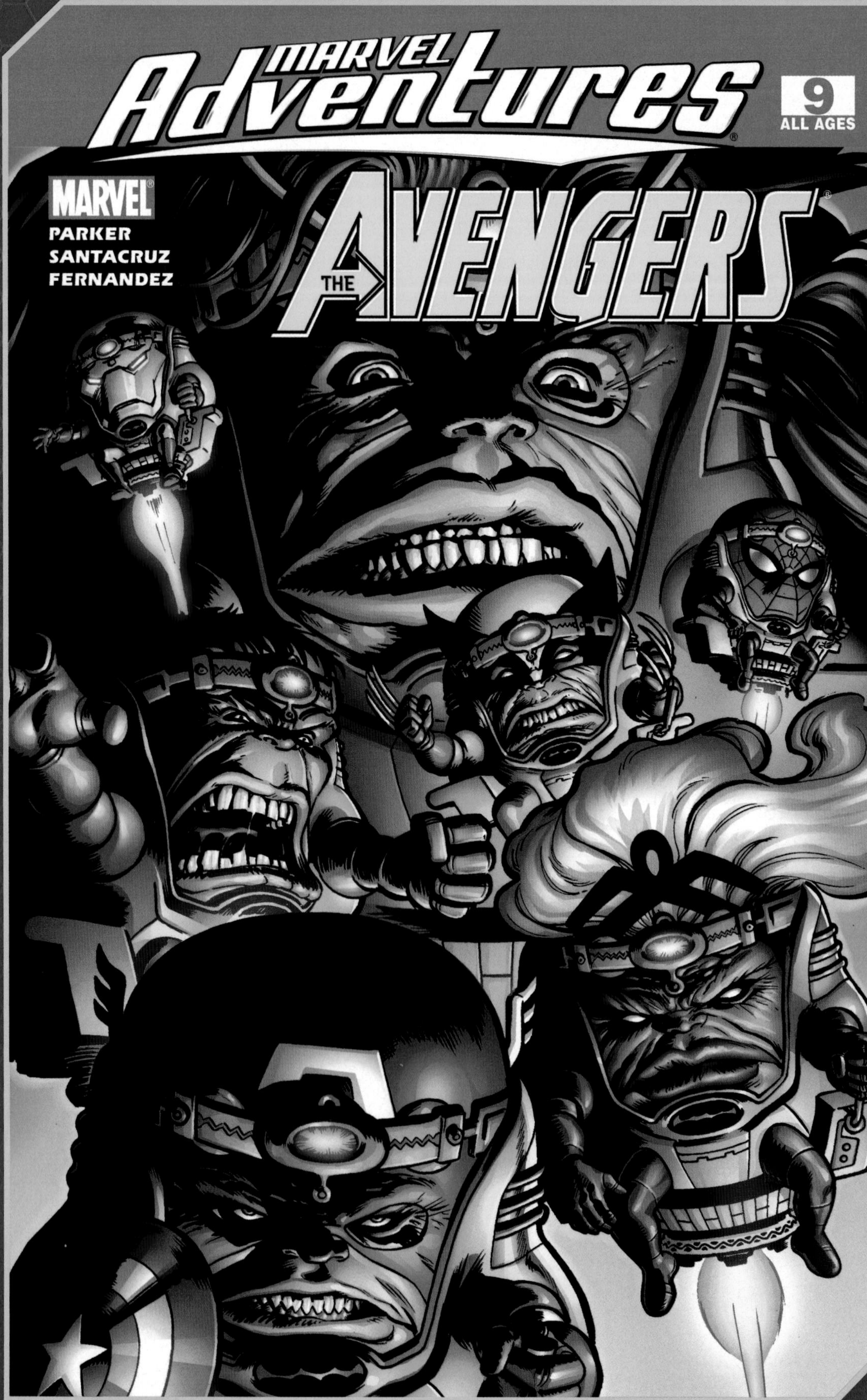

MARVEL
Adventures

MARVEL

PARKER
SANTACRUZ
FERNANDEZ

CAPTAIN AMERICA
STORM
HULK
SPIDER-MAN
GIANT-GIRL
IRON MAN
WOLVERINE
You were right, Iron Man! This has to be the secret base.
Now we know who stole all of that equipment from Stark Industries... A.I.M.!
Seems too easy...
RRAAHHRR!
It's the Avengers! They've found us!
JEFF
MARK
A NOT-SO-BEAUTIFUL MIND
SUPER-SOLDIER FROM WORLD WAR II. WEATHER GODDESS. SUPER-STRONG ALTER EGO OF SCIENTIST BRUCE BANNER. SPIDER-POWERED WEB-SLINGER. GIANT-SIZED CRIMEFIGHTER. BRILLIANT ARMORED INVENTOR. FERAL MUTANT BRAWLER. TOGETHER THEY ARE THE WORLD'S MIGHTIEST HEROES, BATTLING THE FOES THAT NO SINGLE SUPER HERO COULD WITHSTAND!
AVENGERS

"A.I.M." must not refer to their skills. Are these guys bee-keepers or some-thing?
It stands for *Advanced Idea Mechanics.*
They use dangerously experimental technology to further their criminal organization.
Firing sonics!
We are not criminals! We are pure scientists who want no restraints on our sacred research!
Funny how all of your research makes things that destroy.
Like so.
Yeah, you could use your smarts to make better honey!
Spidey, they're *not* beekeepeRUNK!!
HA!
I BELIEVE THE SAYING IS HITTING TWO BIRDS WITH ONE--

--BRAINBLAST!!!
NATE
M.O.D.O.C.!
What is... that?
M.O.D.O.C., duh.
Okay, I don't know what I'm looking at either. Who is this guy?
IF YOU'RE ATTEMPTING A DISTRACTION BY COAXING AN ORIGIN STORY FROM ME...
...IT WILL NOT WORK. STILL, I LIKE TELLING MY ORIGIN, SO I SHALL WIDEN MY BRAINBLAST.
THERE. NOW I CAN TALK WITHOUT HEROIC INTERRUPTION.
I WAS ONCE ONE OF THESE BRILLIANT BUT ORDINARY SCIENTISTS YOU SEE IN THE RADIATION SUITS.

WE WORKED FOR YEARS TO UNLEASH THE FULL POTENTIAL OF THE HUMAN BRAIN--TO CREATE A PERFECT MENTAL ORGANISM.
FINALLY WE'D BUILT A CELLULAR RESTRUCTURER THAT WOULD ALLOW ONE'S GRAY MATTER TO REACH THE GREATEST MASS HUMANLY POSSIBLE.
YET FOR ALL THE TALK OF HOW SUPERIOR AN ALTERED PERSON WOULD BE, NO ONE WAS WILLING TO VOLUNTEER TO BE THE TEST SUBJECT!
IT SEEMS THAT I WASN'T THE MOST POPULAR WITH THE GROUP--NO DOUBT BECAUSE I DIDN'T BRING THE RIGHT KINDS OF SNACKS TO A.I.M. BARBECUES--AND THEY CONSPIRED TO MAKE ME THE FIRST SUBJECT.
MY TRANSFORMATION WAS MORE PROFOUND THAN ANYONE IMAGINED. I EMERGED ABLE TO OVERPOWER THE MINDS OF THE OTHERS.
I MADE THEM BUILD MY HOVERCHAIR, FOR MY BODY CANNOT SUPPORT THE WEIGHT OF MY HEAD. NEXT THEY FASHIONED THE CEREBRAL CHANNELER THAT ALLOWS ME TO ATTACK EVEN YOUR MOST POWERFUL MEMBERS!
NOW I AM TRULY THE *MENTAL ORGANISM DESIGNED ONLY FOR CONQUEST!*
CONQUERING YOUR SMALL MINDS IS EASY ENOUGH AT CLOSE RANGE.
Think again, Humpty-Dumpty.
I have defenses against freaks like you.

SCRRRING!
Hey!!! Wolverine, what are you doing?!
Spidey--come on, guys! Shake it off! M.O.D.O.C.'s thinking for you!
EXCELLENT. PERHAPS YOU SHOULD HAVE BUILT ALL OF YOUR TEAMMATES SUCH ADVANCED SUITS, IRON MAN.
Hulk would just break his.
You can't make the Avengers do your bidding forever, M.O.D.O.C.!
CORRECT. SOMEONE WOULD EVENTUALLY GET OUT OF MY RANGE AND REBEL.
NO, I NEED YOU TO SEE THINGS THE WAY I DO. THAT THE WORLD IS FULL OF MENTAL INFERIORS NOT CAPABLE OF MAKING DECISIONS FOR THEMSELVES.
AND THERE IS ONLY ONE WAY YOU COULD POSSIBLY THINK LIKE M.O.D.O.C...

TO THAT END, I HAVE MADE MY LOYAL WORKERS BUILD A MUCH LARGER CELLULAR RESTRUCTURER.
No way...you can't mean...
JUST THINK! YOUR ENORMOUS PHYSICAL POWERS WILL NOW HAVE AN EQUALLY POWERFUL MIND TO BALANCE THEM!
No, this is sick! You can't DO this!
HEH-HEH-- SOUND FAMILIAR?
He doesn't realize the gift you are giving, sir.
Initiate reformation sequence.
BWEEP
DNA chains unlocking...
Commencing cerebral expansion.

Sir! The Restructurer is overloading!
WHAT?!
The bodies of the Hulk and Giant-Girl are stressing the system!
IMPOSSIBLE! I ANTICIPATED THAT PROBLEM AND ASSIGNED IT TO BE DEALT WITH BY...
...KARL?!
uh...
KARL
KARL
Dude, I thought I was supposed to work on the hoverchairs!
IDIOT!
KARL
Sir, what do we do?
Where-- where are you going?
I AM LEAVING BEFORE THE BASE EXPLODES.
YOU MICROCEPHALICS CAN DO WHATEVER YOU WANT.
KARL
RUN!

PING PING PING PING PING PING PING PING PING PING
PING PING PING PING PING PING
PING PING PING
WHAT *IS* THAT INFERNAL SOUND?
A DISTRESS CALL, COMING FROM MY ARMOR. SOME PATHETIC OFFICIAL IS CRYING FOR OUR HELP.
THOUGH ALTERED, MY ARMOR STILL MANIFESTED A FORCE FIELD TO PROTECT US, SO YOU SHOULD ALL PRAISE ME!
BAH! JUST SEE WHAT THE CALL IS ABOUT!
-vengers, we need your help! Boston is under attack!
WHAT! WHO DARES?
The merman warlord Attuma has invaded our city!
He not only has his aquatic army, but also several giant monsters following orders! We're severely outmatched-- **please help!**
HMM. GOOD PLAN.
YET THEY WILL FAIL! THEY HAVE MADE A FATAL CALCULATION INVADING *OUR* DOMAIN!
Governor! Did the Avengers get the message?
I...think so. I think our connection was bad. They looked a little...distorted.

Run, you miserable air-breathers!
Retreat, men!
Look at them flee from our sea monster assault!
I'd forgotten how much fun it is to attack the surface world!
BZRRAP!
TRI-GORR!
Who could do this?!

ATTENTION AQUATIC INVADERS! RESISTANCE IS USELESS!
YOUR COMBINED FORCES WILL BE DEFEATED IN 4.5352228 MINUTES!

BY THE ASSEMBLED BRAINPOWER OF... THE M.O.D.AVENGERS!
SUBTERRANEAN MONSTERS: KLEE--GOK! SWAH-KROG--NEE! SEH-BUL-SKI!
CAPDOC
STORMDOC
SPIDOC
HULKDOC
GI-DOC
IRONDOC
WOLDOC

Sire, they're crushing our invasion force!
My beasts will compensate!
Rommbu! Eat them!
HA. MY MULTIPLIED ARACHNOID SENSE BEGAN TINGLING BEFORE YOU EVEN SPOKE, ATTUMA.
HALT, CREATURE!
THESE BEASTS' MINDS ARE SIMPLICITY ITSELF TO CONTROL!
ROMMBU, YOU WILL FOLLOW MY ORDERS NOW.
ATTACK YOUR FORMER MASTER!!!
GOHRRAARR!
NOOOO

This cannot be happening! The entire might of my military is being vanquished!
THE ENTIRE MILITARY?
THAT MEANS HIS REALM IS COMPLETELY UNGUARDED.
VULNERABLE FOR CONQUEST.
What...no! You can't...you can't invade my home!
It appears the invasion of Boston has been crushed by the, um...Avengers, I guess...

THIS BACKUP HIDDEN BASE LEAKS! WHO FOUND THIS?
Hey, the computer said this was the best secret location in the state!
STOP WATCHING THAT TRIPE AND GET BACK TO WORK, KARL!
I think you'll want to see this, sir.
Your restructuring process worked!
...heroes seem to have taken on a new look--and attitude.
ATTUMA WILL BOTHER YOU NO LONGER--HIS UNDERSEA KINGDOM IS *OURS!*
THE GAMMA-ENHANCED VILLAIN, **THE LEADER**....
I CALCULATE THAT HE HAS FIGURED OUT HOW TO ESCAPE HIS PRISON CELL.
LET US GO CRUSH HIS PLANS...
AND HIS SPIRIT!
It looks like they're still fighting crime...in a more *conquery* sort of way. Should we contact them?
AHH... NO.
I NEED TO...OVERSEE WORK ON OUR NEW BASE! YOU KEEP AN EYE ON THEM, KARL. BACK TO WORK EVERYONE!

Look, the... Avengers are... back.
When...when do you think they'll leave again?
I WILL FOCUS MY BESTIAL SENSES INTO A CONTINENT-WIDE SCAN... FOUND HIM.
HE IS UPSTATE.
HA HA HA!!! SIMPLE-MINDED VILLAIN. EVEN WOLDOC CAN FIND HIM.
WHY...IF MY CLAWS COULD REACH BEYOND MY FACE...
I TIRE OF YOU TWO BICKERING-- AND BLOCKING MY VIEW!
BESIDES, YOU ARE VILLAGE IDIOTS WHEN COMPARED TO MY GARGANTUAN BRAIN!
RAAHHHAR!!
THE SUPREME HEAD BUTT!
CEASE INTER-TEAM HOSTILITIES! WE MUST FIND AN UNDERGROUND ACCESS THAT WE CAN FIT THROUGH!

Those dull-witted guards at the prison are still fooled by those androids in our cells, Abomination.
By the time they realize we're gone, your exo-enhancer will be complete!
Aw, that'll be great.
Hulk's gonna wish he'd stayed Bruce Banner when I get done with him.
I'm already more powerful than him...if he doesn't get really mad.
Yes, my boy, but now you will thoroughly over-whelm the Avengers!
That'll show the world who the true Master of Evil is!
THE LEADER!
And the Abomination.
Did you say something?
YOU ARE MASTER OF NOTHING!

I don't... how...
OF COURSE YOU DO NOT.
FOOLISH VILLAIN. YOU THINK YOUR RUSE COULD OUTWIT US?
OF COURSE HE WOULD THINK THAT, WITH HIS PUNY HEAD.
HE CAN BARELY COMPUTE THE VALUE OF PI WITH THAT TINY BRAIN.
No...I'm the Leader... I'm really smart...
HAH! YOU'LL NEVER RULE THE WORLD, SIMPLETON. PERHAPS GO INTO TEACHING.
FAH. HE WOULD BARELY MAKE TENURE WITH THAT WEE SKULL.
Stop picking on him!
He does too have a big head!
SCRRRRRRR

MY CHAIR IS FLAWED--I'VE COME LOOSE!
MINE IS DESTROYED-- BUT IT IS NO MATTER! HULDOC'S BODY CAN EASILY SUPPORT SUCH HEAD WEIGHT!
AND USE IT IN A MANNER...
...THIS PRIMITIVE WILL UNDERSTAND!
KTHOOOMM
IF HE EVER WAKES UP!
KZZZRZZZZAAAPPP!

I must correct the flaw in this hoverchair.
THE FLAW IS WITH YOU! YOU ARE LOSING PRECIOUS BRAIN MASS!
My cranium!
YOU ARE LOSING HUNDREDS OF I.Q. POINTS BY THE SECOND--IF YOU WEREN'T SO STUPID NOW, YOU COULD TELL WHAT'S HAPPENING!
YOUR MUTANT HEALING POWER IS CAUSING YOU TO REVERT TO YOUR ORIGINAL FORM.
IF HIS BODY IS REJECTING THE M.O.D.O.C. PROCESS...
...THIS MEANS THE CONVERSION ISN'T PERMANENT! WE'LL ALL EVENTUALLY REVERT TO DRIBBLING IDIOTS!
Ya think I'm down, fat heads?!
I'm just gettin' started!
MMMMMRRRRR--
Aw man, I'm going to get blamed for this too.
KARL

OF COURSE WE'RE NEXT TO THE LEADER'S SECRET BASE.
Huh?
KARL
Great minds think alike?
M.O.D.O.C.! OUR TRANSFORMATION ISN'T PERMANENT!
WE'RE GOING TO REVERT TO SUB-BRILLIANT!
YES...THE CHAMBER EXPLODED BEFORE IT COULD FINISH THE SEQUENCE.
YOU CAN THANK KARL FOR THAT.
CAN YOU HALT THE REVERSION?
YES... IF YOU HELP ME CONQUER THE WORLD.
OUR MISSION IS TO KEEP THE PEACE AND SAVE LIVES!
THEN HOW BETTER TO HAVE ORDER THAN RUN THE PLANET?
TRUE, THAT WILL MAKE EVERYONE SAFER.
WE WOULD BE EXCELLENT MASTERS.
THEN COME BEFORE THIS DISPERSAL UNIT. A SPECIFIC SEQUENCE OF MEGAVOLT BURSTS IS WHAT WILL SEAL THE CELLULAR BONDS.
What...? No...

IT WILL ONLY TAKE A FEW SECONDS, MY ALLIES.
NOOOOO!
KKZZZ ZZZZZZZZZZZ
-verine...
He's coming to!
At last!

We wasted a couple of hours trying to rebuild the equipment.
But Karl was helping us, so w
failed and turne
back to normal
KAR
Where's M.O.D.O.C.?
He's on his way to prison, nursing the world's largest headache.
Thanks for electrocuting yourself!
Had you not stopped the process, we'd all be super-villains by now--and ugly!
That was my next question. If the process reversed itself...
...how come Banner's head hasn't shrunk back down?
What?! No, is...
Oh.
Jerk.
The End

The Multiverse was destroyed! The heroes of Earth-616 and Earth-1610 were powerless to save it! Now, all that remains...is BATTLEWORLD! A massive, patchwork planet composed of the fragments of worlds that no longer exist, maintained by the iron will of its god and master, VICTOR VON DOOM! Each region is a domain unto itself — and the domain of KILLVILLE is protected by its deadliest citizen...

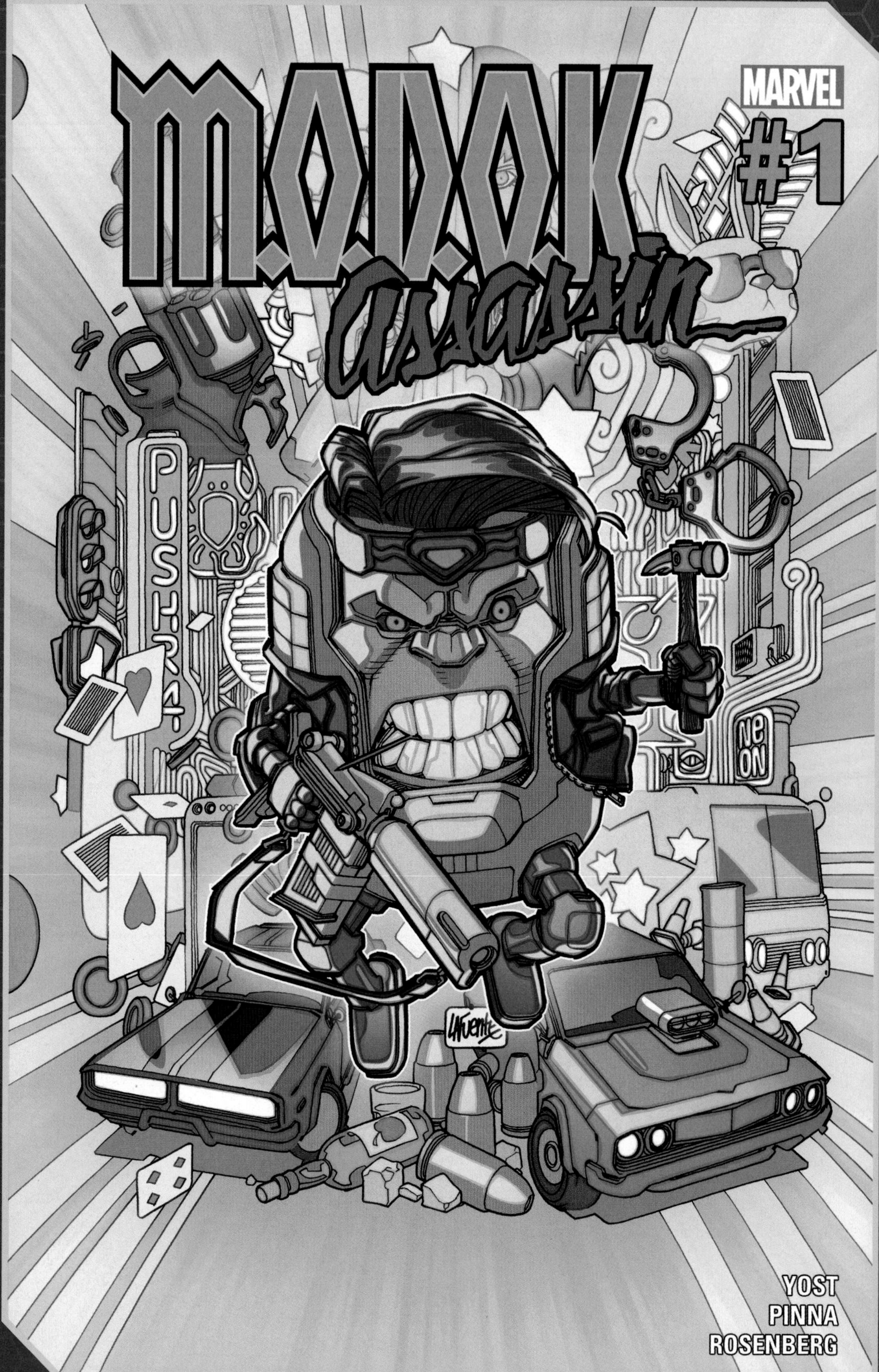

IN THE BEGINNING, THERE WAS NOTHING.
NOTHING EXCEPT THE LORD GOD DOOM. >>>UNACCEPTABLE>>>

DOOM SAVED US ALL, IT IS KNOWN/// UNKNOWN.
THE SCIENCE BEHIND THIS IS UNACCEPTABLE/// BEYOND QUESTION.

LORD DOOM WATCHES OVER US, RULING WITH AN IRON FIST. HIS COUNCIL AT HIS SIDE.
>>>UNACCEPTABLE>>>

THIS IS BATTLEWORLD.
<<<ACCEPTABLE<<<

THESE LARGER QUESTIONS OF COSMOGONY AND THE RULE OF DOOM <<KILL>> ARE NOT THE PURPOSE OF MY DESIGN.
ALTHOUGH AS THE LIVING EMBODIMENT OF SCIENCE, THEY ARE IMPOSSIBLE TO IGNORE.

TODAY I AM FOCUSED ON AN INTELLECT NAMED *OTTO OCTAVIUS*.
NOTE!! WHEN I SAY "INTELLECT," THIS IS <<<SARCASM<<<.
THERE IS A 100% CHANCE HE WILL DIE TODAY.

OCTAVIUS HAS BEEN TARGETED BY THE ASSASSINS GUILD AND AN OPERATIVE HAS ALREADY BEEN DISPATCHED.
THOK
THOK

THE ASSASSIN'S NAME IS *BULLSEYE*, AND HE NEVER MISSES HIS TARGET. <<INCORRECT>>
BUT THAT IS NOT WHY HIS DEATH IS A CERTAINTY.

THUS, WE COME BACK TO THE QUESTION OF *PURPOSE*.
NOT TO SERVE. <<KILL>> NOT TO PHILOSOPHIZE. <<KILL>>
I WAS DESIGNED FOR ONLY ONE THING.

BOOM
I AM THE MENTAL ORGANISM DESIGNED ONLY FOR KILLING!
I AM M.O.D.O.K.!

TAK TAK TAK TAK
WHAT ARE YOU DOING, YOU GIANT FREAK?!
THIS IS A SANCTIONED HIT!!

PATHETIC LITTLE MAN...YOU BELIEVE YOU CAN KILL ME WITH A *KNIFE?* WATCH AS I SEIZE IT IN MIDAIR!!
I AM *M.O.D.O.K.!* I KNOW EVERYTHING THERE IS TO KNOW ABOUT KILLING! I AM--

SLIK
AN IDIOT WHO TALKS TOO MUCH.
GAAAH!!

YOU'RE BREAKING THE RULES HERE, NOT ME. YOU'RE INTERFERING WITH THE *ASSASSINS GUILD.*
AND WORSE THAN THAT... YOU MADE ME *MISS.*

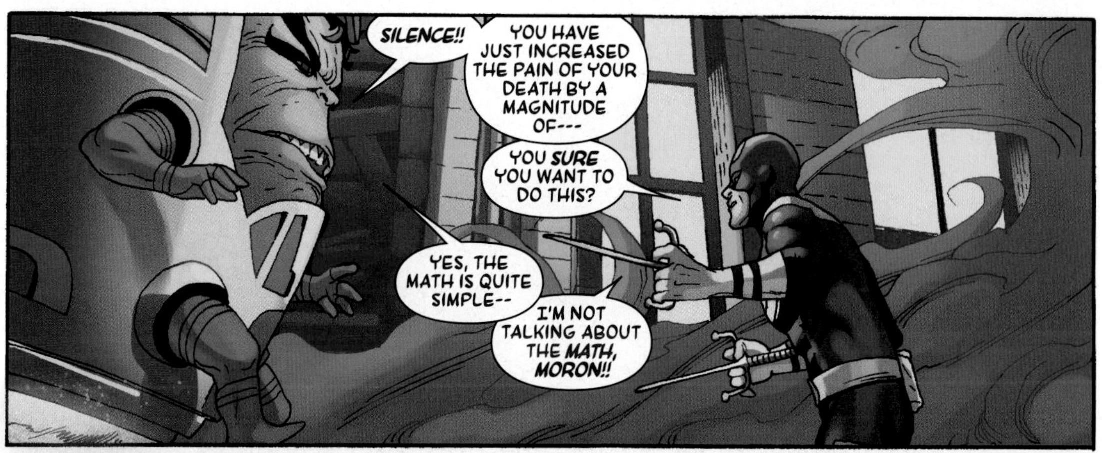
SILENCE!!
YOU HAVE JUST INCREASED THE PAIN OF YOUR DEATH BY A MAGNITUDE OF---
YOU SURE YOU WANT TO DO THIS?
YES, THE MATH IS QUITE SIMPLE--
I'M NOT TALKING ABOUT THE MATH, MORON!!

I'M TALKING ABOUT ME PUTTING A BLADE IN THAT GIANT SKULL OF YOURS!!
DIEE!!!!

HA HA! YOU MISSED YET AGAIN, ONCE MORE MAKING YOUR CLAIMS OF NEVER MISSING INCREASINGLY <<<STUPID<<<!
SPAK
WHAT?!
MY FORCE FIELD INTERCEPTS THE CHILDISH PLAYING CARD, WHILE THE SAI...HAD A VARIABLE AMOUNT OF SPIN ON IT, CONFOUNDING MY CALCULATIONS.

RRAAA!
IT IS POSSIBLE HIS DISMEMBERED BRAIN WILL PROVE VALUABLE.
CHUNK
THIS IS <<<UNACCEPTABLE<<<.

BUT WHILE YOUR STRIKE WAS MARGINALLY SUCCESSFUL, MINE WAS MUCH MORE SO.
HMM. AN INTERESTING PROJECTION OF FUTURE EVENTS.
UHHNN... GONNA KILL... YOU...

LET ME OFFER YOU A MORE >>>SCIENTIFIC>>> ESTIMATION.
THE POWER OF MY UNPARALLELED MIND WILL FOCUS ON YOUR MUCH MORE LIMITED BRAIN. I WILL UNLEASH THAT POWER...
YOU CAN'T--!
AND YOU WILL DIE!
YYEARRGHH!!

IT WOULD SEEM MY ESTIMATION WAS MUCH MORE ACCURATE.
LOOK AT THE EXPRESSION ON HIS FACE. IT IS <<<HYSTERICAL<<<.

OH, GOD, THANK YOU, THANK YOU, THANK YOU...YOU SAVED MY LIFE--
THIS IS <<<OBVIOUS>>>. THE ASSASSINS GUILD'S CLIENT WANTED THE SENTINEL TECHNOLOGY YOU STOLE FROM THE LABS OF ADVANCED IDEA MECHANICS.
MY LABS.
OH, NO.

SPAF
100% CERTAINTY OF DEATH.

OCTAVIUS WAS NO MATCH FOR MY >>>GENIUS>>>. I ALLOWED HIM TO LEAVE WITH THE S-TECH SO THAT I COULD IDENTIFY HIS PAYMASTERS.
BULLSEYE'S INVOLVEMENT COMPLICATED THINGS. THE TECHNOLOGY CANNOT BE ALLOWED ON THE OPEN MARKET AS IT WOULD INCRIMINATE ME.

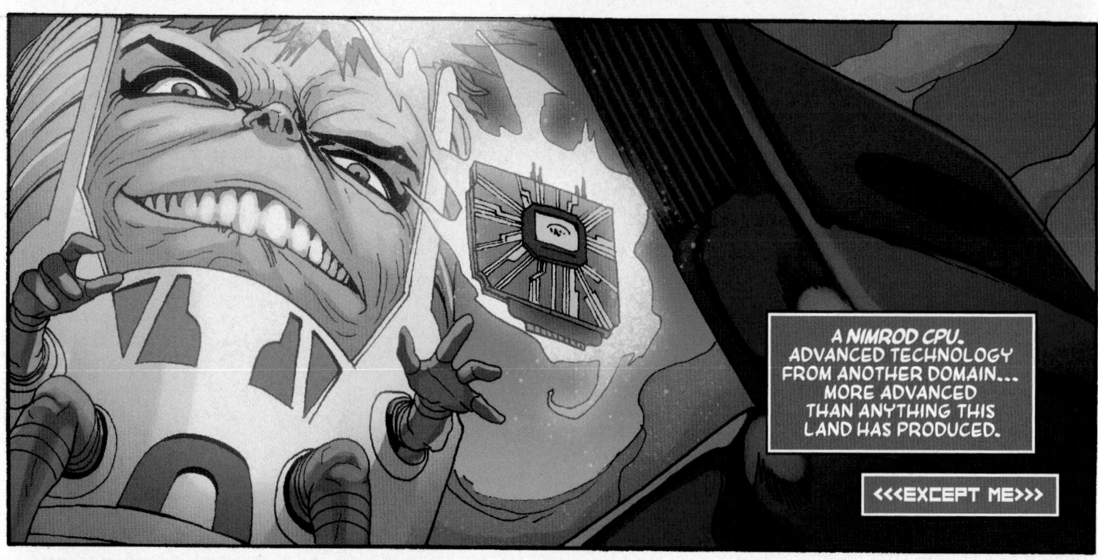
A NIMROD CPU. ADVANCED TECHNOLOGY FROM ANOTHER DOMAIN... MORE ADVANCED THAN ANYTHING THIS LAND HAS PRODUCED.
<<<EXCEPT ME>>>

THE TECHNOLOGY'S PRESENCE IS ILLEGAL, OF COURSE.
THE LAW, IF SUCH A THING EXISTS HERE, AS ENFORCED BY...
OH, HELLO, KARL...OR SHOULD I SAY...
M.O.D.O.K.!!

BARON MORDO!
YOU TRULY DO LOVE TO HEAR YOURSELF TALK, DON'T YOU, MONSTER?
BE QUICK ABOUT THIS, MY BARON. I CANNOT STOMACH LOOKING AT THIS ABOMINATION OF SCIENCE.
YOUR INSULTS ARE MEANINGLESS, CLEA.
AND AS TO YOUR TAUNTS, BARON...
<<<KILL<<<
HOW MAY I SERVE YOU?

DO NOT PLAY GAMES WITH ME, ***M.O.D.O.K.*** AS BARON, I TOLERATE YOU... BUT ONLY JUST.
INCORRECT. YOU ***NEED*** ME.
AND YET, YOU ARE DETERMINED TO FIND YOURSELF ATOP THE ***SHIELD*** OR UNDER THE HAMMERS OF THE ***THORS.***
THEY ARE WELCOME TO ***TRY.***

THE ASSASSINS GUILD WILL NOT LET THIS STAND. BULLSEYE WAS MUCH LOVED BY THE TRIUMVIRATE. THEY WILL HAVE YOUR HEAD, ASSUMING THEY COULD FIND A WALL BIG ENOUGH TO MOUNT IT ON.
BUT I AM MORE CURIOUS ABOUT THEIR TARGET. WHY DID THEY WANT THE ***OCTOPUS?***

YOU WILL HAVE TO ASK ***BULLSEYE.*** ***OH! ERROR!*** YOU <<<CANNOT<<<.

FUNNY.
CORRECT.
>>>IT WAS!>>>

ENOUGH. I FEEL THE BILE RISING IN MY THROAT JUST LOOKING AT THIS THING.
YOU THINK YOU ARE ABOVE THE LAW, ***M.O.D.O.K.,*** BUT YOU ARE ***NOT.***
I AM THE LAW HERE. I AM THE HAND OF ***DOOM.*** AND SHOULD YOU EVER THINK TO CROSS ME...
...YOU WILL FEEL MY ***WRATH.***

MAIM. EXPLODE. DISMEMBER. EVISCERATE.
<<<KILL<<<
WHAT ELSE WOULD I PLAN FOR ***MORDO?*** FOR HIS LOVER? FOR ***ALL*** OF THEM?
AFTER ALL...

...THIS IS KILLVILLE.

THE SHEEP GO ABOUT THEIR BUSINESS, LIVING IN FEAR.
THEY KNOW BETTER THAN TO COME OUT AT NIGHT.
<<<FACT!<<< STATISTICALLY, THE DAY IS NO BETTER.
KILL

THEY HIDE BEHIND DOORS THAT WILL NOT SAVE THEM, THEY COWER BEHIND BARS THAT GIVE THEM NO COMFORT.
THIS CITY IS FILLED WITH KILLERS AND VILLAINS AND <<<MONSTERS<<< WAGING WAR AMONGST THEMSELVES, THE COLLATERAL DAMAGE IS IMPRESSIVE.
THE PEOPLE HAVE NO HEROES LEFT TO PROTECT THEM.

BECAUSE I KILLED THEM ALL.

THE OCEAN TO THE NORTH STILL SHOWS GRAVITATIONAL DISTORTION FROM THAT TIME I KILLED GRAVITRON. IT TURNS OUT HE WAS NOT MORE POWERFUL THAN A BLACK HOLE.
HE WAS VERY SURPRISED, WHICH WAS A <<<DELIGHT>>>.

TO THE WEST, THE MONARCHY OF M...A WORLD FILLED WITH AND RULED BY GENETIC ANOMALIES.
THEY CALL THEMSELVES HOMO SUPERIOR, BUT <<<NONE ARE SUPERIOR TO M.O.D.O.K.<<<.

TO THE SOUTH, A CITY DROWNING IN <<<TEMPORAL STUPIDITY<<<.
DESPITE THEIR INABILITY TO USE CALENDARS, THE FUTURE-CATTLE OF 2099 KNOW BETTER THAN TO INFRINGE ON MY TERRITORY.

AND TO THE EAST...

...THE SENTINEL TERRITORIES.

A LAND OCCUPIED BY GIANT ROBOTS.
THE SENTINELS ARE TECHNOLOGICALLY ADVANCED BUT PATHETICALLY >>>LIMITED>>> IN THEIR DESIGN.
THEY KILL ONLY <<<MUTANTS<<<.

THEY CAN SENSE THE MONARCHY OF M. THEY FEEL THE MUTANTS THERE. THEY *HUNGER* TO KILL EACH AND EVERY ONE OF THEM.
BUT THEY DARE NOT! FOR TO CROSS OVER INTO KILLVILLE IS TO INCUR MY WRATH!

IN THIS, THEY SHOW THEIR INTELLIGENCE.
FOR THE MOST PART.
MUTANT SIGNATURE DETECTED.

BOOOM

THE MONARCHY OF M, HOWEVER, FEELS THE NEED TO SHOW THEIR <<<LACK<<< OF INTELLIGENCE.

THEY TOO ARE AWARE OF THE *SENTINEL TERRITORIES*, AND WILL OCCASIONALLY SEND ONE OF THEIR OWN TO *INVESTIGATE*.

IN THIS CASE... A *THIEF*.

IMPRESSIVE.

CAS

HE MADE IT OUT OF THE SENTINEL TERRITORIES AND BACK INTO *KILLVILLE*.

AN INTERESTING QUESTION ARISES...THE SENTINELS FEAR ME, BUT THEY LIVE ONLY TO KILL MUTANTS.

CAN THEY DENY THEIR NATURE? CAN THEY REJECT THAT WHICH THEY WERE DESIGNED FOR?

>>>THE ANSWER IS NO>>>
THIS MUTANT IS DEAD AS <<<@#$%<<<.

NO LESS THAN A THIEF DESERVES, REALLY.
UHNN!
BOOOM BOOOM BOOOM BOOOM

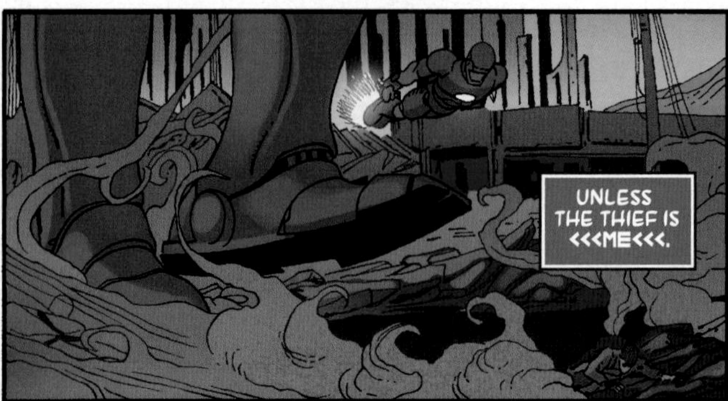
UNLESS THE THIEF IS <<<ME<<<.

TERMINATION OF TARGET LEBEAU, REMY, A.K.A. GAMBIT, IN PROGRESS.

YOU ARE MISTAKEN, ROBOT!

THE ONE KNOWN AS M.O.D.O.K. SHALL NOT INTERFERE!
THE ONES KNOWN AS SENTINELS ARE NO BETTER THAN PROGRAMMABLE <<<TOASTERS<<<.
WHAT HAVE YOU LEARNED ABOUT CROSSING INTO KILLVILLE?
...KILL?

SQWAAARK!!
CHOOOM
EXACTLY.

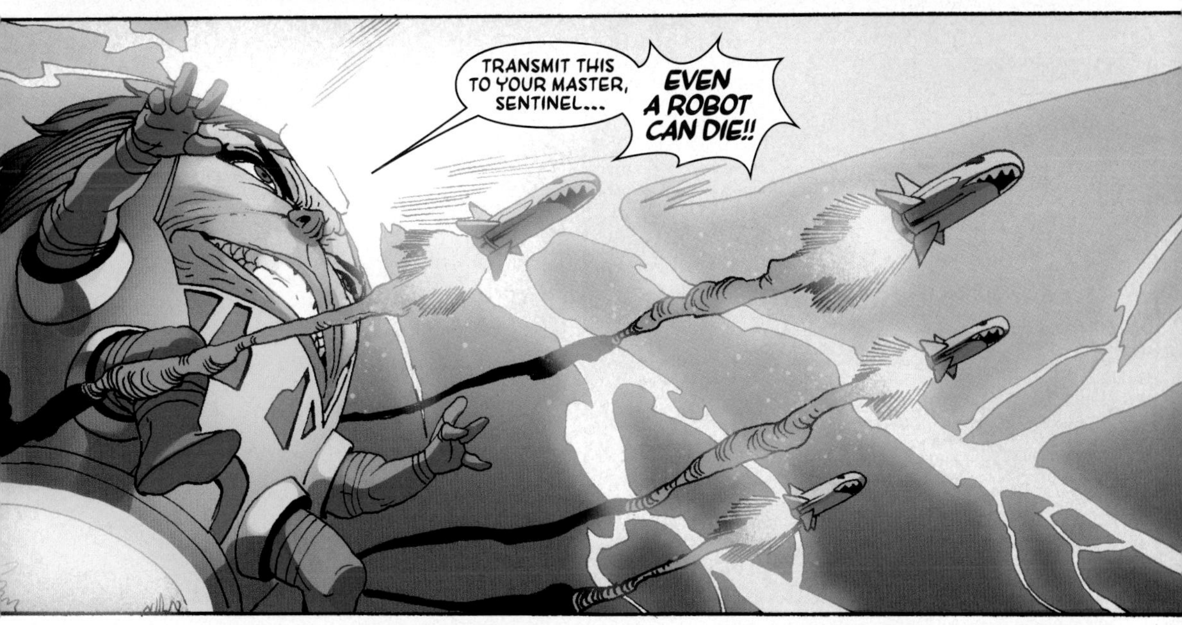
TRANSMIT THIS TO YOUR MASTER, SENTINEL...
EVEN A ROBOT CAN DIE!!

NEW TARGET: M.O.D.O.K.
EXTERMINATE!
THE SENTINELS ARE ADAPTIVE... BUT NOT ADAPTIVE ENOUGH TO OVERCOME ME.
THIS IS WHY BARON MORDO NEEDS ME.

KRA-KOOOM

BE IT MAN OR MACHINE, IT MATTERS NOT.

I AM DESIGNED ONLY FOR KILLING!!

ATTENTION, SENTINEL MAIN "INTELLIGENCE!"
NOTE THAT I AM ONCE MORE USING THE WORD *INTELLIGENCE* WITH QUOTES INDICATING *SARCASM* AND *INSULT!*

IF ANY OF YOUR ODDLY COLORFUL AUTOMATONS *DARE* CROSS INTO KILLVILLE, THEY WILL BE UTTERLY AND COMPLETELY <<<DESTROYED<<<!
AND THEN I WILL FIND YOU, *MASTER MOLD* OR WHATEVER YOU ARE CALLING YOURSELF...

AND I WILL REPROGRAM YOU TO ONLY LOVE MUTANTS, AND POSSIBLY TURN YOU INTO MY <<<PET<<<.
IS THIS <<<UNDERSTOOD?!<<<

MON AMI... THANK YOU.
THE HOUSE OF MAGNUS WILL PAY YOU FOR--
I CANNOT HELP BUT NOTICE YOU ARE TRESPASSING IN KILLVILLE.
WHAT?

PAF
HAHAHAHA! THAT NEVER GETS OLD.
TODAY HAS BEEN A GOOD DAY.

UNTIL NOW.
BOOOOOM

THE SKY EXPLODES ABOVE ME.

THE WHOLE WORLD COMES CRASHING DOWN.

SCIENCE DOES NOT ALLOW FOR THE EXISTENCE OF HEAVEN OR HELL.
ONLY DOOM.
SO THIS IS NEITHER DEMON...

...NOR ANGEL.
A THOR HAS JUST FALLEN AT MY FEET.
<<<KILL>>>
<<<KILL>>>
<<<KILL>>>
I HAVE ALWAYS WANTED TO KILL A THOR. SHE IS...SHE...
SHE IS REALLY QUITE >>>LOVELY>>>.

MODOK
MARVEL 002
NOT THE BEES
YOST
PINNA
PALLOT
TADEO
ROSENBERG

THE MONARCHY OF M.
TWO HOURS AGO.
HAVE AT THEE!!

ONE HOUR AGO.
THE HUMAN EXTREMISTS ARE A GROWING PROBLEM, AS ARE THE SENTINEL TERRITORIES.
GOD DOOM *MUST*--
SURELY YOU WOULD NOT SUGGEST THAT THERE IS ANYTHING GOD DOOM ***MUST*** DO, KING MAGNUS?

...OF COURSE NOT. THE MONARCHY CONTINUES TO BE DOOM'S MOST LOYAL SUBJECTS, AS ALWAYS.
YOU HAVE MY FAMILY'S GRATITUDE, THOR.

VERILY.
SHOULD THE MACHINES CROSS YOUR BORDERS, KNOW THAT THEY WILL FACE DOOM'S WRATH.
AND WHAT OF ***KILLVILLE?*** THERE ARE RUMORS OF MONSTERS, OF ***ATROCITIES--***

YOU FEAR THESE ASSASSINS AND MURDERERS? NOT I.
THEY WILL FEAR ME.

THE BORDER BETWEEN THE MONARCHY OF M AND KILLVILLE.
FIVE MINUTES AGO.

SHRACK
YEAAARGH!

SKREEEEEE--

BOOOM

KILLVILLE.
NOW.

HNN... WHAT...

...WHO DARES...

UH. HELLO.
YOU SEEM TO HAVE, ER... >>>FALLEN>>>.
WHO--?

I AM M.O.D.O.K., MENTAL ORGANISM DESIGNED ONLY FOR KILL--

DIE, FOUL MONSTER!!!
GAAHH!!

OOOOOOWOWWWWW-

I CANNOT REACH MY NOSE TO STOP THE BLEEDING. AND WHEREAS I WOULD NORMALLY BE ENRAGED, I FEEL ONLY...

<<<EMBARRASSED<<<.

PERHAPS THIS *THOR* HAS ADDITIONAL EMPATHIC ABILITIES THAT ARE MANIPULATING MY DID YOU SEE HER SWING THAT SWORD IT WAS <<MAGNIFICENT>>--

NO! FOCUS! WHY THE SWORD, NOT THE HAMMER? SOMETHING IS <<<WRONG<<<.

SHE DRIPS WITH POWER AND MAGIC AND <<<LOVELINESS NO NO NO NO UNACCEPTABLE.
KILL HER. KILL HER. NOTE THE WAY HER SKIN GLISTENS--

GAAHH!
PERHAPS WE SHOULD TALK ABOUT THIS, PERHAPS OVER A NICE CHAMOMILE TEA--
AARGH!!

SHRACK
UHN!!
BECAUSE I AM SUCH AN EFFICIENT KILLING MACHINE, I UNLEASH A TELEKINETIC ATTACK. I DO SO WITHOUT EVEN *THINKING.*
IT IS INSTINCT. MY DESIGN.

YET I AM FILLED WITH...WAIT, THERE IS A WORD FOR IT...REGRET?
ONLY FOR KILLING. ONLY FOR KILLING. ONLY FOR--
ARE YOU HURT? I DID NOT MEAN TO HURT YOU EXCEPT THAT YOU WERE TRYING TO KILL ME. DO YOU NEED A <<<BAND-AID<<< I BELIEVE I HAVE ONE--
SHE LOOKS UP, HER RADIANT SCARLET HAIR PARTING TO REVEAL HER EYES. HER EYES, SO FILLED WITH MURDER AND RAGE AND HATE AND KILL.
I HAVE NEVER SEEN ANYTHING SO <<<BEAUTIFUL>>>.
RRRUMMMMBLE
HM.
IT WOULD APPEAR IT IS GOING TO RAIN, PERHAPS WE SHOULD FIND COVER.
THERE IS NO SAFE HAVEN FROM WHAT COMES NOW, GROTESQUERY. FOR NOW COMES THE THUNDER.
TO ME, DEVILSLAYER!
DEVILSLAYER?

SHE NAMED HER HAMMER DEVILSLAYER. SHE IS <<<INCREDIBLE>>>.

BUT AS I SO ACCURATELY OBSERVED, SOMETHING IS INDEED *WRONG*. THE HAMMER IS BEING INTERFERED WITH.

POLICE STATION
POLICE DEPARTMENT
POLICE
KILLVILLE POLICE HEADQUARTERS.
"HKK... CAN'T...CAN'T BREATHE..."

TELL ME HOW HE DIED!!
SHE CAN'T SAY ANYTHING IF SHE'S DEAD.
LET HER TALK...

...THEN KILL HER.

HE DIED...HE DIED OF A MASSIVE BRAIN HEMORRHAGE...
PLEASE... PLEASE DON'T KILL ME.

SO IT'S TRUE. THIS IS M.O.D.O.K.'S WORK.
WAS THERE EVER ANY DOUBT?
OPEN IT, SHROUD. I WANT TO SEE HIM.

I WANT TO SEE WHAT WAS DONE TO *BULLSEYE.*

THE TRIAD OF THE ASSASSINS GUILD.
VIPER.
HE WAS UNDER THE PROTECTION OF THE ASSASSINS GUILD.
KINGPIN.
BARON MORDO WILL NOT ACT. HE STILL FEELS HE NEEDS *M.O.D.O.K.*
THIS CANNOT STAND.
SHROUD.
TO DEFY MORDO IS TO INVITE DOOM.
WE REQUIRE *PATIENCE. M.O.D.O.K.'S* ARROGANCE WILL CAUSE HIM TO CROSS EVERY LINE, AND ON THAT DAY...

...HE WILL *PAY.*

THE DARK DOMAIN
OF MORDO,
BARON OF KILLVILLE.
GRIFFITH PARK.

FINALLY
FINALLY
FINALLY.

ORINI.

SHOOM
THERE
IS NEWS, MY
BARON.

...KARL?

I AM HERE, MY LOVE.
WHAT IS THIS PLACE? WHAT DO YOU DO IN HERE?
YOU FEAR THE DARK, CLEA?
HERE, THE DARK IS CLAY FOR ME TO MOLD. IN THIS PLACE, I BEND IT TO MY WILL.
NOW TELL ME YOUR NEWS.
SOMETHING IS HAPPENING. REPORTS OF A BATTLE... M.O.D.O.K. AND A THOR.
IS THAT SO?

FOR DOOMGARD!!
TIME STANDS STILL <<NOT LITERALLY>>> AS SHE LEAPS ABOVE ME, FULLY INTENT ON DRIVING A SPEAR THROUGH MY FACE.
INSTEAD OF RUNNING THROUGH THE SEVENTY-THREE WAYS I COULD KILL HER, I ADMIRE HER BEAUTY, HER DRIVE...AND WHATEVER THOSE RIBBONS ARE DOING.
RAAA!
FWOOSH
AND FOR THE FIRST TIME IN MY LIFE, I REALIZE I DO NOT WISH TO KILL SOMEONE.
<<<THIS IS A PROBLEM>>>
LADY THOR! THERE IS NO NEED FOR THIS!
NAY. THERE IS A DEEP-ROOTED DESIRE FOR SPLITTING YOUR GIANT, FREAKISH HEAD LIKE A MELON.
YOU THINK WE HAVE NOT HEARD OF YOU, MURDERER? M.O.D.O.K., ASSASSIN?
SHE HAS <<<HEARD OF ME!<<<
ONLY BY DOOM'S GRACE HAVE WE NOT HURLED YOU TO THE DEADLANDS. BUT NOW...YOU HAVE CROSSED THE LINE.
YOU BELIEVE YOU CAN ATTACK A THOR?!
WHAT IF I TOLD YOU THERE HAS BEEN SOME KIND OF TERRIBLE YET <<<POTENTIALLY CHARMING<<< MISUNDERSTANDING HERE?
HM. SHE LOOKS ANGRIER SOMEHOW.

UNDERSTAND THIS!!

OH, LOOK AT THAT. SHE IS COMING TO <<<KILL ME>>>.

I RESPECT THIS.

YOU MUST LISTEN TO ME!

I RECOGNIZE THAT I AM ATTACKING YOU NOW, BUT I DID NOT ATTACK YOU <<<PREVIOUSLY.

YOU LIE!

I AM NOT DESIGNED FOR <<<LYING<<< EXCEPT WHEN IT SUITS MY PURPOSES!

WAIT!! I DID NOT MEAN TO SAY THAT LAST PART OUT LOUD!!

IT WILL BE THE LAST THING YOU EVER SAY.

...I HAVE NO WORDS TO DESCRIBE HOW I FEEL SEEING HER WIELD MY CHAINSAW.

I COULD NOT FOCUS ENOUGH TO <<<EXPLODE HER BRAIN<<< EVEN IF I WANTED TO.

BRRREEEE
LISTEN TO ME!
I DID NOT ATTACK YOU! I DID NOT EVEN KNOW YOU WERE IN KILLVILLE UNTIL YOU CRASHED INTO IT!
KILL

LISTEN TO A KILLER? TO A CORRUPTION OF SCIENCE?
NO, YOU FOUL, REPUGNANT, DISGUSTING--
YOU HAVE MADE YOUR POINT...

NOW THERE IS ONLY BATTLE!
NYEARGH!
SHRAK

WHAT TREACHERY IS THIS?
IT IS MY NULL BOMB, A WEAPON OF MY OWN DESIGN.
IT IS QUITE A PIECE OF WORK, IF I AM BEING HONEST. I CREATED IT TO KILL GRAVITON AND NOW I WILL SEE IF IT CAN KILL A--
KILL

THOR.
NO.

I CANNOT QUITE EXPLAIN WHAT IS TRANSPIRING HERE.
AS THE NULL BOMB EXPLODES, I FIND MYSELF NOT SAVORING THE DEATH OF MY ENEMY, BUT INSTEAD...INSTEAD...
I FIND MYSELF TRYING TO *SAVE* HER.
THE NULL ENERGY FLOWS INTO ME, ANYONE ELSE WOULD BE <<<DEAD>>> BY NOW. BUT I AM M.O.D.O.K. AND--AND--AND--
I HOPE SHE <<<NOTICES.

I...I LIVE.
HOW...
UHNN...
YOU.
THIS ENDS NOW, YOU WRETCHED...
...WRETCHED...
IT IS MY DUTY. YOU ARE A MONSTER, AN ASSASSIN...YOU ATTACKED ME...
SCRAAPE
HNNN...
GAAH!!!
<<<ERROR!>>> ROCKET CHASSIS REBOOTING... I CANNOT MOVE!
THAT IS A VERY BIG <<<AXE<<<.
BUT AS I PREPARE TO DIE, AS THE GREATEST KILLER THIS WORLD HAS EVER KNOWN PREPARE TO BE KILLED...
...EVEN NOW, I CANNOT BE MAD AT HER.

RRAAAA!!!
SHUNK

YOU... MISSED?
<<INCORRECT>>
NO. YOU DID NOT. YOU SPARED ME.

YOU RISKED YOUR OWN LIFE TO SAVE ME.
WHY WOULD YOU DO THIS?
IT...IS COMPLICATED. BUT I DID NOT ATTACK YOU.

NO... I SENSE THE TRUTH IN YOUR WORDS.
BUT IF NOT YOU... THEN WHO? WHO WOULD DARE ATTACK A THOR?

I DO NOT KNOW. BUT TOGETHER... TOGETHER, WE CAN...
COULD YOU PLEASE HELP ME UP?!

THE ASSASSINS GUILD. KILLVILLE.
I UNDERSTAND.
WHAT DID THEY SAY?
EVERYTHING WE HOPED FOR. M.O.DO.K. HAS ANGERED THE WRONG PEOPLE.
AND THE ASSASSINS GUILD HAS BEEN HIRED TO KILL THE INSUFFERABLE BASTARD.
FINALLY!!
WHO DO WE SEND?
IT'S SIMPLE, VIPER.

SEND EVERYONE.

M.O.D.O.K
Assassin
MARVEL
003
LAFUENTE
YOST
PINNA
PALLOT
ROSENBERG

KILLVILLE.
37 MINUTES FROM NOW.
REPAI
ELETRON
OF
THERE IS NOTHING TO BE <<<CONCERNED>>> ABOUT HERE.
JUST A FEW *MINOR* >>>COMPLICATIONS.

NOW!
I AM ANALYZING THOR'S HAMMER TO FIND OUT WHY IT WILL NOT RETURN TO HER STRONG, YET TENDER, HAND.
BUT I AM SECRETLY LOOKING AT THOR HERSELF IN A VERY SUBTLE, "PERIPHERAL VISION" KIND OF WAY. HER POWER, BEAUTY AND WILLINGNESS TO KILL ME WITH AN AXE STIR THINGS WITHIN ME I HAVE NOT FELT SINCE...ANOTHER LIFE.
YOU ARE A THING OF >>>BEAUTY.
...WHAT?
ER, THE HAMMER. I WAS REFERRING TO THE HAMMER.
THIS MAKES NO SENSE. THE OTHER THORS SHOULD HAVE REALIZED THAT I HAVE NOT RETURNED YET. SHOULD BE COMING FOR ME.
HOW WOULD THEY FIND YOU?
BY SCIENCE OR MAGIC, WE ALWAYS FIND A WAY TO PROTECT OUR OWN.
AND THAT IS WHEN I REALIZE I CANNOT SEE HER...THAT IS, I CAN SEE HER. MY TECHNOLOGY CANNOT.
SHE IS CLOAKED.
SOMEONE IS TARGETING YOU.
NONE WOULD DARE.
<<<INCORRECT.>>>
I HAVE RUN MANY SIMULATIONS AND HAVE ATTAINED A 63.76% KILL RATE AGAINST MULTIPLE TH--
SELF EDIT! SELF EDIT!
MULTIPLE WHAT?
IT DOES NOT MATTER! I WILL HELP YOU!
YOU WILL HELP ME?

YOU ARE A MONSTER, A KILLER.
I SAVED YOUR LIFE!
WHAT DO YOU WANT?
I DO NOT UNDERSTAND.
THAK
YOU ARE NOT BARON HERE, IN THIS LAND OF MURDER. YOU REVEL IN KILLING.
>>>KILLING CAN SOLVE MANY PROBLEMS.
IS THERE NO MORE TO YOU THAN THIS?
THOK
SHE FRUSTRATES ME WITH THESE COMPLICATED QUESTIONS. "THERE IS NO MORE TO ME THAN THIS," I WANT TO SCREAM.
BUT WHEN I LOOK AT HER--
WHAT?
LOOK. A >>>PUMPKIN.
I KNOW THAT PUMPKIN. THAT MEANS...
>>>UH-OH.
DOWN!!

DOES EVERYTHING IN THIS DOOM-DAMNED KINGDOM EXPLODE?!
NORMALLY, I QUITE >>>ADMIRE THAT QUALITY ABOUT KILLVILLE.
THEN ENJOY IT WHILE YOU CAN, FATHEAD.
BECAUSE IT'S THE LAST THING YOU'RE EVER GOING TO ENJOY.
YOU KNOW, UNLESS YOU ENJOY DEATH.
DESIGNED ONLY FOR DYING.
JACK O'LANTERN.
BOOMERANG.
SCREAMING MIMI.
ASSASSINS.

YOU ARE ATTACKING M.O.D.O.K.? IS THE ASSASSINS' GUILD AWARE THAT YOU ARE SUICIDAL? BECAUSE THAT AFFECTS YOUR ELIGIBILITY FOR HEALTH INSURANCE.
THE GUILD SENT US, GENIUS.
WHAT?! THEY WOULD NOT-- WAIT, IS THIS BECAUSE OF THE BULLSEYE THING?

NOPE. SOMEONE PUT A HIT OUT ON YOU.
YOU HAD TO HAVE KNOWN THIS WAS COMING.
HIT HIT HIT...

HOW LONG HAVE YOU BEEN RUNNING AROUND HERE, KILLING WHOEVER YOU WANT, THINKING YOU'RE ABOVE THE LAW?
IT WAS ONLY A MATTER OF TIME, AND GUESS WHAT? TIME JUST RAN OUT, FREAKSHOW.

SKRREEEEEEEEE
HNNN!
AAAH!!
IN RETROSPECT, I SET MYSELF UP FOR THAT ONE.
YOU'RE HANGING AROUND WITH THE WRONG PEOPLE, RED. CONTRACT PAYS EXTRA FOR YOU.
YOU WISH ME DEAD?
COME AND GET ME.
BOOM BOOM BOOM
AAAHH!
SHUNK
YOU ARE MAKING A TERRIBLE AND LETHAL <<<MISTAKE>>>, BOOMERANG. LOOK AT HER!!
YOU ARE ATTACKING A THOR.
BOOM
BOOM
YEAH? IF SHE'S A THOR, THEN WHERE'S HER HAMMER?
IT IS RIGHT OVER THERE, YOU IMBECILE!!

HM. BOOMERANG DID NOT APPRECIATE THAT.

THOK

HE WAS ALWAYS **SENSITIVE.**

BOOM

LET GO!!

YOU BELIEVE I NEED MY HAMMER TO DEAL WITH YOU?!

WHAT HAMMER?! WHAT ARE YOU TALKING ABOUT?!

I SPEAK OF YOUR DEATH, VEGETABLE-FACED KILLER!!

AGH!

LEAVE HIM ALONEEE

NYEARRGHH!

THEY SEEM VERY SERIOUS ABOUT THIS. PERHAPS I HAVE BEEN >>>UNKIND TO THE ASSASSINS' GUILD OVER THE YEARS.
THEY ARE JUST SO PATHETIC, THOUGH.
BWAM
UHN!!
BWAM

THOR, LOOK! DID YOU SEE THE EASE WITH WHICH I--
THOR?!
EEEEEE!

PHYSICALLY, SCREAMING MIMI IS NO THREAT TO THOR, BUT HER SONIC POWERS CAN TURN A MIND TO >>>JELL-O.
MIMI ENJOYS HER WORK, WHICH I CAN UNDERSTAND.
BUT SHE CHOSE THE WRONG TARGET TODAY.
SPAF
HURK!

CAN YOU HEAR ME?! THAT WAS VERY LOUD, WAS IT NOT?
I AM GOING TO KILL EVERY LAST ASSASSIN IN THIS KINGDOM, I SWEAR TO DOOM--
IN THIS, WE ARE IN AGREEMENT. BUT MORE WILL COME. IF THE TRIAD IS MOVING AGAINST ME, THEY WILL SEND EVERYTHING--

SPAK
M.O.D.O.K.!!
UHNN!!

BLACK WIDOW.
INTEL WAS CORRECT, TARGETS ACQUIRED.
M.O.D.O.K. IS DOWN, THE FEMALE IS-- BOZHE MOI.

KRSSHHH
AAAHH!

MY NANOBOTS WILL REBUILD MY FOCUSING CRYSTAL, BUT MY POWERS ARE LIMITED WITHOUT IT.
WE HAVE TO GO!
YOU ARE A COWARD.
NO. I AM <<<EXTREMELY INTELLIGENT.>>>
WE NEED TIME TO RECOVER, AND THINGS HERE WILL ONLY GET WORSE.

WE WILL KILL THEM ALL.
OH, YES.
BUT ON OUR TERMS.

DOOMGARD.
SOMETHING IS *WRONG.*

SHE HAS NOT REPORTED IN AFTER LEAVING THE MONARCHY OF M.
OF ALL THE THORS, I BELIEVE SHE CAN TAKE CARE OF HERSELF.

OF COURSE. BUT WE CANNOT *SENSE* HER.
SCIENCE CANNOT *FIND* HER.
SO WE TURN TO YOU.

DOCTOR STEPHEN STRANGE.
SHERIFF OF BATTLEWORLD.
WELL. THAT *IS* INTERESTING.

KILLVILLE.
AAAIIEEE!
NOTE TO SELF: CROSS THAT ONE OFF BUCKET LIST.
THANK YOU, BUSHWACKER.

I SHOULD HAVE GONE TO WAR WITH THE ASSASSINS' GUILD *YEARS* AGO. THIS IS INCREDIBLE.
PERHAPS THE HAND CAN RESURRECT THEM ALL SO I CAN DO IT AGAIN--
<<<OH, NUTS.>>>

THE GHOST.
I AM DRIVING 100 KM PER HOUR AND MY BRAKES ARE WET WITH BLOOD. THIS IS NOT--
HELLO, M.O.D.O.K.
I LIKE YOUR CAR.
BOOOOOM

ENOUGH! I HAVE HAD ENOUGH OF THIS!
WHO IS NEXT?!

CHK-CHK
WHO WOULD DARE--

HIT MONKEY.
AAAK! AK-AAAK!!
--WHAT IN DOOM'S NAME ARE YOU?

I CALL HIS SKULL!!
DO IT, KAINE!
GET OFF ME!! OR YOUR DEATH WILL BE EVEN MORE >>>HORRIBLE.
THANKS FOR THE WARNING.

I'LL TAKE IT INTO CONSIDERATION.
GAAAAHHH!
MY FLESH DOES NOT BURN AT THE SCARLET SPIDER'S TOUCH SO MUCH AS TEAR...HIS "MARK OF KAINE."
I WILL NOT LIE. IT HURTS.
HSSSS
HSSSS
BUT WHAT HURTS MORE IS THE THOUGHT THAT THOR WILL NO LONGER FIND ME <<<ATTRACTIVE.>>>

STAND AND FIGHT, CREATURE!
YOUR BULLETS MEAN NOTHING TO ME!
TNG
TNG
TNG

MAYBE NOT, BUT HE MAKES A GREAT DISTRACTION.
AAAAHH!

UHN!
THAT HURT.
GET UP, CREATURE. YOU HAVE MORE SUFFERING TO DO.

YOU'RE GOING TO PAY FOR KILLING MY HUSBAND.
ELEKTRA?!
I KILL MANY PEOPLE, YOU WILL HAVE TO NARROW IT--
BULLSEYE, YOU IDIOT!!
THE PUNISHER AND TYPHOID MARY, TOO. THESE ARE THE GUILD'S BIG GUNS. I NEED TO GET THOR AND GET OUT--

THOR?!
HNNNN!!
THE GHOST HAS PHASED HIS HAND THROUGH HER BRAIN, HE'S PLAYING WITH HER NOW...I AM NOT CERTAIN SHE CAN SURVIVE THIS...

AW, LOOK... HE'S WORRIED ABOUT HIS LITTLE GIRLFRIEND.
I THINK I'LL SET HER ON FIRE.
NO!

FWOOOSH
HAHAHAHAHA!!

THOR!!

SHOW ME...
SHOW ME WHAT YOU...WERE DESIGNED FOR...
I HAVE BEEN CONSUMED BY CONFUSION, BY THESE...FEELINGS. AND BY A CONSIDERABLE AMOUNT OF <<<PAIN.

BUT SHE HAS NOT FORGOTTEN WHO I AM.

SHE >>>BELIEVES>>> IN ME. SHE REMEMBERS...

SHE REMEMBERS WHAT I AM DESIGNED FOR.

ASSASSINS!!
IN YOUR LAST MOMENTS ON THIS WORLD, ALLOW ME TO REMIND YOU WHO YOU HAVE MESSED WITH!!
I! AM! M.O.D.O.K.!
BOOM
OH, CRAP.
ARE YOU DISTRACTED, SPECTER?
THAT WILL BE YOUR LAST MISTAKE!
SHUNK

AAA--
THIS IS HOW BOOMERANG DIES.
CHOK

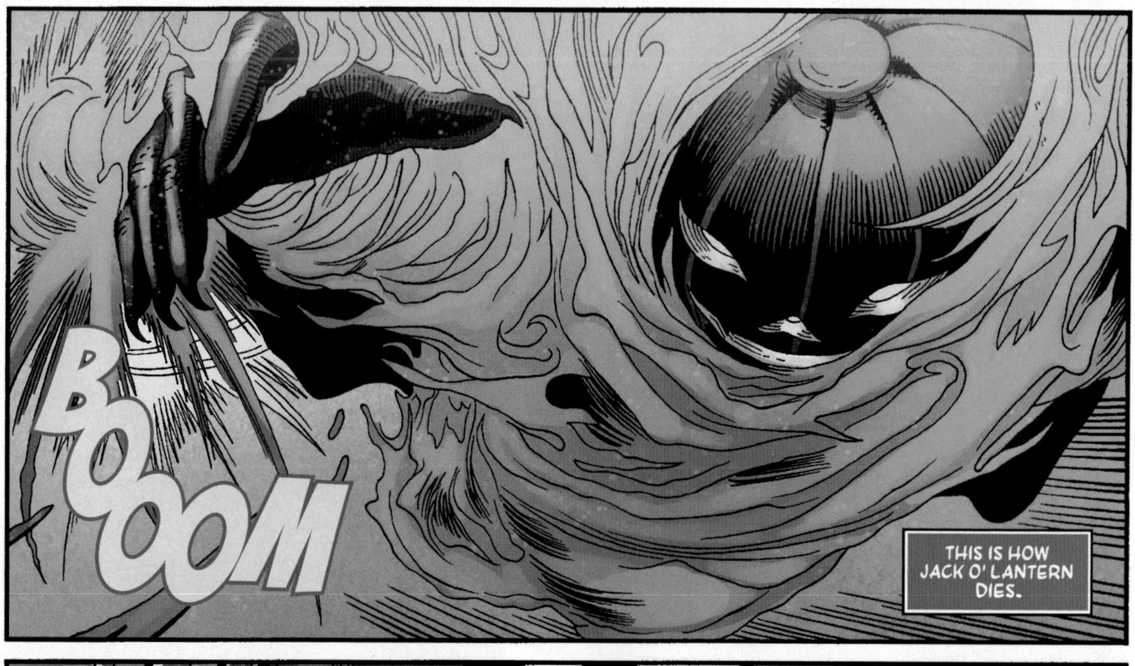

AS PLEASED AS I AM WITH MYSELF RIGHT NOW, THE SIX PLUS CORPSES AT MY FEET ARE NOTHING COMPARED TO THE SIGHT BEFORE ME.
THE MOST BEAUTIFUL THING I'VE EVER SEEN.

SHE'S CRUSHED THE MONKEY'S SKULL WITH HER BARE HANDS.

SHE IS >>>PERFECT.>>>

ARE YOU HUNGRY? I KNOW A PLACE NOT TOO FAR FROM HERE...
HOW MUCH DEATH HAVE WE DEALT THIS DAY?

WELL, LET ME SEE... I KILLED SCREAMING MIMI, THEN YOU KILLED GRIM REAPER, THEN---
IT NEVER ENDS HERE, DOES IT? THE KILLING.
WOULD YOU WANT IT TO? I UNDERSTAND THAT YOU ARE DOOM'S JUSTICE AND ALL, BUT YOU ARE >>>VERY GOOD AT KILLING.
IT CONCERNS ME THAT I ENJOY IT AS MUCH AS I DO.
SNIKT
YOU ARE BEING TRUE TO YOUR NATURE, THERE IS NO SHAME IN--
HURK.

WOLVERINE.
PARTY'S OVER, BUB.
YOU *LOST.*

SABRETOOTH.
M.O.D.O.K.?!
YOU SHOULD WORRY LESS ABOUT HIM, MORE ABOUT YOU.
ENOUGH, CREED.

I WOULD HAVE A WORD WITH M.O.D.O.K. BEFORE YOU KILL THE GIRL.
KINGPIN.
SHROUD.
VIPER.
HOW THE MIGHTY HAVE FALLEN.
WHO ARE YOU?
WE ARE THE LORDS OF THE ASSASSINS GUILD. M.O.D.O.K. WOULD EXPLAIN WHAT THAT MEANS, EXCEPT THAT HE CAN'T SPEAK DUE TO LOGAN'S CLAWS IN THE BASE OF THAT GARGANTUAN SKULL...

NOTE THE EMPHASIS ON "ALMOST."

VMMMMMM

UHN!!

AAH!

HK!

GONNA JUST HAVE TO PUT MY CLAWS IN DEEPER, BIG GUY.

YOU ARE WELCOME TO TRY, MUTANT--

>>>WHOA.>>>

SHRACKK

M.O.D.O.K....
THAT WAS NOT ME, FOR THE RECORD.
WHAT DARKNESS IS THIS?
NO...
WHAT ARE THESE THINGS, MORE ASSASSINS?
NO, THEY ARE... THEY ARE...HM. I CANNOT READ THEM. AS IF THEY ARE >>>MINDLESS.
HAVE YOU GIVEN ANY MORE THOUGHT TO DINNER?

MARVEL | 004
M.O.D.O.K.
Assassin
YOST
PINNA
PALLOT
ROSENBERG

KILLVILLE.
EIGHT YEARS AGO.

GOD EMPEROR DOOM.
SURVEYING HIS KINGDOMS.
KNEEL!

KNEEL BEFORE YOUR GOD!

"KILLVILLE"?
I THOUGHT THAT WAS A TYPO.
VALERIA.
SCIENCE ADVISOR TO GOD DOOM.

THEY MOCK US, MY LOVE.
SILENCE, CLEA. THERE ARE LARGER THINGS AT PLAY HERE.
GOD DOOM WILL SEE HE NEEDS ME. THAT I, BARON MORDO, AM THE GREATEST SORCERER BATTLEWORLD HAS EVER KNOWN AND--

DISTASTEFUL IS WHAT IT IS, VALERIA. A LAND OF KILLERS? IT'S AN ABOMINATION.
STEPHEN STRANGE.
SHERIFF TO GOD DOOM.
YOU ARE MY MOST TRUSTED ADVISOR, STEPHEN, BUT IN THIS WE DISAGREE. ALL THINGS HAVE THEIR USE, EVEN CREATURES SUCH AS THESE.
WHAT THE HECK IS A M.O.D.O.K.?

"MY MOST TRUSTED ADVISOR..."

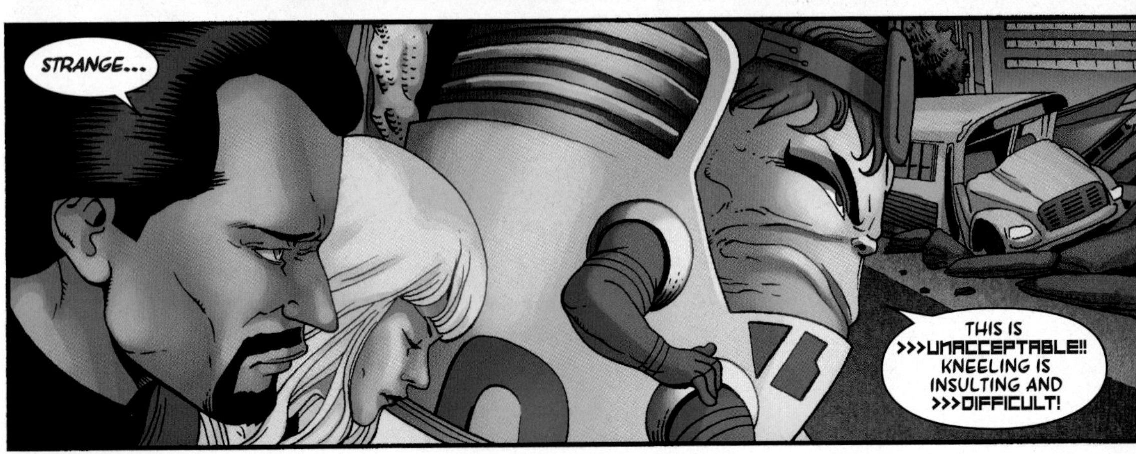
STRANGE...
THIS IS >>>UNACCEPTABLE!! KNEELING IS INSULTING AND >>>DIFFICULT!

NOW.
A LESSER CREATURE WOULD BE TERRIFIED IN THIS SITUATION.
BUT I AM M.O.D.O.K., AND AS SUCH I AM USUALLY EXCITED BY THINGS LIKE THIS.
AS I WATCH THE KINGPIN'S FAT BOIL AWAY FROM HIS BONES, I FEEL ONLY >>>ANGER.
NYEEAAARGH--
ANGER THAT IT WAS NOT I, M.O.D.O.K., THE GREATEST KILLER THE WORLD HAS EVER SEEN, WHO KILLED HIM.
SHRACK
INSTEAD, IT WAS THESE...

...THINGS, WHATEVER THEY ARE.

I AM NOT GETTING ANY STRAY THOUGHTS FROM THESE CREATURES. IT'S AS IF THEIR MINDS ARE *PROTECTED*, OR...

M.O.D.O.K.!

WHAT IN DOOM'S NAME ARE THESE THINGS?!
OH, I SEE. ARE WE ON SPEAKING TERMS NOW, SHROUD?
JUST DEAL WITH THEM!
YOU SENT YOUR ASSASSINS TO KILL ME! LIKE, FIVE MINUTES AGO.

THOOM

MOVE!!

I WATCH AS THE SHROUD'S PATHETIC EXCUSES FOR KILLERS BATTLE THE ONCOMING HORDE OF >>>WHATEVERS.
VIPER WILL PROBABLY DIE FIRST, HER BULLETS AND POISONS AS *USELESS* AS SABRETOOTH'S CLAWS.

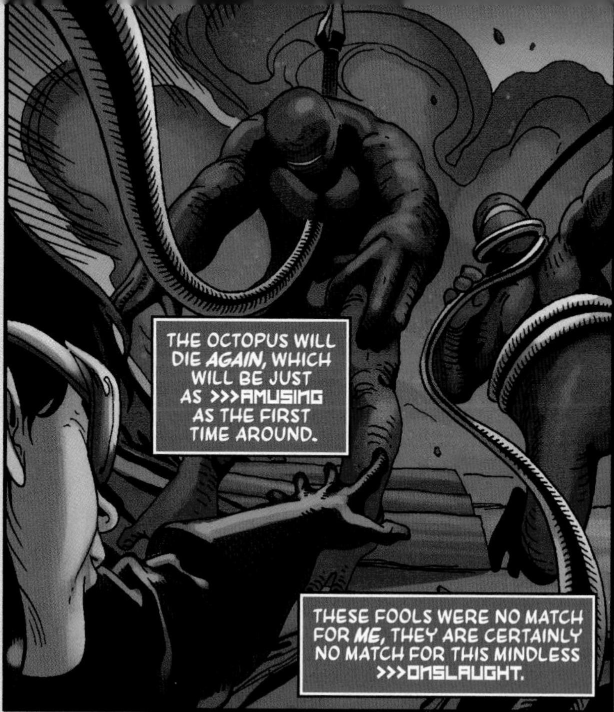
THE OCTOPUS WILL DIE *AGAIN*, WHICH WILL BE JUST AS >>>AMUSING AS THE FIRST TIME AROUND.
THESE FOOLS WERE NO MATCH FOR *ME*, THEY ARE CERTAINLY NO MATCH FOR THIS MINDLESS >>>ONSLAUGHT.

AND THEN THERE IS *THOR*. LOOK AT HER GRACE AND BEAUTY AS SHE LEAPS INTO THE FRAY WITH NO HESITATION, EXCITED BY THE PROSPECT OF *MURDERING* EVERYTHING SHE SEES.
SHE AND I ARE CLEARLY >>>SOULMATES.<<<

LOOK AT THE *SHROUD*. SO >>>SMUG. HE IS JEALOUS OF ME, WHICH HE SHOULD BE.
OUT OF MY WAY, YOU MELON-HEADED BUFFOON!!

THESE GOLEMS WILL NOT PIERCE MY DARKNESS.

YOU'RE DOING IT!
THEY ARE POWERFUL... BUT NO MATCH... FOR...

SPAK

WHAT DID YOU DO?!
I... I...
IT WAS >>>HABIT! I SWEAR!

YOU IDIOT! THE SHROUD WAS THE ONLY THING KEEPING THEM BACK!
IN TRUTH, THIS WAS ILL-PLAYED.
THEY WERE GOING TO BREAK THROUGH ANYWAY, YOU COULD TELL!
SO YOU THOUGHT YOU'D JUST SPEED THINGS UP?! WHY DOES MORDO EVEN LET YOU LIVE?!
<<<DO NOT THINK THAT I WILL NOT KILL--

HM. PERHAPS WE SHOULD TABLE THIS CONVERSATION.

AS WE >>>STRATEGICALLY REPOSITION, I CANNOT HELP BUT ADMIRE THESE MINDLESS ONES.

ZAP

ZAP

ZAP

ZAP

WHILE THEY DO NOT SEEM TO ENJOY THE DELICIOUS SLAUGHTER THEY ARE COMMITTING...

...THEY'RE CERTAINLY *EFFICIENT* ABOUT IT.

I HAVE ALWAYS WANTED TO DECAPITATE VIPER.

I HOLD NO ILL WILL AGAINST SABRETOOTH, BUT CUTTING THROUGH HIS TORSO WITH A >>>LASER SEEMS DELIGHTFUL.

IT IS CLEAR THESE MURDEROUS AUTOMATONS HAVE TO DIE, BUT IN ANOTHER LIFE...WE COULD HAVE BEEN >>>FRIENDS.

WILL YOUR SHIELDS HOLD?

AS LONG AS I AM NOT DISTRACTED.

DIE, M.O.D.O.K.!!

>>>SERIOUSLY? DID YOU NOT HEAR WHAT I JUST SAID?!

DIIEAAACK--
SHUNK

YOU... YOU SAVED MY LIFE.
WHY WOULD YOU DO THAT?
I...I DO NOT ACTUALLY KNOW.
WE SHOULD LEAVE.

>>>AGREED.
AS I EVADE LEAPING MONSTERS AND LASER FIRE, I AM ONLY MAD AT MYSELF.>>>
WHAT IS WRONG WITH ME?! SO MANY BETTER THINGS I COULD HAVE SAID JUST THEN.

BUT SHE IS HOLDING MY HAND.
ADMITTEDLY, SHE WOULD FALL TO A GRISLY DEATH IF SHE DID NOT, BUT THE FACT REMAINS.

THOR AND I FLY OFF INTO THE SUNSET TOGETHER.
PERHAPS THERE IS MORE TO MY DESIGN THAN KILLING.
I SEE NO WAY IN WHICH THIS COULD GO BAD.

CASTLE DOOM.

THIS IS *BAD.*

FINDING THIS ERRANT THOR...IS MORE *DIFFICULT* THAN IT SHOULD BE.

A SQUAD OF THORS AWAIT YOUR COMMAND, SHERIFF.
SHE IS NOT DEAD, BUT THERE'S SOMETHING...
SO ODD... SOMETHING IS OBFUSCATING... WAIT...

THERE.
KILLVILLE.

ALL RIGHT.
YOU HAVE MY INTEREST.

WHERE ARE WE GOING?
YOUR HAMMER. THERE'S SOMETHING ABOUT YOUR CURRENT >>>PREDICAMENT THAT IS NAGGING AT ME.
I BELIEVE--

THOK
UHN!
M.O.D.O.K.?!

I RECOGNIZE THAT SHIELD.
I HAVE FELT IT BREAK MY NOSE BEFORE.

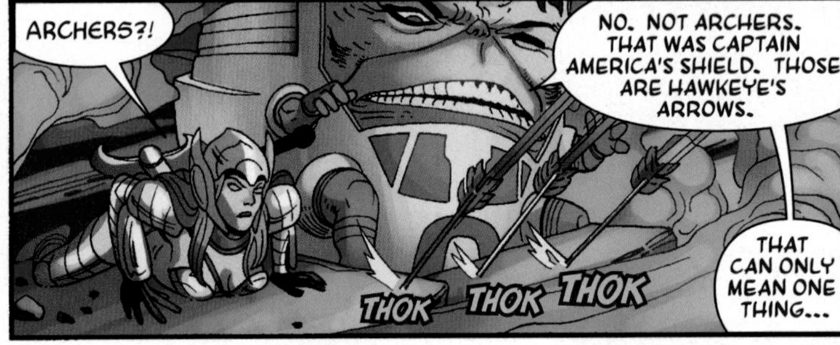
ARCHERS?!
NO. NOT ARCHERS. THAT WAS CAPTAIN AMERICA'S SHIELD. THOSE ARE HAWKEYE'S ARROWS.
THOK THOK THOK
THAT CAN ONLY MEAN ONE THING...

<<<TASKMASTER!!>>>

YOU @#$%^& MORONIC, IMBECILIC, GRINNING BUFFOON!
I WAS IN THE MIDDLE OF THINKING SOMETHING!
WHOA.

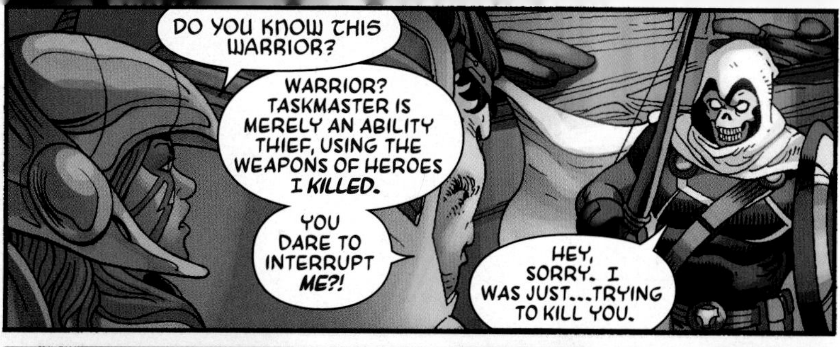
DO YOU KNOW THIS WARRIOR?
WARRIOR? TASKMASTER IS MERELY AN ABILITY THIEF, USING THE WEAPONS OF HEROES I KILLED.
YOU DARE TO INTERRUPT ME?!
HEY, SORRY. I WAS JUST...TRYING TO KILL YOU.

WHATEVER. NOW WHERE WAS I? THE ENERGY SPHERE OVER YOUR HAMMER... THE BOLT THAT TOOK YOU DOWN...
MAYBE YOU DIDN'T HEAR ME, I'M GOING TO KILL--
BE SILENT, MORTAL! M.O.D.O.K. IS THINKING.

IT WAS BARON MORDO!

I DO NOT KNOW WHY HE DID IT, BUT I KNOW IT WAS HIM.
HEY! EXCUSE ME! CAN WE FOCUS HERE?
NO BARON WOULD DARE ATTACK A THOR.
YOU ARE NOT FAMILIAR WITH MORDO OR THE DEPTHS OF HIS >>>ARROGANCE/IDIOCY.

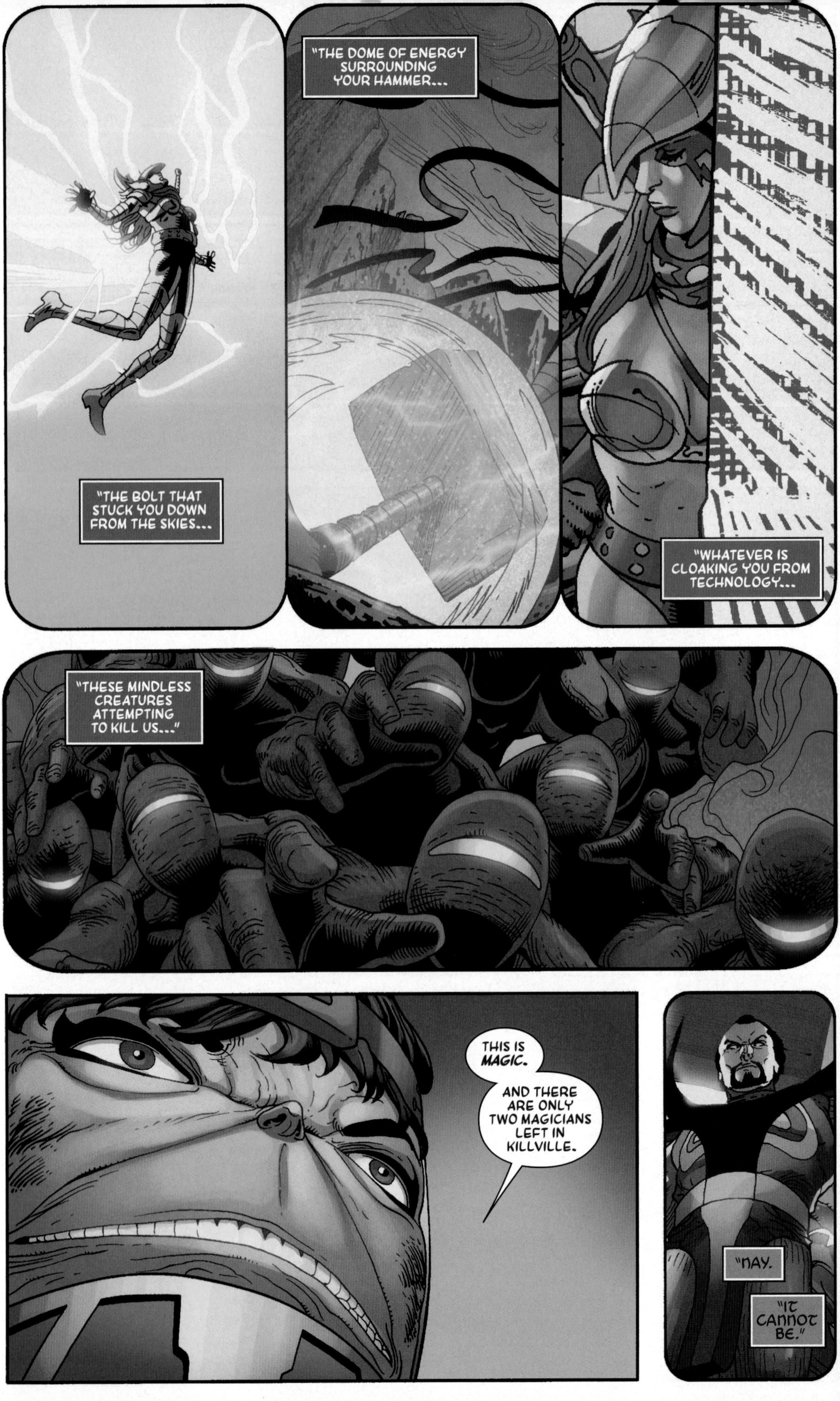

"THE BOLT THAT STUCK YOU DOWN FROM THE SKIES...

"THE DOME OF ENERGY SURROUNDING YOUR HAMMER...

"WHATEVER IS CLOAKING YOU FROM TECHNOLOGY...

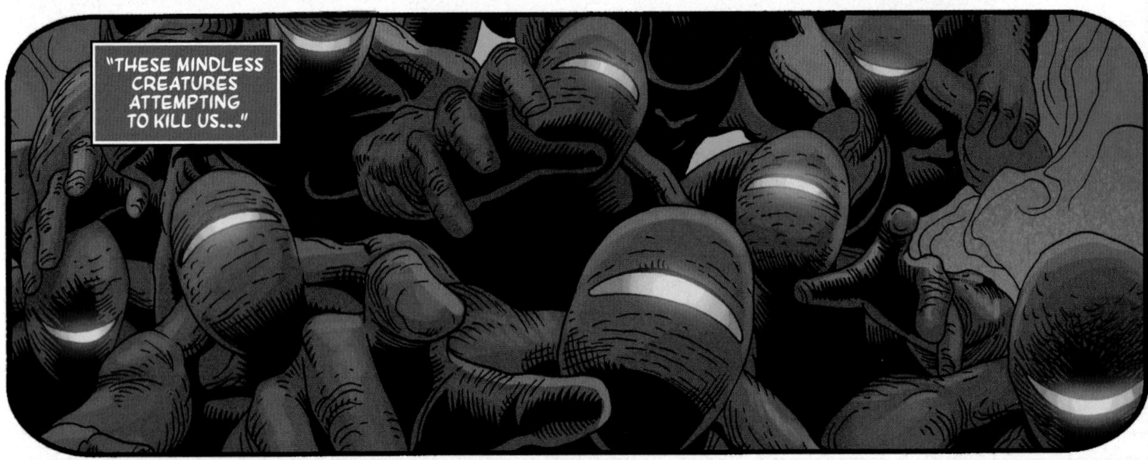

"THESE MINDLESS CREATURES ATTEMPTING TO KILL US..."

THIS IS MAGIC.
AND THERE ARE ONLY TWO MAGICIANS LEFT IN KILLVILLE.

"NAY.
"IT CANNOT BE."

ALL KNOW THE CONSEQUENCES OF SUCH TREACHERY.
THE SHIELD, THEN THE DEADLANDS.
BUT WHAT IF NO ONE KNEW MORDO WAS RESPONSIBLE?
ALL RIGHT, THAT'S IT. YOU'RE DEAD.

IF THIS IS TRUE, M.O.D.O.K., THEN YOU WOULD KNOW.
THAK
WHAT THE--
>>>I AM STILL WORKING OUT THE DETAILS.

COME HERE, TASKMASTER... I HAVE NEED OF YOU AFTER ALL.
VMM
URK!

SHRACK
I LIVE TO SERVE M.O.D.O.K.! I LIVE TO--
AHHH--!

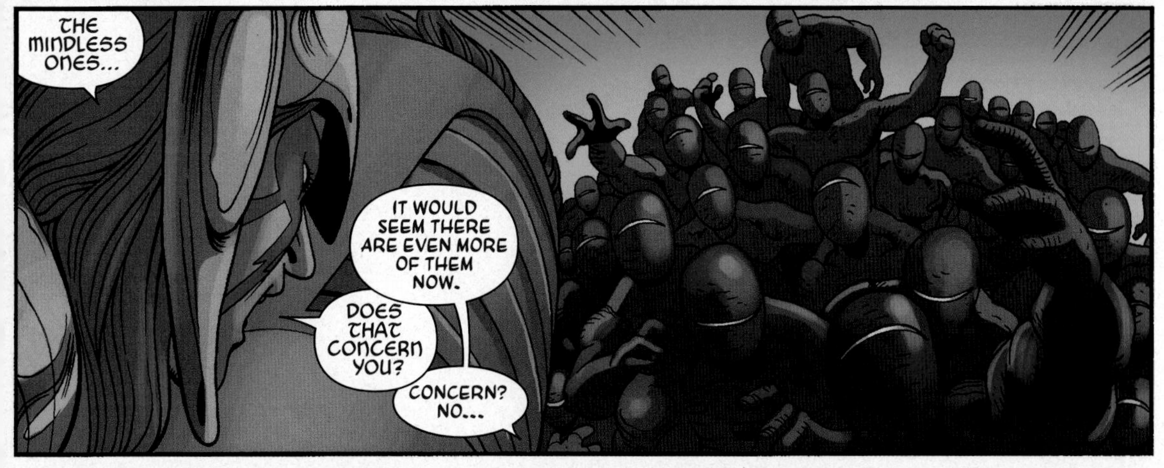
THE MINDLESS ONES...
IT WOULD SEEM THERE ARE EVEN MORE OF THEM NOW.
DOES THAT CONCERN YOU?
CONCERN? NO...

EXCITE.
HAVE AT THEE!!
KILL

DEVILSLAYER IS NEAR! WE MUST CLEAR A PATH!
KILL THEM ALL!!

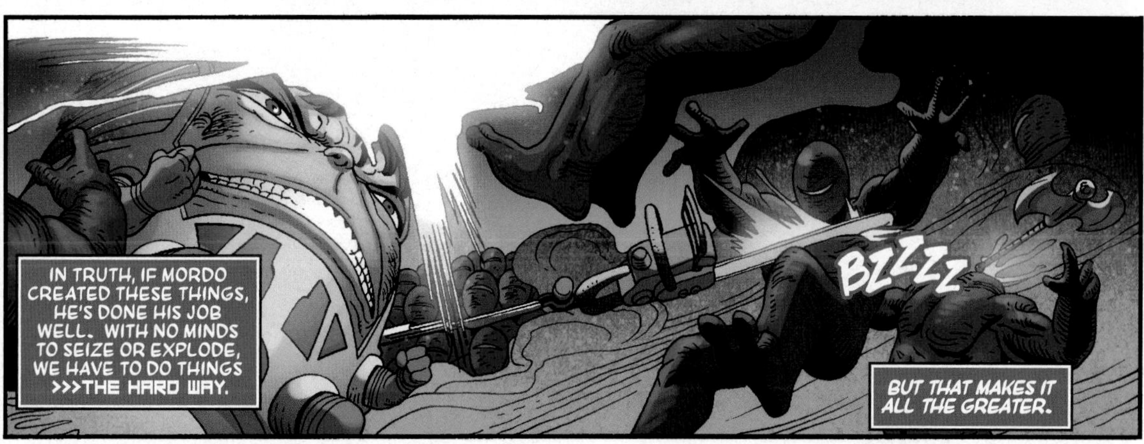
IN TRUTH, IF MORDO CREATED THESE THINGS, HE'S DONE HIS JOB WELL. WITH NO MINDS TO SEIZE OR EXPLODE, WE HAVE TO DO THINGS >>>THE HARD WAY.
BZZZZ
BUT THAT MAKES IT ALL THE GREATER.

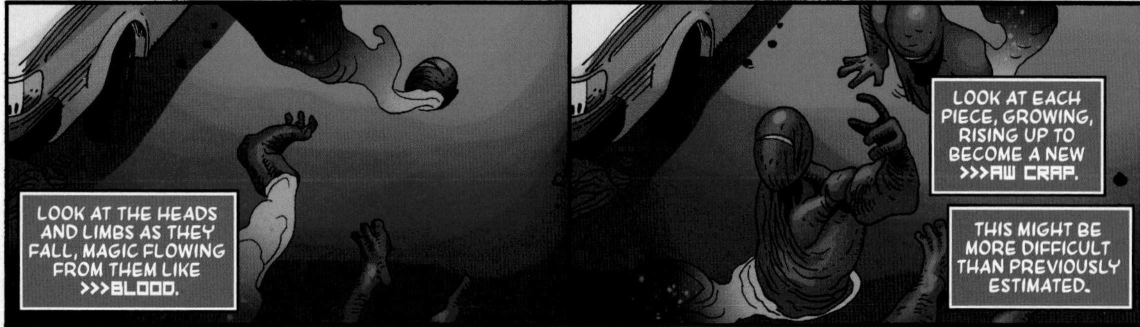
LOOK AT THE HEADS AND LIMBS AS THEY FALL, MAGIC FLOWING FROM THEM LIKE >>>BLOOD.
LOOK AT EACH PIECE, GROWING, RISING UP TO BECOME A NEW >>>AW CRAP.
THIS MIGHT BE MORE DIFFICULT THAN PREVIOUSLY ESTIMATED.

WE HAVE A PROBLEM.
NAY... ONLY MORE THINGS TO KILL.

THERE...MY HAMMER...

EXCUSE ME, THOR? YOU SEEM TO BE >>>LEAVING ME TO DIE.
HOLD THEM OFF!
THOR?!
"HOLD THEM OFF," SHE SAYS.

A THOUSAND UNKILLABLE DEATH MACHINES, AND SHE SAYS "HOLD THEM OFF."
>>>SHE BELIEVES IN ME!
AND I WILL NOT LET HER DOWN!

I WILL KILL EVERYTHING IN THIS DOOM-FORSAKEN KINGDOM TO PROVE MYSELF TO HER.

LUCKILY, THIS IS WHAT I WAS DESIGNED FOR.

IF THIS TRULY BE DARK MAGIC STANDING BETWEEN US... THEN IT SHALL STAND NO MORE.

HNNN!!
KRAAK
SHE PUSHES HER HAND INTO THE ENERGY FIELD. I CANNOT IMAGINE THE WILL IT TAKES...OR THE PAIN.
THOR! THOR!!
MY SENSORS CANNOT EVEN CALCULATE THE POWER IN PLAY HERE.
IN PART BECAUSE OF THESE THINGS CRAWLING ALL OVER ME.

BUT SHE DOES NOT STOP.
NYYEAARGH!!

THOOOOOORR!!

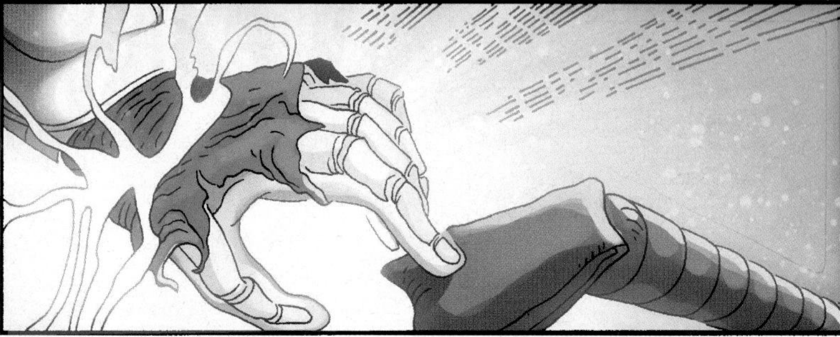

KRA-KOOOOOOOOOM!

FROM THE >>>MIGRAINE>>> I HAVE, I CAN INFER THAT I AM STILL ALIVE.
WHATEVER THAT WAS, IT GAVE ME RESPITE FROM THE MINDLESS ONES.
WHERE IS--

THOR.
ALIVE, THANK DOOM, BUT UNCONSCIOUS. HER HAND IS FLAYED...

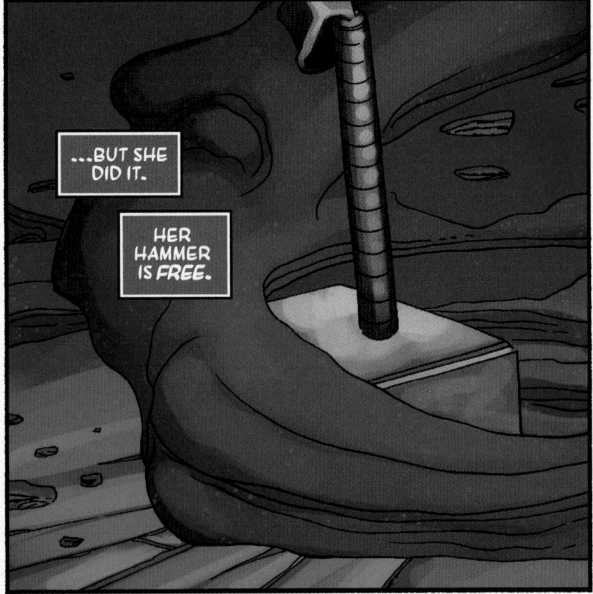
...BUT SHE DID IT.
HER HAMMER IS FREE.

WHICH LEAVES ME WITH A PROBLEM.

THOR! *THOR!*

IT WOULD BE CONVENIENT IF YOU WERE TO WAKE UP NOW AND SAVE OUR LIVES!

EVEN IN UNCONSCIOUSNESS AND/OR A POTENTIAL COMA, SHE IS TRULY BEAUTIFUL.

BUT NOW IT IS I WHO MUST SAVE HER.

THE HAMMER LIES THERE, WAITING TO BE HELD. TO BE USED. IT WANTS TO KILL, JUST LIKE *ME*.

I CAN DO THIS.

I AM WORTHY OF KILLING THINGS WITH THIS HAMMER.
I CAN--

HURNN!
THIS HAMMER IS VERY >>>HEAVY.
YOU POOR, PATHETIC MONSTER.
EH?!
THE ONLY THING YOU ARE WORTHY OF...
...IS DEATH.

MARVEL | 005

M.O.D.O.K. Assassin

YOST
PINNA
PALLOT
ROSENBERG

I AM LOST IN HER BEAUTY.
IT WAS HER EYES I FIRST NOTICED, LOOKING BACK TO >>>TWO HOURS AGO WHEN WE MET.
THEY WERE SO FILLED WITH THE DESIRE TO *KILL*.
HER HAIR, THE COLOR OF FIRE. >>>WHICH CAN KILL.
IT SWIRLS EVER SO, AS IF FLOATING IN BLOOD. >>>BLOOD THAT IS ON *FIRE*.
AND WHATEVER IT IS THOSE RIBBONS DO. >>>I ASSUME THEY KILL PEOPLE.
HER MOUTH, SPECIFICALLY HER LIPS...THEY GLISTEN LIKE BLOOD.
FOR REAL, AS SHE IS CURRENTLY BLEEDING.
I AM NOT SURE IF HER LIPS CAN KILL, BUT I CAN PICTURE HER KILLING SOMEONE WITH HER *TEETH* AND IT IS *GLORIOUS*.
HER SUPPLE HAND, CHARRED DOWN TO THE BONE AS IF SHE WERE DEATH HERSELF.
WHILE OTHERS MIGHT BE ASHAMED OF SUCH A DISFIGURING WOUND, I KNOW SHE WILL JUST >>KILL PEOPLE WITH IT.
HER NAME IS *THOR*, AND I CAN NO LONGER IGNORE THE FACT THAT <<<I LOVE HER.>>>

DIE, YOU MISSHAPEN BEAST!
HAHAHA!!
YEAARGHH!
THIS NEWFOUND REALIZATION GOES AGAINST THE VERY NATURE OF MY BEING, AGAINST MY VERY >>>PURPOSE. FOR I AM M.O.D.O.K., MENTAL ORGANISM DESIGNED ONLY FOR KILLING.
THE POINT MAY BE MOOT, HOWEVER...
...AS IT SEEMS WE ARE BOTH ABOUT TO >>>DIE AT THE HANDS OF KARL MORDO, BARON OF >>>KILLVILLE.

GAAAHH!
DO YOU KNOW HOW LONG I'VE WAITED FOR THIS MOMENT TO COME, YOU HIDEOUS CREATURE?
DO YOU KNOW HOW HARD I'VE WORKED?!
LOOK AT HIM FLAIL!

GROUNDING A THOR IS NO EASY FEAT. SEPARATING HER FROM HER HAMMER, HAVING HER LAND AT YOUR MINISCULE FEET...
...ALL WHILE CUTTING HER OFF FROM HER FELLOW THORS AND DOOM'S SCIENCE? BUT I FOUND A WAY.
I FOUND A WAY TO BRING SHERIFF STRANGE HERE AND YOU RUINED IT.

YOU WERE SUPPOSED TO KILL HER, YOU MONSTROUS FREAK!
KILL THE THOR AND LURE THE SHERIFF HERE TO AVENGE HER!
HRRNN!!
MY SUPERIOR BRAIN KNEW IT WAS YOU AND CLEA BEHIND ALL THIS, BUT YOUR MOTIVES ARE BAFFLING AND PROBABY >>>STUPID.
WHY WOULD YOU WANT STRANGE TO COME TO KILLVILLE?

"WHY"? "WHY"?
BECAUSE I DESERVE TO BE DOOM'S SHERIFF, YOU FOUL, REPUGNANT ATROCITY! NOT HIM!
STRANGE IS NOTHING COMPARED TO BARON MORDO!!

>>>I AM NOT FOLLOWING. AND ALSO, ARE THE PERSONAL ATTACKS REALLY NECESSARY?

TELL ME, "MENTAL ORGANISM DESIGNED ONLY FOR KILLING"...

WHAT WOULD YOU DO IF STRANGE CAME HERE AND ATTACKED YOU?

PAF

HURK--!

REALLY? *THAT'S* YOUR PLAN? BECAUSE THAT IS THE SINGLE **DUMBEST>>>** THING I HAVE EVER HEARD.
WHAT?!
THIS *"PLAN,"* AND NOTE THE SARCASM AS I CALL IT THAT, IS FILLED WITH LOGIC ERRORS. **>>>STUPIDITY.**
SHUT UP!!
THE LEAST OF WHICH IS THE STRONG POSSIBILITY THAT DOOM WOULD JUST **>>>KILL YOU** FOR FAILING TO PROTECT STRANGE FROM ME.
WHAT IF STRANGE DOESN'T COME? WHAT IF THOR KILLED *ME* INSTEAD? I ASSUME YOU HIRED THE ASSASSINS GUILD--WHAT IF *THEY* KILLED ME?
<<<DO YOU WISH ME TO GO ON?>>>
NOT TO MENTION YOUR MINDLESS ONES, THEY LOOK INCREDIBLY--
UHN!
STRANGE *WILL* COME. HE WILL NOT BE ABLE TO RESIST.
AND IF YOU WON'T KILL THIS *THOR...*
NO!
...THEN I'LL DO IT *MYSELF.*

NO!!
HAHAHHAA!
LOOK AT HIM, KARL... HE'S IN LOVE WITH HER.

LOVE? I DIDN'T THINK YOU WERE CAPABLE OF ANYTHING OTHER THAN BEING A THORN IN MY SIDE, M.O.D.O.K.
BUT I'M GLAD. YOU CAN HAVE YOUR MISSHAPEN HEART TORN OUT BEFORE YOU DIE.

>>>CURSES. YOU HAVE DEFEATED ME, BARON MORDO. WHATEVER WILL I DO?
OH, WAIT, >>>I KNOW. I WILL MANIPULATE YOU INTO WASTING TIME WHILE I ENGINEER YOUR >>>DESTRUCTION.

WHAT IS HE TALKING ABOUT, KARL--
SHRACK
AAHH!

OH, @#$%.
AN APPROPRIATE RESPONSE.
YOU SEE, YOU NEVER TRIED TO KILL ME BECAUSE I WAS >>>USEFUL. BECAUSE YOU WERE AFRAID OF THE MACHINES, AND THEY WERE AFRAID OF ME.
ERGO, YOU ARE AFRAID OF ME.

ZZZAR
LET ME SHOW YOU WHAT I AM DESIGNED FOR!!!
ZZA

IT'S KILLING, BY THE WAY.
MY >>>INCREDIBLE MIND CONTROLS THE SENTINELS, UNLEASHING THEIR DISINTEGRATION BEAMS AGAINST MORDO'S MINDLESS ONES.

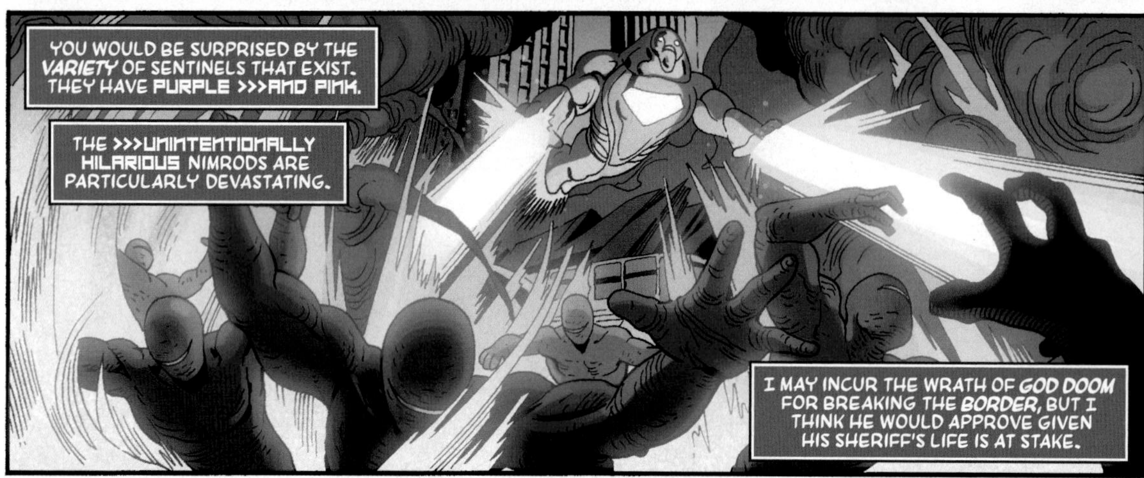
YOU WOULD BE SURPRISED BY THE VARIETY OF SENTINELS THAT EXIST. THEY HAVE PURPLE >>>AND PINK.
THE >>>UNINTENTIONALLY HILARIOUS NIMRODS ARE PARTICULARLY DEVASTATING.
I MAY INCUR THE WRATH OF GOD DOOM FOR BREAKING THE BORDER, BUT I THINK HE WOULD APPROVE GIVEN HIS SHERIFF'S LIFE IS AT STAKE.

AND WHEN THE MINDLESS ONES FINALLY REMEMBER THEY CAN FIGHT BACK, JOINING TOGETHER TO ACTUALLY DESTROY ONE OF MY METAL PUPPETS...
...THAT'S WHEN THE FUN >>>KICKS IT UP A NOTCH.

THEY ARE CALLED WILD SENTINELS.
ONE OF THEM HAS A GUN INSIDE ITS FACE AND IT IS >>>ADORABLE.

NO! NO! WHAT ARE YOU DOING?!
KARL! STOP THEM! DO SOMETHING!
I AM!
DESTROY THE ROBOTS, MY CHILDREN!!
YOU HAVE BIGGER PROBLEMS, "KARL."
REEEEEE
KILL

BUDDA BUDDA BUDDA
SHRACK
YOU ARE AN ITCH I HAVE WANTED TO SCRATCH FOR A VERY LONG TIME.
TO BE CLEAR, IN THIS METAPHOR "SCRATCHING" YOU MEANS >>>KILL YOU.

CLEA, JOIN YOUR POWER WITH MINE! FOCUS EVERYTHING ON M.O.D.O.K.!
KILL
UHNN!!
WHAT ABOUT THE GIANT ROBOTS?!

NO...I WILL NOT DIE LIKE THIS.
I AM KARL AMADEUS MORDO...

AND I WILL NOT BE DEFEATED BY YOU!!
CHOOOM
UHM!
VMMM

PLEASE...FORGIVE ME... DID NOT KNOW...YOUR MIDDLE NAME WAS >>>AMADEUS.
IT ALL MAKES SENSE NOW, WHY YOU ARE SUCH AN >>>IDIOT.

LAUGH ALL YOU WANT, "GEORGE."
I'M GOING TO USE YOUR CORPSE TO KILL STRANGE WHEN HE ARRIVES. EVEN IN DEATH, I WILL OWN YOU.
CLEA... END IT.

I'VE ALWAYS HATED YOU, MONSTER.
DO YOU HEAR THAT?
...WHAT?
>>>THUNDER.

KRA-KOOOM
AAAIIIEEE--!
...I NEED TO CHANGE MY CHASSIS.
CLEA... NO.
HOW IS THIS POSSIBLE?
MORDO, BARON OF KILLVILLE!
BY THE AUTHORITY OF LORD GOD DOOM, FOR THE CRIME OF TREASON...
...I SENTENCE YOU TO DEATH!!

YOU HAVE MADE >>>POOR LIFE CHOICES.
BEFORE YOU DIE, CONFIRM FOR ME...SHE IS AMAZING, RIGHT?
MINDLESS ONES...KILL THEM ALL!

I THINK NOT! FLY, DEVILSLAYER!!

BOOM

BOOM

BOOM

M.O.D.O.K., WHILE I DEAL WITH THE REST OF THESE GOLEMS...
...KILL BARON MORDO.

I BELIEVE THERE WAS >>>ROMANTIC INTENT BEHIND THAT STATEMENT.
SHRACK
AAAHH!

DO NOT RESIST, KARL... WAIT, NO, ON SECOND THOUGHT, DO.
IT WILL BE MUCH MORE >>>ENTERTAINING.
AS EVER, YOUR ARROGANCE WILL BE YOUR DOWNFALL!

BEHOLD, THE BOLTS OF BALTHAKKK!
SHLIK
GAAAHH!

YOUR SCIENCE... IS NOTHING BEFORE ME. YOU WERE DESIGNED ONLY FOR KILLING?
I AM DEATH ITSELF, COME FOR YOU!

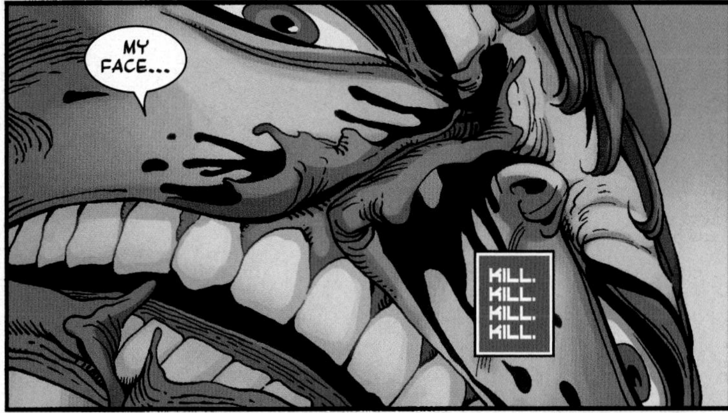
MY FACE...
KILL. KILL. KILL. KILL.

I SUMMON THE FLAMES OF--
GAAAHH!
KILL
REEEEEE

YOU CANNOT WIN... HNN. MY FACE HURTS. DOES IT LOOK ALL RIGHT?
KILL YOU. I'M GOING TO KILL YOU. I...I CAN'T FEEL MY ARM.
>>>SHOULD WE TAKE A BREAK?
YOU WERE NOTHING... A TOOL, A WEAPON FOR ME TO POINT...
NO! I AM MORE THAN THAT!
THERE IS MORE TO ME THAN KILLING!
YOU WILL DIE AS YOU LIVED, M.O.D.O.K.
I NEED ONLY ONE HAND TO KILL--
WHAM
KARL AMADEUS MORDO, BARON OF KILLVILLE, HITS THE GROUND, HIS EYES ROLLING BACK INTO HIS HEAD.
NOT DEAD, BUT UNCONSCIOUS.
NOT KILLED, BUT DEFEATED.

WHAT ARE YOU WAITING FOR?

WHY HAVE YOU NOT KILLED HIM?
I SERIOUSLY CONSIDERED IT. EVERYTHING IN ME SCREAMED OUT TO KILL HIM.
BUT HE MUST FACE JUSTICE FOR WHAT HE HAS DONE. THE JUSTICE OF **DOOM.**

FOR I AM MORE THAN MERELY A KILLING MACHINE AND SCIENTIFIC GENIUS AND CRIMINAL MASTERMIND AND LORD OF MACHINES AND DOMINATOR OF MEN'S WILLS!!
...I WOULD HAVE JUST KILLED HIM.
KRA-KOOM
CHOOM
SHRACK
KABOOOM

>>>UH-OH.
FINALLY.

THOR.

THAT IS A LOT OF >>>THORS.

NONE SO BEAUTIFUL AS *MINE*, I MIGHT POINT OUT.

WHAT HAS TRANSPIRED HERE? YOU COULD NOT BE DETECTED BY NORMAL MEANS. IT TOOK SHERIFF STRANGE TO--

IT WAS THE SHERIFF THAT WAS IN DANGER, NOT ME. BARON MORDO PLOTTED TO KILL HIM. IS STRANGE HERE?

NO. HE DECIDED HE WAS TOO BUSY TO COME HIMSELF.

TOO BUSY? *TOO BUSY?!*

RBBT!

ALL OF THIS WAS FOR NOTHING!!

I'LL KILL YOU *ALL--*

M.O.D.O.K.!!
IN THE NAME OF LORD GOD DOOM, YOU ARE ORDERED TO SURRENDER!!

YOU WISH A FIGHT? THEN A FIGHT YOU SHALL--
WAIT!!

DO NOT KILL HIM.
HE IS A MONSTER!
NO. HE SAVED MY LIFE.

WERE IT NOT FOR M.O.D.O.K., I WOULD BE DEAD MANY TIMES OVER.
IT WAS HE WHO PROTECTED ME, AND UNCOVERED THE PLOT AGAINST THE SHERIFF.
...REALLY?

YOU HAVE DONE A GREAT SERVICE TO BATTLEWORLD, M.O.D.O.K.
I WILL INFORM THE SHERIFF WHAT YOU HAVE DONE THIS DAY, AND RECOMMEND YOU BE MADE THE NEW ***BARON*** OF KILLVILLE.
...REALLY?

THE REMAINING THORS LEAVE, AND I AM FINALLY ALONE WITH...RED-HEADED THOR? KILLER THOR? HM.
WHEN I FIRST SAW YOU, I MUST ADMIT... I THOUGHT YOU A MONSTER AS WELL. BUT I SEE NOW, THERE WAS MORE TO YOU.
NOT MUCH, BUT STILL. YOU HAVE MY GRATITUDE.

THIS IS IT.
MY MOMENT. THERE IS BLOOD ON MY FACE, BUT I THINK THAT WILL MAKE THE EXPERIENCE >>>ALL THE SWEETER.
...WHAT ARE YOU DOING?
ARE YOU ALL RIGHT? IS YOUR FACE HAVING A CONVULSION?
I WOULD KISS YOU NOW.

WHAM
YOU PRESUME TOO MUCH, KILLER!!

WAIT! AT LEAST TELL ME YOUR NAME!

...MY NAME IS ANGELA.

SHE SMILED AT ME.
ANGELA SMILED AT ME.

ONE WAY
I AM M.O.D.O.K.
MENTAL ORGANISM DESIGNED FOR BUT NOT STRICTLY LIMITED TO KILLING.
AND AS I KILL EVERYONE I SEE IN MY DUTIES AS BARON OF KILLVILLE, I DO SO WITH LOVE IN MY HEART.
FOR IN THE END, WHAT ELSE IS THERE?
B.W.
KILLING... AND LOVE.
>>>JUST THOSE THINGS.
KILL
YOU HAVE BEEN READING
M.O.D.O.K.! BARON OF KILLVILLE
MARVEL

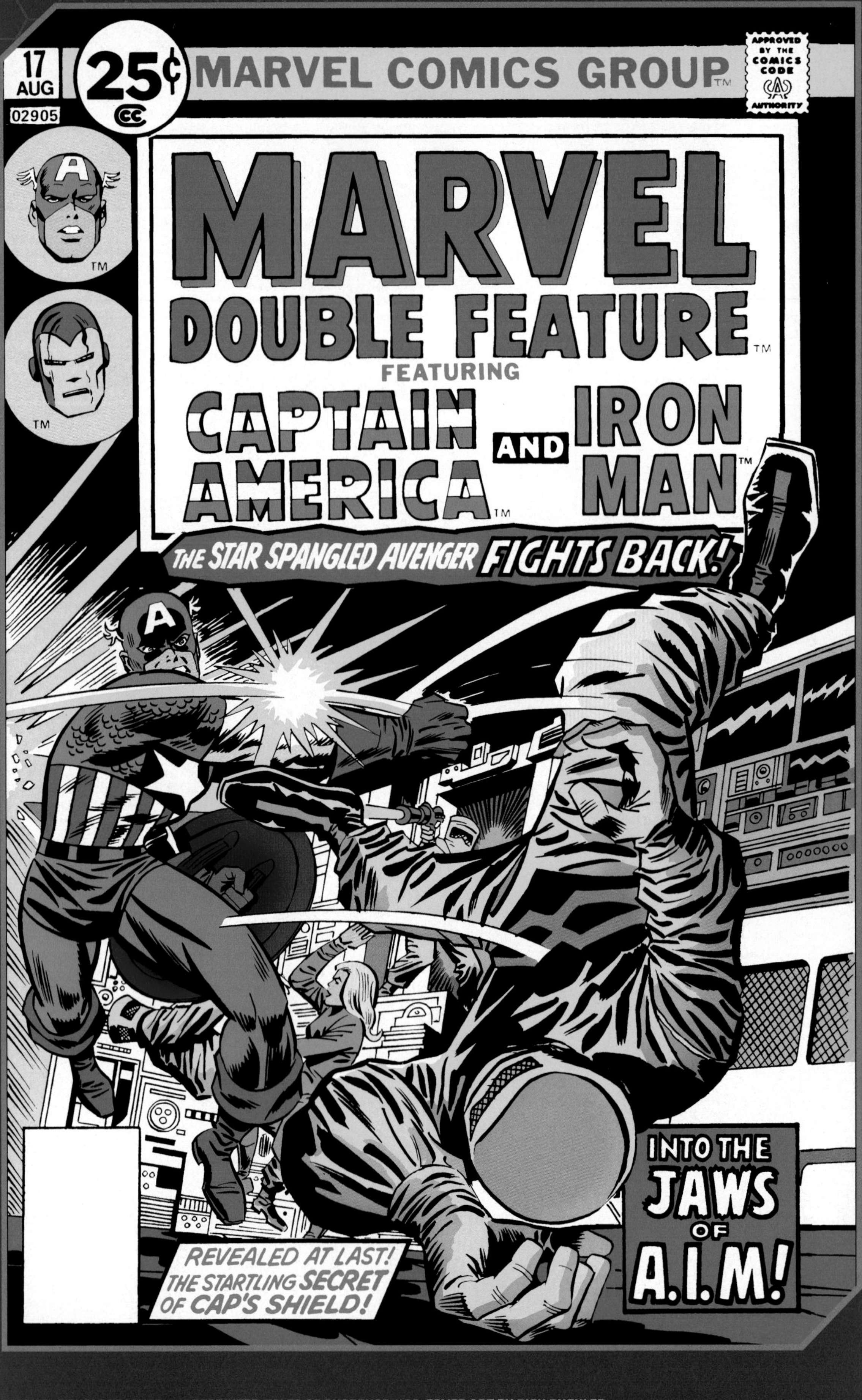

17
AUG
02905

25¢

CC

MARVEL COMICS GROUP™

APPROVED BY THE COMICS CODE AUTHORITY

MARVEL DOUBLE FEATURE™

FEATURING

CAPTAIN AMERICA™ AND IRON MAN™

THE STAR SPANGLED AVENGER FIGHTS BACK!

REVEALED AT LAST! THE STARTLING SECRET OF CAP'S SHIELD!

INTO THE JAWS OF A.I.M.!

MARVEL DOUBLE FEATURE #17 REPRINTED *TALES OF SUSPENSE #93*. COVER ART BY RICH BUCKLER

MARVEL DOUBLE FEATURE #18 REPRINTED *TALES OF SUSPENSE #94*. COVER ART BY JACK KIRBY

TALES OF SUSPENSE 94

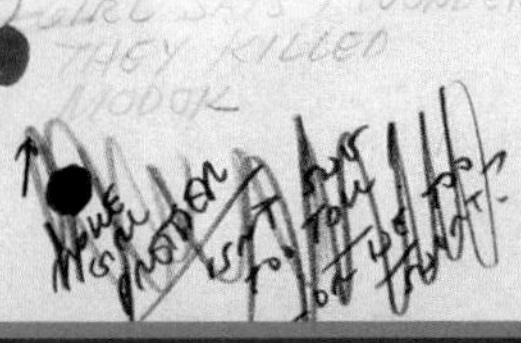

TALES OF SUSPENSE #94, PAGE 22 ART BY JACK KIRBY & JOE SINNOTT

COURTESY OF HERITAGEAUCTIONS.COM

INCREDIBLE HULK #288 COVER ART BY RON WILSON & JOE SINNOTT
COURTESY OF HERITAGEAUCTIONS.COM

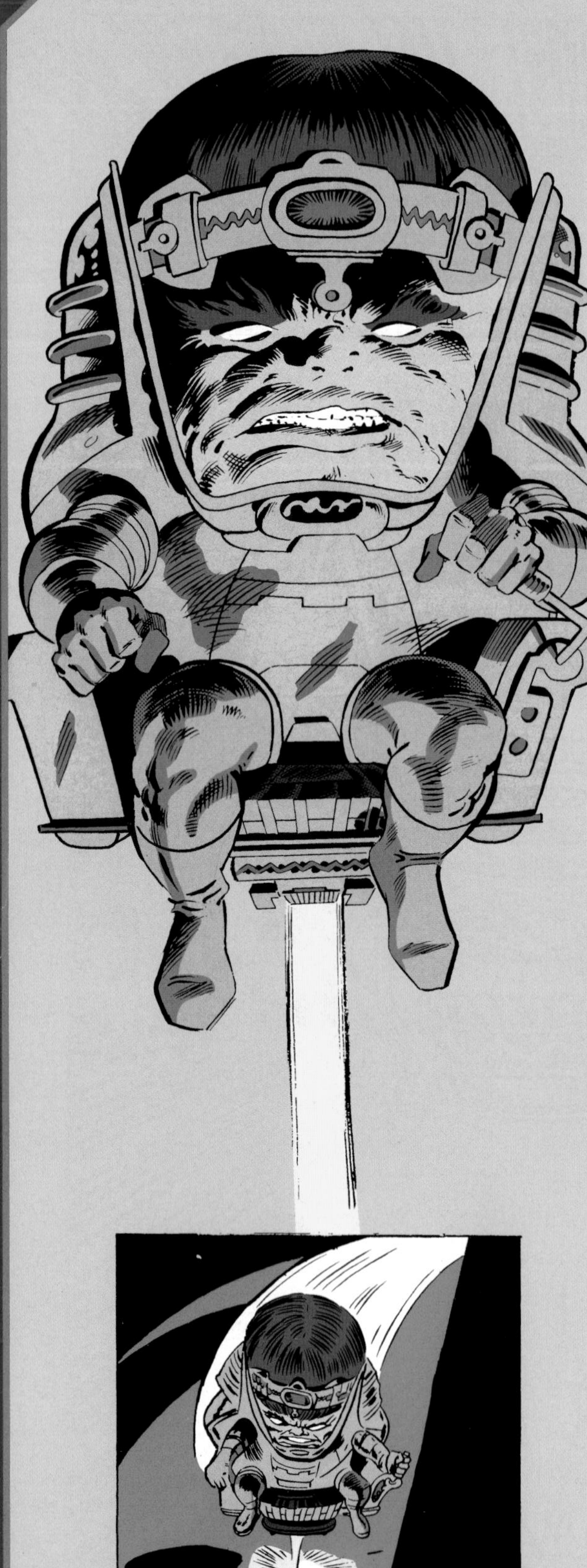

MODOK

Real Name: George Tarleton
Occupation: Supreme leader of the Advanced Idea Mechanics (A.I.M.)
Identity: Secret
Legal status: Citizen of the United States with no criminal record as yet
Former aliases: None
Place of birth: Bangor, Maine
Marital status: Single
Known relatives: None
Group affiliation: Advanced Idea Mechanics
Base of operations: Mobile
First appearance: TALES OF SUSPENSE #94
Origin: George Tarleton was an agent-technician of average intelligence employed by A.I.M. who was chosen at random by A.I.M.'s scientist supreme, Lyle Getz, to be a subject for an experiment in controlled mutation. Placed against his will in the "alteration chamber," Tarleton underwent extensive cellular irradiation and physical bio-engineering to be transformed into a massive-headed being of superhuman intelligence. Enraged by his hideous condition, Tarleton used his new psionic powers to slay the scientist supreme who subjected him to the treatment, earning the name Modok: Mental Organism Designed Only for Killing. Modok then seized control of the entire A.I.M. organization and eliminated opposition within the ranks. The leader of A.I.M. ever since, he has on numerous occasions supervised the construction of lethal weaponry with which to foster A.I.M.'s goal of a technological conquest of the world.
Height: 12' **Weight:** 750 lbs
Eyes: White **Hair:** Brown
Unusual features: Modok's head is of greater mass than his body, necessitating the use of artificial devices, such as his hover-chair, to support his great weight.
Powers: Modok possesses superhuman mental and psionic powers. He has an organic, computer-like brain which can calculate probabilities, formulate strategies, and solve complex equations. His mind has total recall and has absorbed all available knowledge about the physical sciences and technology. Although he possesses a genius I.Q. many times over, Modok still has only the creative capacity of his former human self.

Modok can project psionic force from his brain for a variety of effects. He can project a concussive blast, capable of killing a human being from the force, or puncturing a 2-inch thick steel plate with a single blast. He can also use psionic energy to increase the motion of molecules in his vicinity, creating heat. He can form globular fields of psionic force capable of protecting him from the effects of the detonation of a small nuclear weapon (500 kilotons) at a range of as little as 100 feet from the center of the blast. He can also use his psionic powers to scan the brain engrams of others: although he cannot "read" thoughts, he can recognize specific engrams. Modok is able to employ his psionic powers within a maximum radius of about 5 miles. He can perform up to two different psionic feats at one time, and use various psionic abilities in succession for 1 hour before suffering any fatigue.
Weapons: Modok has designed and supervised the construction of numerous weapons. He has used a robotic body proportional to his oversized head, armed with various offensive weaponry. He has used an "ultra-ray" gun capable of felling the Hulk. He has employed various androids, robots, and cyborgs. He has also used various brainwashing devices to subjugate the will of others to his own.

M.O.D.O.K.: ASSASSIN #1 VARIANT BY GABRIEL HERNANDEZ WALTA

M.O.D.O.K.: ASSASSIN #2 VARIANT BY CHRISTIAN WARD